Intercultural Education Woven into Theory and Praxis

Karma M. Chukdong B.Ed, M.A., M.Ed

authorHOUSE

AuthorHouse™
1663 Liberty Drive
Bloomington, IN 47403
www.authorhouse.com
Phone: 833-262-8899

Published by AuthorHouse 09/24/2020

ISBN: 978-1-6655-0039-5 (sc)
ISBN: 978-1-6655-0038-8 (e)

Print information available on the last page.

*Any people depicted in stock imagery provided by Getty Images are models,
and such images are being used for illustrative purposes only.
Certain stock imagery © Getty Images.*

This book is printed on acid-free paper.

CONTENTS

Foreword vii

Acknowledgements ix

Dedication xi

Chapter 1—Communicating Online and Student Self-Care 1

Chapter 2—Self-Care and the Digital Classroom 6

Chapter 3—Social Justice and Digital Learning 14

Chapter 4—Empathy and Educational Policy 18

Chapter 5—Multi-Cultural Student Wellness 25

Chapter 6—Emotional Intelligence in a Robotic System 53

Chapter 7—Self-Care Age and Education 62

Chapter 8—Post-Colonial Lens for Educators 66

Chapter 9—Infusing Art Therapy into the Digital Classroom (Revised) 123

Chapter 10—Weaving the Self-Care Age with Modern Education 129

Chapter 11—An Elder's Wellness Advice to Students 131

Appendix: Academic Calendars, Lesson Plan Templates, Grading Sheets 137

About the Artist: Jim Oskineegish 215

About the Author: Karma Chukdong 219

Bibliography 221

FOREWORD

This text looks at Wellness and Empowerment from the student, parent and teacher perspective. It addresses the obstacles diverse student populations encounter in school systems and sees how we as educators, administrators and academic leaders can transform schools, classrooms, and departments into safe, inclusive, culturally responsible, and positive spaces for our students. The text has framework exemplars from Elementary, Secondary, College and University sectors. Specifically, this text looks at Indigenous Student Success, International Student Success and Domestic Student Success. This e-book will be available to parents, teachers, vice-principals, principals, academic deans and policy makers through many digital platforms. What is amazing is that this Intercultural Education e-learning text will be available worldwide and especially in remote fly-in reservation computer labs and homes at all times once downloaded. These Intercultural Educational frameworks will be available will be accessible through Apple e-books, Kobo e-books, Rakuten, Kindle and many more.

Student Wellness, Empowerment and e- Learning is more than a trend in education. As we will see that in Indigenous school systems Student Wellness and Empowerment was the core purpose of the education system.

This e-Book looks how a business model or factory model of education should be altered to a more human approach in order for our next generation to thrive.

This text takes the reader on a journey from Indigenous Educational Models, to the Agricultural Age, Industrial Age, Digital Age and into the future Self-Care Age. This Self-Care Age will focus on Wellness, Empowerment, and our next generation will be the ones who help us unplug and have pathways to an authentic digital detox through Indigenous Pedagogy.

Indigenous and Holistic approaches see trends, phenomenon from a cyclical perspective. Contrary to viewing phenomenon in a hierarchical way where humanity and technology are advancing to greater, and great heights; Indigenous holistic approaches see a world where everything must come back down to the center to achieve a natural balance.

Our students were born into the Digital Age, living their entire life thus far connected to the Digital World. They will be the ones who help us all disconnect and return to having more human ways of interacting, educating, communicating, and returning to the original ways of education. Education was seen as a medicine, and in this way this latest dynamic text "**Intercultural Education Woven into Theory and Praxis**" will empower the next generation of educational leaders re-establish a balance, harmony for their students. In an increasingly impersonal, competitive, and machine-like world, this factory model of existence has seeped into all fields of our lives: education, economics, health-care, natural environment, sports, spirituality, family, parenting, and communication.

This timely text will assist the practicing educational leader share pathways for their students to re-connect to their innate human nature that is naturally balanced, whole and happy; this is the purpose and aim of the education models outlined in the pages within.

Since the dawn of the Industrial Revolution our education system was modelled on the factory model of conforming children as unified product throughout an assembly line if you will to be distributed to the masses. This revelation has shocked and angered many policy makers, curriculum designers, and administrators, and parents in time.

This business model is inherent in our educational system. The student is seen as a customer the parents are viewed as shareholders, and financial aid departments are the stakeholders. So, where is the child left in all this complicated system of education? This is the main topic we will examine and reveal how education management must change to view the student as much more than a customer. Furthermore, education systems must put the student first, and we will see why the student is seen as having the least power or voice because of this business model of education. Our children are not customers but are sacred human beings who will be the ones who will shape our next generation. If, our education systems are linked to consumerism then it is difficult to have a peaceful happy society.

How can we integrate Native Science our Natural Laws of Interdependence rooted in Quantum Physics into our classrooms? Land-Based Learning Science "Kis Kin Ha Ma Ki Win" in the Cree Language into outdoor learning classrooms? How can we integrate Medicine Walks into the school day on a permanent basis? What about meditation for students rooted in Vipassana and Shamatha living traditions? What about "Karma Yoga" which looks at the importance of selfless community service into our long- range planning? These Traditional Student Wellness Practices can be weaved into theory and praxis, and are highly necessary for the well-being and mental health of students in our school systems today.

ACKNOWLEDGEMENTS

❖

I would like to thank Authorhouse publications who believed in this "Intercultural Education Woven into Theory and Praxis " text from the very beginning. I want to thank my parents Nyima Chukdong, Susan Chukdong, and sister Dechen Chukdong.

My mentors: Dr. Narendra Wagle, Dr. Leonard Priestley, Dr. Sarkar, Dr. Grace Feuerverger, Dr. Reva Joshee and Choje Lama Namse Rinpoche for his compassionate guidance in my formative years.

I am certain that this text will be an invaluable online resource for Deans, principals, vice-principals, curriculum advisors, parents and teachers helping them with their sacred mission of educating the next generation of our children.

DEDICATION

To His Holiness the Dalai Lama who requested academics globally to research Traditional Indigenous educational practices and frameworks. We were requested then to weave them into our Modern Education System for the next generation of students.

© Office of His Holiness the Dalai Lama

CHAPTER ONE

Communicating Online and Student Self-Care

⌘

Naturally Joyful:

~ Fire element
Keeps us warm
Water element
Keeps us hydrated
Earth element
Keeps us whole
Wind Element
Keeps us moving
Space Element
Keeps us aware
These Sacred Elements
Are in us at all times
Perfect
Pure
Pristine
This knowledge
Keeps us
Naturally Joyful ~

Author Teaching on Remote Fly-in First Nation Community: (Kitchenmaykoosib Innuwagan)

Communicating online and internet publishing seems like a given since we are directly situated in the Digital Age. However, if we really think about it before the Digital Age our communication was very robotic in nature to which this book addresses the root causes in later chapters. Now, being forced to adapt to the e-Learning environments how can we communicate effectively online when our communication during face to face interactions was far from genuine or authentic in most cases? Especially, parents and students trying to communicate and publish their work online for their teachers and professors how can we improve or at least prepare our parents who are teaching from home and students whose grades are now totally dependent on communicating effectively and publishing online?

Write Intention:

- ✓ Review your email messages very diligently before sending a reply
- ✓ If the note is very important, complicated, or can be open to misunderstandings request an online digital conference instead
- ✓ Review to make sure you are sending your messages to the right person or group of people.
- ✓ Make sure if cc'ing certain people is necessary and perhaps write each person a separate note maybe more suitable.
- ✓ Try to avoid sending and forward messages to make another party look tardy, or unprofessional. Intention in physical interactions and digital communication still apply.

Assist Others in Understanding:

Your note or email is not the only one being received by your colleague, teacher, or supervisor.

- ➢ In the " Subject Line" try to clearly state the theme or topic of your note
- ➢ Try not to be confusing, write in a style that is attractive, logical and kind
- ➢ Write in bite sized paragraphs- space it out and separate each point with spacing

Publishing Online:

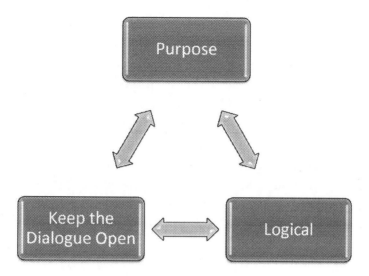

Be purposeful, logical and make to stay away from one-sided conversations online by keeping the dialogue open and ask questions to the reader online.

Unplug from the Digital World: Working online is quite efficient and six hours is not necessary when your teacher has prepared specific time slots for each lesson. You must make your own "recess" and breaks are just as important as the academic content itself for your health and wellness.

Seeing obstacles and road-blocks before they occur:

"There is currently a 'crisis' in education. This centers on the basic standards and the adequacy of progressive teaching methods. The controversy which is developing (and which is most noticeable for the virtual absence of the views of classroom teachers and complete absence of the views of the kids) is really a supremely ideological battle which only partially and through many distortions represents the real processes of class conflict, the reproduction of labor force, the cultural and general social processes of reproduction taking place on the site of the school." (Willis, 1977)

On this front not much has changed from this point since the teachers most likely have roots in the Middle Class and have greater amounts of Cultural Capital than certain segments of our population. Cultural Capital as defined as sharing the dominant cultural norms of a society being born in a Middle Class family, speaking English as our first language, having networks with other Middle Class and Upper Class members of our society, and live in Middle Class or Upper Class neighbourhoods. This cultural capital give an advantage to certain members of our society over other marginalized and low-socio-economic members of our society. These social assets are out of reach for the marginalized and low socio-economic students and these inequities are further amplified in the school setting

Parent and Student Wellness:

There is a whole new thrust in education and studies in business of the importance of Emotional Intelligence for our future students and workers entering the modern workforce. This chapter will look at Traditional education frameworks and curriculum from Indigenous societies to provide more perspective for future research.

From the Indigenous perspective everything is viewed in a Sacred Circle model so what is happening in our schools and workforce is quite natural to Indigenous Pedagogical lenses. This is because modern education and our modern education has hit the peak the climax of efficiency and results from the material perspective. So, according to all Indigenous Pedagogical Frameworks what "goes up, must come down" but not losing all that we have acquired in modern education and modern economies but we must adapt and keep the Sacred Circle going.

The highest running educational system and work system has us working very efficiently and achieving tremendous results. School and our Economy is results driven and the numbers tell the story. However, this was not sustainable. This text throughout its chapters will assist the modern educator, and parent combine Emotional Intelligence rooted in Indigenous Knowledge with Modern results oriented frameworks. After all we are human and not robots so using the analogy of recharging or restarting our education, our economies must look at emotional intelligence rooted in a new distinct age.

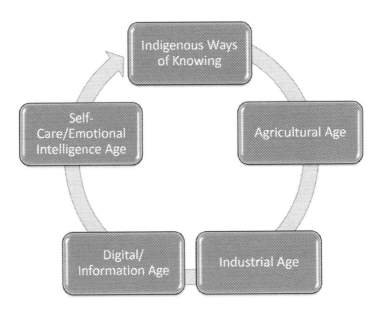

What we find is each Age does not disappear but it builds upon the next age. So, this Digital Age with Virtual Learning, online learning, the digital classroom must be blended with the Self- Care Age. Thus, the Self-Care Age must rely heavily on the original Indigenous Pedagogical Age which its education was very successful devoid of technology.

Our modern education system was already still frozen in time being developed during the Industrial Age. The students and workers who could act and perform like "robots" mechanical and who were able to memorize and download software by rote learning into their memory chips excelled in industrial age learning styles. But, what of our students who could not, or would not conform to this robotic " banking concept" of learning?

Now educators and parents have a vast array of resources to see what learning styles mesh well with their child and student. The "One Size Fits All" we all know now does not fit in the new age of Self-Care.

Emotional Intelligence is argued in this chapter as one having the ability to be conscience of, recognize, and share one's emotions, and in this way handle interpersonal relationships, school and work life making good life decisions and respond to others empathetically.

Emotional Intelligence in Action:

- Recognize, understand and manage our own emotions
- Recognize, understand and influence the emotions of others
    In practical terms, this means being aware that emotions can drive our behavior and impact people (positively and negatively), and learning how to manage those emotions – both our own and others – especially when we are under pressure.

When would I need to manage my Emotional Intelligence?

- Giving and receiving feedback
- Meeting tight deadlines
- Dealing with challenging relationships
- Not having enough resources
- Dealing with change
- Dealing with setbacks and failure (Destructive Emotions, Goleman).

CHAPTER TWO

Self-Care and the Digital Classroom

⌘

Thriving in the Digital Classroom: Creating Your Medicine Bundle

Traditionally in Indigenous societies a Medicine Bundle is where precious items were placed in pouch made of leather or strong material. This Medicine Bundles would have precious items in there from Elders, Knowledge Keepers and items placed that would protect your spirit, mind, and body. Here these frameworks are a Medicine Bundle or framework that can ground and keep one focused when trying to implement Intercultural Education today that will enhance education student success outcomes especially in this new age of online learning.

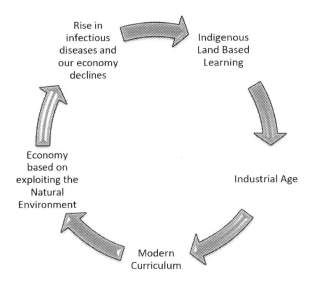

<u>Your Medicine Bundle:</u>

Teachers, Principals and Administration all most work together in all aspects of the school day and operation. The new teacher will rightfully focus a lot of her or his time on classroom management strategies. The three rules that I utilized as a new teacher were: 1. Respect yourself, 2. Respect others, and 3. Respect property. These three rules for our classroom worked very well and after time I realized these were vital to be expressed in the first day and enforced all year long. As long time education experts and parents reading this we all know how important classroom management has been throughout the years. But, as a reflective practitioner can we see historically classroom management as punitive in nature, meaning taking away privileges and punishing for incorrect behaviour. I want us to reflect on the root or the foundation of school and our systems, we take these for granted as timeless. In this first section we will look at: Indigenous Classroom Management rooted in Indigenous Restorative Justice Practices. The reason for this, is because myself as a new teacher and an experienced educator now I realize that I was more comfortable and naturally had the historic Western classroom management style but initially was connected to Indigenous Best Practices in Classroom Management.

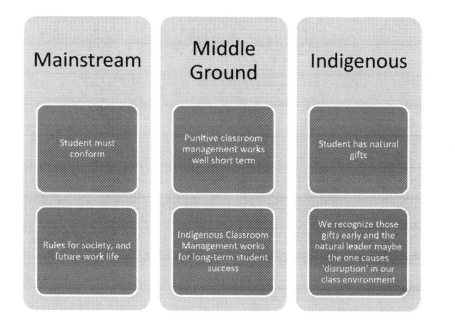

Indigenous Programming Quality Assurance Model:

What are the specific goals of classroom management? The ultimate goal is to create an environment that maximizes student learning.

Allocated versus Engaged Time:

One way you as a teacher can determine the results of your classroom management effectiveness is to critically examine how much time your students really have for learning in the classroom environment. Allocated time is the time you set aside and plan to utilize for learning. Engaged time is the time that students actually spend on learning. How does this relate to Emotional Intelligence? Throughout this text we will weave a web that connects Emotional Intelligence to all aspects of student wellness, learning and success.

"The brain is the last organ of the body to become anatomically mature; the progressive mental and social milestones of a child's development reflect its continued growth. The prefrontal areas are the last parts of the human brain to become fully mature, continuing to show anatomically growth into the mid-twenties and making life's early years a key window of opportunity to help younger people master the most helpful lessons of life." (Goldman, Destructive Emotions (2008).

In previous research we used these scientific findings to discredit the streaming system of our grade eight students when their emotional intelligence, brain development has not fully occurs until the their later years in high school. Having grown up in the school system and taught for many years in the system we all know of students who had the " light turn on" and excel in education in the later part of their high school career.

The Power of Circle Theory and Process: Cultural Wellness with Students Online

Indigenous People worldwide use the structure of the circle for education, council meetings, spiritual ceremonies, healing, sharing, learning and teaching.

The circle is holistic in that everyone has an equal opportunity to participate and each voice is valued and respected; what one individual shares in the circle is equally as important as any other.

In many Indigenous cultures, silence indicates respect; therefore, full participation requires an understanding of both oral and aural functions.

When a person shares in the circle, there is no interruption. Non-interference and the value of holistic active listening is most important.

Indigenous Academic Programming Quality Assurance Standards
Source: Aboriginal Healing Foundation (2005)

Indigenous Educational Practice Utilized in Program and Classroom Setting	Never	Regularly	Every Day
Healing Circles:			
When used in educational programs, the function of the circle is to re-connect learners with parts of themselves that have been injured and to connect with others. The most sacred learning arise out of the collective insights of those who fully participate in the circle of learning in a good way.			
Is a sacred practice using medicine such as sage, sweetgrass, cedar or tobacco, to cleanse people, the classroom, food and learning objects. Depending on the preference of the Elder or traditional healer, elements such as fire and water may be placed in the centre of the classroom circle to help the learners stay focused. Fire in the centre of a circle symbolizes and connects students to their own inherent inner sacred potential (fire).			

Indigenous Educational Practice Utilized in Program and Classroom Setting	Never	Regularly	Every Day

Giving Thanks Meditations:

Once all learners have been cleansed an Elder or traditional person may offer up an expression of thankfulness and hope for the gifts of Creation, affirming for those within the Circle their shared commitment to speaking, thinking and behaving in a good way.

Sacred Items:

Traditional People and Elders often use sacred objects, such as an eagle feather or talking stick, to guide the circle process. Other sacred objects used in the classroom are: the drum, pipe, drumstick and rattle.

Art and Dance Therapy:

In Inuit, Metis, and First Nation cultures, dance is a form of non-verbal expression that defines and strengthens at a personal level, while also honouring connections with community. Mainstream educational institutions are now recognizing dance as a form of therapy and a powerful way to destress and rejuvenate the mind, body and spirit.

Indigenous Best Practices

Indigenous Best Practices	This Practice is Absent	Regularly Implemented	Everyday

Physical Empowerment:

Is restored in healthy ways through

✓ Breathing and rest/relaxation techniques in Circle

    ✓ Medicine Walks

    ✓ Therapeutic Dance

    ✓ Support to manage wellness

✓ Traditional medicine that reduces anxiety and hyper-arousal

Mental Empowerment:

Is restored in healthy ways through

    ✓ Traditional Teachings

✓ Cognitive strategies, such as identifying symptoms and triggers and using daily journals, reflections, meditations or diaries to chart them

✓ Visualizing innovative and more hopeful outcomes of challenges in the learner's life

Emotional Empowerment:

Is restored in healthy ways through:

✓ Anger release and anger management techniques

    ✓ Art therapy

✓ Restoring pride in Indigenous identity, history and culture; and continuous affirmations of the learner's unique gifts, strengths and inherent dignity.

Indigenous Best Practices	This Practice is Absent	Regularly Implemented	Everyday

Spiritual Empowerment:
Is restored in healthy ways through any
opportunity to re-connect with the life
force or power of Creation through
✓ Meditation or prayer and giving thanks
   ✓ Participation in ceremonies;
✓ Consultation with respected Elders and/ or
Traditional People;
   ✓ Storytelling and legends;
  ✓ Chanting, singing or drum-dancing;
    ✓ Healing circles;
  ✓ Workshops for drum-making, wood
or stone carving, beading and craft-
making and
✓ Hunting or spending time on the land.

Indigenous Best Practices Check List
*Source: Aboriginal Healing Foundation (2005)

Faculty, Staff, Helpers, including Traditional People follow these essential protocols when relating to colleagues, clients, prospective parents, guardians, and learners:

- ✓ Offer unconditional compassion and support within a safe, confidential environment
- ✓ Understand holistic needs: provide resources for students that are culturally appropriate and support all aspects of well-being: mental, physical, spiritual, and emotional.
- ✓ Understand and role-model the Seven Teachings with learners and co-workers: love, trust, courage, honesty, bravery, respect, and honour.
- ✓ Use learner-centered approaches, the learner directs the healing journey, not the Faculty; move at the learner's pace trusting them to know their needs, and respect their choices.
- ✓ It is important that learners do not have to repeat the details of their trauma over and over again; becoming active listeners and more aware of their feelings will lead to positive change.
- ✓ Faculty, Staff and Traditional Peoples must walk their talk: we can only take our learners as far as we have gone on our own healing journeys.
- ✓ Active listening, positive feedback and attention to body language are crucial aspects of helping learners feel safe in the classroom.
- ✓ Minimize power imbalances between colleagues, staff, and learners.
- ✓ Respect diversity: understand different cultures and faiths, know your own roots. Assumptions and stereotypes based on gender, race, culture, sexuality, age and/or physical and mental ability serve to dis-empower and re-victimize clients and diminish the helper's effectiveness.

✓ Each staff member and learner is an individual: although patterns exist, it is important to recognize the unique resilience of each individual staff member, colleague, and learner.

✓ Every organization should have a Code of Ethics that all staff sign and agree to abide to. (The Seven Teachings can be used as guide.)

✓ Every organization should re-view its service environment through new eyes to assess whether, from an Indigenous perspective, it is a place of hope and belonging, (i.e., whether Inuit, Metis and First Nation People are represented, respected and welcomed there).

✓ Healing work is sacred work: learners deserve Faculty and Staff who honour their own healing paths and can model self-care and respect of the body, mind, heart and spirit.

Most experienced teachers arrive at the realization that our curriculum is a generic one, but an essential one that gives us a measuring stick a standard that gives us results. What really stands out is that our students are not generic they are all unique, and gifted in the real sense in so many ways. This is the crux of this text: how do we educate the whole child and how can we help administrators understand that the student must always be first in education systems? Through the monumental work of Bowles and Gintis(1976) Schooling in Capitalistic America states without hesitation that our school systems is founded on the business model, in fact they state our schools are based on the Factory-Model meaning our students are customers, and their parents are shareholders. If there groundbreaking thesis is correct we the educator, the police maker, the curriculum designer, the administrator really need to re-think education.

We can all agree that Mental Health and wellness is something our School Improvement strategies must embrace and there is a real sense of urgency of infusing Mental Health and Wellness in our Curriculum as soon as possible. The growing rates of perpetual bullying, anxiety, and depression in our students today. What is unique about this ground breaking academic text is that it only contains practical School Improvement Frameworks that have proven to work. Theory and practice are combined and a new pathway to school improvement is precisely displayed in a clear and concise way that any administrator, staff member, teacher or Faculty member can keep with them during their long career in the educational field.

Review Reflection:

1. In the box below sketch a mainstream standard classroom with desks, chairs and position of Teachers, and Educational Assistants. Has your perspectives on classroom management changed from reviewing this chapter?

2. In the box below sketch an Indigenous classroom format. Where is the teacher situated? Where are the educational assistants? Is there a Medicine Bundle in the middle of the class. Are the desks in straight lines or are the desks and chairs formed into a circle? How does this impact classroom management long-term, how does this impact genuine communication long-term for the entirety of the school year? How does this improve classroom attendance and engaged learning on a daily basis? What is your Medicine Bundle?

Notes:

_____

_____

_____

_____

_____

CHAPTER THREE

Social Justice and Digital Learning

⌘

Digital Learning has created an even more larger road block for marginalized and low economic students. Home environment and access to technology and internet are all major concerns facing this online learning trend.

In the mainstream studies of Paul Willis he argued that our school system really reinforce, the histories, and backgrounds of the student in school. The student will have a difficult chance if any to move beyond her or his current station in life in our school systems. In his highly influential research paper entitled: Learning To Labor: How Working Class Kids Get Working Class Jobs (1977) he adds weight to our assertion that the sociology of education needs to be taken more seriously in academia today. The social background of the student will greatly determine their future in the school systems they enter. The social economic background of the student will be in fact be largely predetermined to where they will land in the 'assembly line' of the school system. The school system regulates how they will perform in their school experience. This is why we argue we must foster and cultivate a spirit of love of learning and create welcoming spaces for our low-socio economic, marginalized, and Indigenous students. Our school systems for generations have failed these families in their long histories. This is why we truly celebrate a student who is the first one to enter college or university from their family; this is because they survived incredible odds. What if this marginalized student decides now to enter the teaching profession? These marginalized students who decide to enter the educational profession and become teachers will naturally help remedy many of the 'broken' school practices we have today.

From the Structural Functionalist Perspective: Teachers are the problem. As teachers we have made it through the system by being the most compliant to the system and by being such good students we have now actually became teachers. Teachers, who can now mold and colonize the future generations as well. We are colonized and we are assimilated. Now, people like the First Nations and other marginalized peoples who are not as easily integrated, how can we help them?

In my classes I had an important theme to share: we are all immigrants. We all have origins in other countries, the true Canadian or first people are the First Nations of this land. From this starting point it is amazing how much we can cover, discover and learn with our students.

"The teaching profession is portrayed as one which seeks to help children learn what they will need to know when they reach maturity. But its role in perpetuating the social relations of educational and economic production are seldom discussed or recognized by teachers or students." Rothstein(1991), pg.6[17]

Capitalism is inherently linked with our school systems and the hierarchical structure of our system creates many issues we have in education. If we are aware of the inherent conflict of power and control dynamics we can better prepare ourselves for a long and rewarding career in teaching.

If we are aware of the structures and forces that are arrayed against us we can not only teach our children but teach our peers, colleagues and supervisors.

"Children and teachers are unconscious robots who cannot understand what they are doing in their classrooms." Rothstein(1991) p.56 [19]

Unfortunately, this accounts for the conflict of Department Heads, Vice-Principals and Principals with teachers. Each one of us can only see from our own limited perspective.

Teachers Still Succeed Against All Odds:

From this Structural Perspective position of teachers, students, and parents are trapped into a caste like status and our school systems reproduce their status in our schools. What is most important according to this perspective was cultural capital. Depending on one's cultural capital will have the greatest influence on the success of the student in his or her future life.

"Streaming, grading, selecting, stigmatizing slow learners, and the rest are not pedagogically sound practices. They can only be understood when linked to the kind of social relations that exist in the workplace and social world of adults, when they assume their places in the social system's efforts to reproduce its economic and social relations."

Rothstein (1991), pg.149 [21]

In curriculum studies we investigate the statement: "Whose knowledge counts?" or what is the "hidden curriculum?" Is the hidden curriculum set out to silence the voice of the "other"? Rothstein arrives at this conclusion when he stated:

"Curriculum is presented to students as valid knowledge that has been legitimated by the best people in the state and society. These ideological presentation are presented as science, even though they have little to do with the scientific method and rest primarily on the traditions and mores of the more dominant classes in society."14 Rothstein, (1991), p.143 [22]

Emile Durkheim and Pierre Bourdieu both agreed that those individuals who were from the dominant group who shared the same language and culture of the educational system had the best prospects of doing well in our schools. They agreed that this was a structure where the school system sustained its structures and culture that it was meant to re-create.

This is why the quote below is so profound. If a teacher or administrator is not aware or has limited knowledge they can create much symbolic violence in our classrooms and schools. Niyozov (2009), Zine (2001).

Globalization: Education, Economy, Politics and Power

The so-called 'global culture' has largely reproduced the colonial structures of inequalities, with the postcolonial elite playing a major role in their reproduction.

The focus in on the cultural identity after colonization has taken place. The process of nations trying to create a national identity and the complex issues of trying to severe their history with the colonizer and the colonization that has taken place. The example of British India when the British left and India had to recreate its identity. Before British invasion India was able to exist with many diverse identities, world-views and religions. This diversity and rich cultural pluralism was the identity of India before colonization, however after the British Empire the divisions were magnified, by a divide and rule strategy that left India divided which lead to the partition on India.

The main aim of post-colonialism for educators is for us to see the side-effects of imperialism on people, countries and cultures. We are not only concerned with history, but how we can reconcile what has happened and create a world of mutual respect. The marginalized world-view, voice or people that have been invisible, need to be made visible and not only seen but understood. This is what it means to be an educator, the ability to really understand our students, our society and our world.

Imperialism is a method by which a people can use the words like 'liberating' people from a 'tyrannical' rule or by introducing the policies of a new 'superior' way of life. The foundation of imperialism is: greed, power and control.

Once we recognize these intricacies the Post-Colonial Perspective in education specifically it becomes a positive view-point. But only if teachers, policy makers, principals, directors of education, school board officials all work together. If we take this literally post means it is over or we have learnt something from the past era. We must move forward but also we must continue to educate so we are all aware of what has happened and to make sure this oppression is rectified. It recognizes a truth based in science and in our common understanding; we are one race: the human race. There is only one human family. Post-colonialism fights to decolonize our future and to recognize that we are all members of the human family and all problems are workable because we are the creator of these problems.

Summary:

The intent of this research was for us as educators to see how power, control, and politics shape our profession and schooling systems. What has happened because of this capitalistic creed that has permeated our modern culture; is that we constantly look down on each other, selfish motives, and are in constant competition with each other. This competitive nature can now be found between countries, states, provinces, school boards, schools, family members, siblings, and even between spouses in the realm of individual salaries. What is the meaning of this? All this competition and all this striving for material gain, fame, status and wealth we accumulate will all have to be left behind when one leaves the earth. From the individual level, or national level Mother Earth seen in a holistic way does not have lines differentiating countries. We should see one world, a world that is simple and natural but we humans have made this life more problematic and more confusing.

This is why as postcolonial educators we must stress the unifying principle of the human family and we must work together to solve educational, societal, and international problems. This higher awakening or consciousness arms us and our students with the wisdom and compassion to genuinely see that all human problems can be rectified because all human problems are human created from the beginning.

CHAPTER FOUR

Empathy and Educational Policy

⌘

Traditional Knowledge applied to policy studies: The intricate power dynamics that are at the core of policy studies and what perspectives are shared in policy should be researched more in depth. Policy is power and whose values and teachings are voiced in our policies today? Peoples and communities who possess this Traditional Knowledge should write, and control their own policy so this unequal power struggle can be healed in a progressive policy discourse. Traditional Knowledge is naturally inclusive. So many gaps in educational policy are remedied when Traditional Knowledge is applied to our academic policies.

For instance while teaching and taking the quantitative data from my year in the remote fly in community of Kasabonika Lake, First Nation, Ontario we discovered some real solutions to policy studies and curriculum studies.

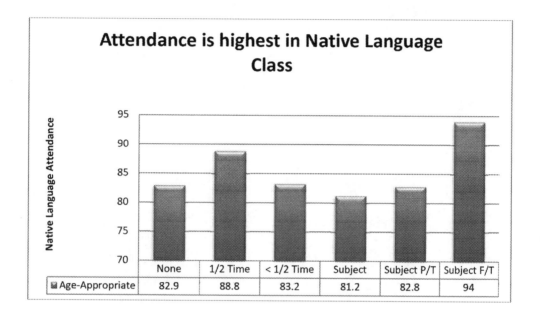

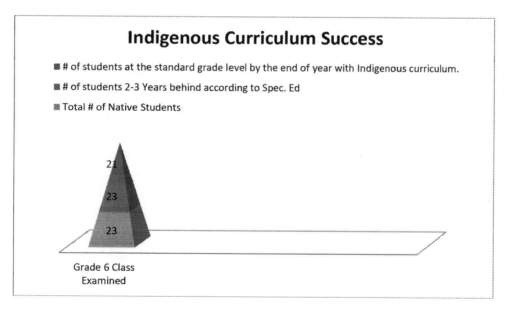

Creating Success and Breaking Barriers:

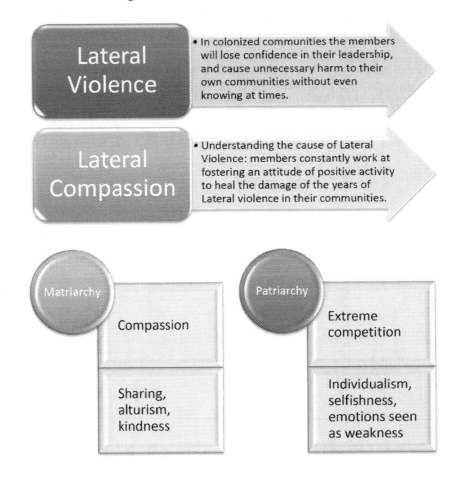

For decades First Nation, Metis and Inuit academics, and political leaders have been working for control of their own education system. This they believe will also secure self-determination for their peoples. In policy studies we know that policy is power, and if the Indigenous peoples are not able to control policy or at least have a voice in the creating and finalizing policy then they will be left out, not understood, or at worse the policy could actually cause more harm than good for their peoples. Policy as placebo is discussed in all higher learning institutes, and especially at OISE University of Toronto. Michelle Goldberg lectured on this extensively, and when I presented an Ontario First Nation Education Policy Framework document and used her Policy Placebo framework for this document it was a very enlightening experience. Policy Placebo essentially makes it look like the powers that be, were trying to understand the issue. In fact my mentor Michelle Goldberg stated policy is only created when there is problem to be remedied. So, policy will continue to be placebo for First Nations, Metis and Inuit until Indigenous voices are heard in the documents, and when the Indigenous have ultimate control over their own education systems, then they can write their own authentic policies for their own peoples.

Imagine First Nation, Inuit and Metis educational leadership in our schools today. Education would be seen in a new light. This begs the question to the modern practicing academic, policy maker or curriculum designer: What is education?

In present day academia there is not much scholarship on Indigenous knowledge and, the implementation of Indigenous knowledge, or emphasis on its importance in today's school or society. So, most graduate students in education will rely on the writings of Paulo Freire for citing scholarly citations in your work, and then expand on his thesis when directly relating to your specific field of school improvement strategies. This has much to do with his thesis where he depends on three main themes: Power, Control, and Role of Organizations play in structuring school systems. From there we can find answers to why some students historically do not do well in our school systems for generations. Here we can stop looking at the student as failing, but begin to look at the school that is failing certain important members of our student population for generations.

Here we see that leadership has an important role to play when discussing change and policy development in school systems. Leadership is directly linked to administration, community, power, authority, change, diversity, and value systems. The six types of leadership are: Instructional, transformational, moral, participative, managerial, and contingent forms of school leadership. (Leithwood,1999)

Pedagogy of the Oppressed by Paulo Freire was a monumental book written for administrators, policy-makers and teachers. He looked at leadership but also more importantly the necessity to change attitudes and find genuine solutions that are needed for students today. In that text Paulo Freire gives his definition of what education truly is. Essentially one must recognize that one is oppressed. One must also ultimately understand that the oppressors are also oppressed. The goal of true education is to recognize that one is oppressed and work toward gaining genuine liberation. But the education does not stop there, once you are thus liberated your true work is just beginning. Now as a true educator you must work to help others achieve the very liberation you have achieved and free everyone from the oppressive nature of our human created societies.

Paulo Friere was born on the northeastern coast of Brazil in the city of Recife in 1921. His family were devout Catholics. In his youth he was involved with social justice and joined the Catholic Action Movement in 1944. He was later employed by the National Literacy Program in Brazil. He had great influence there and inspired his students to such a degree that they became impassioned to change their society. Later the military gained control of the government in 1964, and he went into exile in Chile. Paulo Freire wrote this book for any human being who wanted to gain awareness of the oppressive nature we have in our societies. Specifically calling on administrators, and educators who hold power to transform and fix our world for the better. He wrote this book in the 1960s when he was a professor at Harvard.

The book had four chapters. Freire, commences his work by stating the rationale behind the Pedagogy of the Oppressed. He discovered the root cause of the oppression as our deterioration of our human values, human integrity and divine nature as human beings. Paulo Freire acts like a physician of the human condition where he diagnoses the ailment of our society. First, one must arrive at the realization that our schools are broken, and that our society is ill. Once one recognizes that our society is ill we must then seek out the cure. If one does not recognize that we are ill then one will not seek to find the antidote to the sickness. After he discovered the cure he gave us his diagnosis. He prescribed his diagnoses in four distinct but interconnected chapters.

Chapter One: You are Oppressed. This important chapter diagnosed the problem. Outlines why we are oppressed and how we can transcend this dichotomy of oppressor and the oppressed.

Chapter Two: Our School Perpetuate The Oppression. Here he described the 'banking' concept of education. Our schools actually perpetuate the inequality we have in our world. Education should be a quest to understand the world and the systems that create our suffering. Education is now viewed as a path to reclaim our humanity.

Chapter Three: The Awakening. Humanity awakens to the nature of reality. We arrive at this realization through critical reasoning, reflection, and investigation.

Chapter Four: There Is A Path To Freedom. Directly pin-points the methods utilized by the oppressor to keep the conquered oppressed. Thirst of Conquest, Divide and Rule, Manipulation and Cultural Invasion (Assimilation).

The Pedagogy of the Oppressed is unique because it is written from the perspective of the oppressed. However, it gives power to the oppressed because their voice is heard and articulated in an academic text. The teaching helps the oppressed, educators who teach the oppressed, and the privileged elites who are far removed from these everyday sufferings to see outside of themselves. One who is committed to human liberation, constantly seeks freedom within the systematic prison of this existence. However, to Freire, liberation is not an escape, but he advises us to live within it, in order to gain he wisdom to better transform it.

There has been much scholarship discussing the critiques of this work. Which lead Paulo Freire to write a follow-up book entitled: "Pedagogy of Hope" to address some of these critiques and to elaborate on his thought and teaching. Some of the critique is focused on gender and that his language was from a masculine perspective (Sandra Tan, 1998 OISE UT). However, the main point of the his argument was that we are ALL oppressed and interdependent. No matter if you are a woman, man, black, white, marginalized, or a member of the privileged class- we are all oppressed.

This work however, does utilize the same language as the colonizer or the oppressor. Even though Freire was against colonization and imperialism he still utilized the same terminology as the imperialists. The key term: "Liberation." This term is the word used by the imperialists as a justification to rule and conquer the people indigenous to the lands. The imperialists who view other cultures and peoples from a limited own point of view. They view themselves as the liberator to save the "savages" from their ignorant ways and beliefs.

Paulo Freire was heavily influenced by a school of theology within Christianity, particularly the Roman Catholic Church called Liberation Theology. The teaching of Jesus Christ is rooted in social justice and the duty to transform the world. Christ who preached that one should love your enemies and to perform virtue to those who wrongfully hurt you. (Matthew 5:44). Liberation Theology is founded on the Christian mission or duty to bring justice to the marginalized or oppressed. This was the worldview of the author, however the author failed to address the fact that imperialism utilized a distorted form of Christianity to legitimize conquest, rule and brutal occupation of people and land. (Martin Carnoy, 1974). Christian missionaries believed they were on a divine mission to civilize the world. These activities were directly responsible for oppression, and exploitation of humans and natural environment. The Christian missionary work coupled with the exploitative creed of capitalism has created the problem of oppressive structures, class struggle, stratified society, and economic disparities we see today.

Paulo Freire literary style is conversational in nature and the reader gets a genuine sense of the author. However, using this style of dialogue he chooses the direction the conversation goes. As mentioned earlier, the role organized religion was also utilized wrongly by humans to rule over others, and how religion viewed in the wrong way is seen as a tool to further divide us still. Along these same lines one wishes that he would have addressed the propaganda, and media that perpetuate this first world nation status versus the third world status dichotomy. Today our society has the wrong-view that third world poverty as a timeless condition. The wrong belief that third-world countries are poor, infertile, and peoples unproductive and lazy. This is incorrect. Third world countries in the continents of Africa, Asia, and South America have long been rich with abundantly wealthy with precious minerals, precious stones and abundant natural resources. This is the reason imperialists went through all the trouble to steal and plunder them. The author should have outlined that developing nations are now impoverished but it was not always this way.

So what are administrators, policy-makers, educators and people of conscience to take away from this book written by Paulo Freire? Well for specific examples of oppression, social stratification, and colonialism one should refer to Martin Carnoy, Ellwood Cubberly and Richard Scott. However, the purpose of this author was to talk directly to the reader and discuss in general terms to include all peoples. No matter if one is rich or poor, believer or non-believer, black or white, man or woman. He wanted us to recognize our oppression. This book will remain a classic as he discovered the major illness of our human predicament. The human sickness of: greed, thirst for power, status and control. Colonization has created the injustices in the world and American imperialism is in full power today. However, no longer using Christianity as its liberating tool, but now using the new catch phrase of spreading "democracy" throughout the world. So, this work is highly relevant as the bullies of the world are still looking to stay on top of this human created hierarchy.

"In cultural invasion it is essential that those who are invaded come to see their reality with the outlook of the invaders rather than their own; for the more they mimic the invaders, the more stable the position of the latter becomes. For cultural invasion to succeed, it is essential that those invaded become convinced of their intrinsic inferiority."

The divisions, war, deception, injustice, pollution, poverty, racism, bigotry, human slavery, discrimination, and bullying we see from one person to person and nation to nation are totally human created. Freire, focused on the root cause of our society as the deterioration of our fundamental human values. Our natural divinity as human beings has been obscured by our greed, manipulation, exploitation, injustice, violence and oppression. Through these systematic methods to gain power, the oppressor erases the human dignity of the oppressed. This has a cyclical effect: the oppressed do not see any viable alternative way to get 'power' and control, but to emulate the oppressor. However, we must have compassion for the oppressors because their behavior is a learned one as well. Freire asked us to wake up and inform both separate but connected groups of oppressed and oppressor to see their true reality. In order to be truly free and to have true power which is freedom one must reclaim their humanity. The responsibility is one the oppressed to liberate themselves and also to liberate their oppressor.

Main Stream Worldview: Is Human-Centered

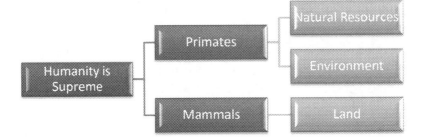

Indigenous Knowledge: Everything is Connected and Equal

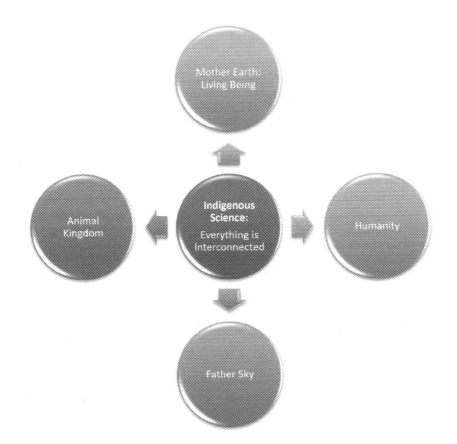

CHAPTER FIVE

Multi-Cultural Student Wellness

First Published in: The Human Family (2008)

Faculty and International Department Quality Assurance Checklist:

International Learning Outcomes (ILO's) International Quality Assurance.

International Cultural Practices introduced in Curriculum, Classroom or International Departments	Never	Regularly	Everyday Priority
International Role Models International Worldviews: Quotes, sayings, teachings, biographies. Cultural significant days, months, and importance recognized.			
Cultural Potlucks with diverse Nations cuisine.			
Invite International Cultural Leaders into the campus or online environments engage in meditation, Traditional Teachings and Practices.			

Art and Dance Therapy: These are forms of non-verbal expression that defines and strengthens at a personal level, while also honouring connections with community. Mainstream educational settings are now recognizing dance as a form of therapy and a powerful way to distress and rejuvenate the mind, body and spirit.			
International Cultural Symbolism visually seen in classrooms and digital classrooms, throughout the digital platforms.			
Lead breathing meditation focusing on diverse cultural practices: Jain, Sikh, Hindu, Buddhist, Muslim practices.			
Flags visible in International Platforms.			

Questions:

1. What is a worldview?

2. How can we consistently implement these international learning outcomes on a monthly basis?

3. What is the International Education Model?

4. How does this model guarantee International Student Success, Retention, Graduation Rates and Increased Enrollment Rates?

Notes:

_____

_____

_____

_____

_____

_____

_____

_____

_____

_____

The rise in international students enrolling in our high schools, colleges and universities in Canada for instance is a relatively new phenomenon. Our international students pay three times the amount as our domestic students in our schools here in Canada. This could add weight to the argument that schools have becoming more and more seen as businesses but, are our teachers and schools prepared for our new international students? We need professional development for our Canadian teachers, professors and deans. This chapter is designed to help the Canadian educator who most likely has never left the shores of Canada, and may have a difficult time connecting with their international students in their classrooms. The main points are that even though our international students speak another language, their reading and writing could be better and equal to our domestic students. Why is this so? Colonization once again, since Britain colonized most of the lands where our international student originate from, their home nations have adopted the British or French systems long ago, since Britain and France where the main colonizers of the early 19th century. In this way issues of academic integrity will not come into play, since our international students for the most part have already embraced English educational models from their home country. Academic integrity was a huge issue before the arrival of international students, where institutions accused African American and African Canadian students of academic integrity throughout campuses in North America many of the claims were fought and won, and essentially the bias and discrimination of the teacher was the key factor in the false claims against students of colour.

Professional Development for Faculty and Staff:

A Glimpse Into The Muslim World

Sir Sayyid Ahmad Khan is an excellent life to study when seeing a successful Muslim leader who blended modern and traditional ways of knowing in his life journey. What are the obstacles facing Muslim International students today? From the historical point of view the main obstacle facing Muslim leadership was during British Rule in India. Two worlds collided at this time and this research shows how his leadership helped secure Muslim identity during this trying time in India's history. This research will examine how Sayyid Ahmad Khan protected Islam and made it stronger by using those tenets found in the Koran that meshed with modern scientific development. We will also analyze Sayyid Ahmad's contributions to the growth of Muslim self-consciousness and identity in British India in the late nineteenth century. This research will be three-fold in organization, these three phases are a) Religion, b) Muslim Reformer, and c) British Imperialism. He wanted to rationalize Islam so they could compete against the constant attacks of the British Imperialists. Rationalism was needed in order for the Muslims in the sub-continent to survive.

a) As a student of comparative religion, Sir Sayyid Ahmad Khan had a great understanding and admiration for all religious doctrines. We will now broadly examine his belief or concept and purpose of religion. From his contact with Christian and Hindus, Sir Sayyid Ahmad Khan learned to see beyond the realm of his own religious tradition. He knew very well that what was true for him was not necessarily true for others. But through his vast wisdom he knew what the purpose of religion was. This is clearly seen when he stated:

"Religion is important because it is natural to man, because it helps man, reforms him, if it does not serve this purpose it cannot be true." 28

He was aware that there are many different religions in this world, but each of them has its own special qualities, its own unique way of presenting the spiritual path. The aim of developing true friendship, brotherhood, love and respect for others is something, which is the essence to be found in all religions. Religion contributes toward achieving peace of mind and tranquility, but it is not necessary for a person to be a follower of a particular religion in order to achieve it. All religions have the same potential to help humankind although they differ in philosophy. This rational way of thinking is clearly seen when he stated:

"Religion is the name of that differentiation which relates to the conduct of human beings. In the light of which human actions are judged right or wrong or neither right or wrong. Without the judgment of human action there can be no religion, what people call religion is man's inborn nature, so there is no person without it, nor is, nor will be."29

He believed religion to be natural to humanity or part of one's inborn nature. The idea of religion is not learned or acquired; it is inherent. Religion has been viewed by Sayyid Ahmad Khan as innate in human nature and essential for one's moral well being.

b) Sayyid Ahmad Khan as Muslim Reformer: He had a very modernist interpretation of Islam. In this second phase we will examine and give reasons for his unique interpretation. We will also examine Sir Sayyid Ahmad Khan's great contributions to the growth of Muslim self-consciousness, leadership and identity in British India in the late nineteenth century. Ultimately, we will understand how his findings can contribute to the appreciation and respect deserved to true practitioners of the Muslim faith around the world. Just as the Lord Jesus Christ was attacked unjustly during his ministry, today the Muslim is being attacked unjustly and we as educated and enlightened people must stand up for our Muslim brothers and sisters.

In religious matters, the Koran, the Hadith and the Shari'a (Islamic Holy Law) should be re-examined to see if they relate to the changing modern world. His main aim was to attain an interpretation of Islam, which, could withstand the attacks on religion from the side of modern scholarship. This development of Ahmad Khan's religious thought can be seen after his steadily increasing contact with the West. There is no doubt that Ahmad Khan held human reason as supreme. He was looking for a new interpretation of Islam, which would make it possible for the Muslim youth to remain faithful to their religious convictions. Although Sayyid Ahmad Khan's reformative movement was socio-ethical and educational, he fully realized that the reformation of Muslim India required a change in the religious attitudes of the people. His main task was of religious reforms and this also depended on, social, educational, moral, cultural, and scientific revival, reformation and awakening of the Muslims of India. Sir Sayyid Ahmad Khan stated:

"The idea called religion is born in the heart without any external causes, experience or examination or without any rational proof. The heart is its base and the belief in it is more certain that in objects perceived." 30

He disliked dogmatism of the Muslim scholars, which he believed was hindering the progress of the Muslim community and the nineteenth century youth who were exposed to Western scientific development and learning. He wanted to save his future brethren from dogmatism. If they did not accept the scientific knowledge that the West had to offer then, the Muslims would continue to decline and will continue to be viewed as "backward" peoples. He wanted them to be educated, civilized, tolerant but to live as Muslims. His question, then was not, which philosophy of Islam is true, but which philosophical outlook would help Muslims of India to rise above the state of decadence. To Ahmad Khan humans are at the center of the universe. So, his thought revolves around humankind and our problems. Firstly, as a society, the Indian Muslims were faced with many problems. He therefore examined their problems and to identify the internal and external causes of their degeneration and gave them a path to rise and excel. He fully realized the problems were fundamentally cultural and social in essence.

"Thinking that man has much more to do than animals, I thought the Great Creator who created man more helpless than even animals, with such a lot of difficulties in his way, must have given him something to overcome all these difficulties. My heart named it 'Reason'." 31

Reason, understanding and free will are the main capabilities, potentialities or talents of humanity as we have examined earlier. His respect for reason and understanding remained constant throughout his life. He stated:

"After a lot of thinking. And meditation about what it is that is acquired by reason. I got the idea that it is knowledge, which means cognition. At this stage I understood that what I have to do above all other animals is to know the reality of all things. I realized that knowledge and certainty/belief (Yageen) are necessary for each other. When I have knowledge of something I can be certain about it. And what I am certain of is known to me. So I decided that there can be no certainty without knowledge and knowledge without certainty."29

Again nothing can be accepted out of blind-faith. Knowledge is held supreme and this clearly seen when one studies the Koran. In various lectures and writings he tried to prove that in its essence the Koran, the word of God, was entirely consistent with the laws of nature, which was created ultimately by God. He tried to show his contemporary Muslim brethren that new scientific knowledge was directly related to the teaching of Islam. The core of Sayyid Ahmad Khan's views about human capabilities however is his concept of open-mindedness and understanding. Reason is important, but it is already there as human's inborn natural faculty, knowledge is acquired by humankind but what is important to know is, how to use this faculty of reason, to apply the knowledge acquired. This practical and applied form of reason is what Sayyid Ahmad Khan deemed important. This is what he believed his peoples lacked and this is what was needed most for their development and reform.

"Just an understanding or wisdom is distinctive perfection, hypocrisy is the greatest evil. The climax of goodness is understanding and the climax of evil is hypocrisy."30

A person of understanding dislikes wrong views, deceitfulness, superstition and blind-faith. He believed his people had to take the knowledge of their ancestors and progress naturally with the times and not remain stagnant, they had to stop living in Islam's glorious past.

"This idea is very mis-leading. Our ancestors also had their ancestors. But they with their efforts achieved more than their ancestors before them. They strived and put hard work, researched and discovered many treasures of knowledge on their own. They modified and developed what they discovered and made their treasures beautiful and attractive. If those people were still alive or we who are their inheritors, were busy in developed their arts and sciences, we would have taken their knowledge and culture to a very high level. We would have discovered many new treasures from the deep ocean of knowledge. But we have done nothing. We have lost their possessions also. So that when we are awake again and attend to our progress and development, first of all we should find out what other people have done when we were in our slumbers of ignorance. What levels have been reached in the development of knowledge and culture. Whatsoever nation is the master and possessor of the wealth of knowledge, we should extend our hand toward it." 32

They had to move on and be leaders of tomorrow. So, the model of a cultured society that he had in mind was naturally of the British nation. Since, Sir Sayyid Ahmad Khan was an optimistic and rational person he believed since they had access to this Western learning, they could learn from them easily. Through visionaries like Sayyid Ahmad Khan, Indian thinkers found a window to western thought, from which they were isolated thus far. This was a new phenomenon in an area which has been too traditional, too conservative and too authoritarian in thought. Naturally, he generated an immediate reaction amongst the orthodox Muslims, still, he opened the way for a critical approach to Islamic and with him started an attempt to assimilate the modern western thought with Islamic thinking. Through his leadership abilities he created a new Muslim Identity, and he rationalized Islam so it could compete not just with the British, but ultimately with the modern world. Today we see so much hatred and animosity with the Muslim world and the Western world, but if we are rational we must see we are all interconnected. We only have one planet to share and must learn to live with each other. This is his vision of his times and needs to be achieved for the betterment of the world as a whole. Humanity's greatest guide is reason which enables us to differentiate between what is positive and what is negative. There is no doubt religion is based on an institution of faith, but it would be incorrect to think that reason is no use in religious concerns. During Sayyid Ahmad's time there was an anti-rational tendency among the orthodox ulema, which criticized the application of reason in comprehending religious problems. Their argument was that human reason is imperfect and therefore, what God and the Prophet reveal are without a doubt perfect. He did not agree to this outlook and he was fully conscious of the growing discontent among the educated younger generation of Muslims who were more likely to believe only what satisfied their reason. Besides as we noted earlier, religion's purpose is to help us sentient beings cope with this harsh world, if the religion cannot guide us through reason then it is ultimately powerless. Sayyid Ahmad Khan believed that times had changed and even the illiterate were eager to comprehend the problems with the aid of reason to common sense, and therefore only a rationalistic explanation could help in the precarious situation in which the Muslims were living. Reason liberates us from the bonds of tradition and custom, it enables one to create a new path consistent with the demands of one's inherent nature, and endows one with an independence, which otherwise would have been impossible. He was a great admirer of science and scientific knowledge and he believed that this knowledge is essential for the advancement of communities. European nations have become great on account of their reliance on science. As a pious Muslim, he could not reject the compelling superiority of faith and reason. The Prophet himself said " Knowledge is the heritage of the believer, and that he should acquire it wherever he can find it." [33]

The Prophet Muhammad also said that the Muslims should seek knowledge even in China to find it. So rationally the Muslims should seek knowledge from the British. So, as a modern reformer, he could not deny that scientific knowledge was essential for the rise and development of a community. His attempt was to reconcile the two and preached that religion is not opposed to science but its completion.

c) The Importance of British Rule: Hindu and Muslim peaceful co-existence only possible under British Rule. By examining the writings and speeches of Sir Sayyid we can conclude that he never used the word nation in the technical sense of the term, and never considered the Muslims and Hindus as two separate nations. One can clearly see, that there is no speech of Sir Sayyid which reveals that he ever thought Hindus and Muslims are separate nations. He sincerely wanted them to live in unity.

"The English nation came into this conquered country of ours like a friend, not a foe. It is our earnest desire that the English Rule in India should last not only for a long, long time but that it should be everlasting and eternal. The desire of ours is not for the sake of the English nation itself, but for the sake of our own country; it is not for the sake of the English people but its is for the prosperity and welfare of our own country" [34]

When discussing the necessity of the unity of the Muslim and Hindu nations he asserted:

"One cannot live without the cooperation of the other. If united, we can sustain each other, if we are disunited, it would lead to the destruction and downfall of both." [35]

He feared that great horrors would occur if the British were to leave India to govern herself. That is why Sir Sayyid was against the nationalistic aims of the Indian National Congress Party. He believed that the highest progress, could only be achieved through peaceful relationships between the Muslims and Hindus under continued British Rule. So essentially, he believed that British rule in India was fate an act of God. It was nothing negative, now Islam and the Hindus could progress and learn from what Western education had to offer.

He asserted:

"The adoption of the new system of education does not mean the renunciation of Islam it means its protection." [35]

But, the Muslims at this time would not cooperate with their English rulers. He again stated:

"If we go with our present obstinacy in neglecting it (Western education), we shall be left far behind. How can we remain true Muslims or serve Islam, if we sink into ignorance." [36]

His plan was two-fold: he wanted to show the British that the Muslims were loyal and to educate his own people that it was in their best interest to learn from the West. He believed such continued resistance on the part of the Muslims would only weaken them, therefore, in order to make the Muslims progress and advance, he asked them to change their traditional ways and support liberal ideas. He wanted the assimilation of Western ideas and education. Now with the development of science, things began to be tested with reason and even religion could not escape examination. He himself did not accept Islam because he was born a Muslim but because he tested it with reason, and had he had even the slightest doubt about the truth of Islam, he would have deserted it.

Here we have examined a positive outlook on how to deal with imperialism. The essence of all religion is to be endowed with the ability to turn a negative situation into a positive one. This is what Sir Sayyid was able to achieve for his Muslim brothers and sisters under the British Rule in India. His goal was to rationalize Islam so they could compete with the modern scientific world. The Muslims had to stop living in the past and move on. To him, it was a shame that both Hindus and Muslim nations whose ancestors had been so enlightened and educated had disgraced their ancestors by their ignorance. To him they lived under the protection of the English which has given them security. They should be thankful to their government which had given them unique opportunities in the realm of education. The truth is, Islam would prosper greatly if its believers were well educated in the matters of the modern world; it would decline if its followers were not willing to change with the times.

The Hindu World

Most have not heard of Ram Mohan Roy. Ram Mohan Roy is an another excellent example in how his traditional world embraced the modern world. Why did the Brahmo Samaj and Ram Mohan Roy fail to achieve world historical status? Why did they maintain only a modest or marginal social presence throughout its history? We will examine and give a sociological explanation of the social-historical trajectory of the Brhamo Samaj. This research will examine the Brahmo's contributions to the growth of Hindu self-consciousness, leadership and identity in British India in the nineteenth century. This research will be four-fold in organization, these four phases are a) A basic history of the Brahmo Samaj, b) Religion, c) Hindu Rationalism and d) The reason for the marginal social presence throughout its history. The Brahmo Samaj wanted to rationalize Hinduism so that it could compete with the influx of British Imperialism and thus the modern scientific world.

a) Basic History of the Brahmo Samaj: This Hindu religious sect was founded by Ram Mohan Roy. The members of the sect, the faith of which is based on the ancient text of the Vedas, they believed in the worship of one God and were against superstition and idol worship. He was a social reformer as well as a religious leader, Ram Mohan Roy assisted in the abolition of the practice of sati(widow burning) in India.

What made Ram Mohan Roy stand above his peers, was his rationalistic mind and strong leadership qualities. He studied many religions, and worked for social reform and women's rights. He was the founder of the Brahmo Samaj in 1828, which was originally called the "Brahmo Sabha". It rejected idol worship and the worship of many gods and goddesses of traditional Hindu beliefs. Ram Mohan Roy was influenced by western thinking, especially Sufism and Christianity.

His successor as leader of the Brahmo Samaj was Debendranath Tagore, he laid down the principles that the Vedas are not perfect, that true religious faith is based on intuition and nature, that moral righteousness is most vital, and that rituals, and caste distinctions have no religious value. Debendranath Tagore took leadership of the Brahmo Samaj after the passing of Ram Mohan Roy. Tagore took an active interest in the Brahmo Samaj, and began to transform the Brahmo Samaj into spiritual organization. His main focus was on the Upanishads one of Hinduism's ancient books.

b) The Religious Beliefs of the Brahmo Samaj: As a student of comparative religion, Ram Mohan Roy had a great understanding and admiration for all religious doctrines. We will now broadly examine his belief or concept and purpose of religion. From his direct contact with Christians, Muslims and Buddhists, Ram Mohan Roy learned to see beyond the realm of his own religious tradition. He knew very well that what was true for him was not necessarily true for others. But through his vast wisdom he knew what the purpose of religion was. This is clearly seen when he stated:

"That the true system of religion is what leads its observers to a knowledge and love of God, and to a friendly inclination towards their fellow-creators, impressing their hearts at the same time with humility and charity, accompanied by independence of mind and pure sincerity." [37]

He was well aware that there are many different religions in this world. But, each of them has its own special qualities, its own unique way of presenting the spiritual path.

The purpose of religion is to develop a kind heart, a feeling of closeness for all human beings. The goal of developing genuine friendship, love, brotherhood, and respect for others is something, which is the essence to be found in all religions. Religion contributes toward achieving peace of mind and tranquility, but is not necessary for a person to be a follower of a particular religion in order to achieve it. To Ram Mohan Roy, these inner qualities are really human qualities. If we have these--- compassion, love and respect for others, honesty and humility—then we can call ourselves genuine human beings. Basically all major religions of the world carry the same message, therefore harmony between different religions is both important and necessary. All religions have the same potential to help humankind although they differ in philosophy. This rational way of thinking is clearly seen when he stated:

"Moral doctrines, tending evidently to the maintenance of the peace and harmony of mankind at large, are beyond the reach of metaphysical perversion, and intelligible alike to the learned and to the unlearned. This simple code of religion and morality is so admirably calculated to elevate men's ideas to high and liberal notions of one God, who has equally subjected all living creatures, without distinction of cast, rank, or wealth, to change, disappointment, pain, and death, and has equally admitted all to be partakers of bountiful mercies which he has lavished over nature, and is also so well fitted to regulate the conduct of the human race..." [38]

Thus, he believed in religion as natural to humanity's or part of one's inborn nature. The idea of religion is not learned or acquired; it is inherent. Religion has been viewed by Ram Mohan Roy as innate in human nature and essential for one's moral well-being. There are different religions among different peoples, and everyone believes that one's religion is the only true one. Ram Mohan Roy believed that true religion does not hinder the progress and development of humanity because God would not desire that His creations should degenerate and decline. If He the Creator had wanted to degrade humanity, then there would be no reason to create humans. So this sets the foundation for the next topic, that of Ram Mohan Roy's role as Hindu reformer.

As we know India had a very early confrontation with Imperialism. The imperialism of the British in India was very cruel and demeaning. Indian intellectuals had to find a way to defend their views, identity and spirituality against this onslaught of capitalism masked in the form of 'Christianity'. Today Muslims need to find ways to ways to meaningful defend themselves from the Imperialism of America. We only hope the true religious leaders of Islam start to make their voices heard an provide solace for their people. We do not need to look to far to see the plight of our First Nation brothers and sisters in Canada and America. Here is an example how a Hindu successfully defended his beliefs and spirituality in the face of British invasion of his country.

Roy was a man before his times. He contributed to the growth of Hindu self-consciousness and identity in British India in the late nineteenth century. The leaders of all the different branches of the Brahmo Samaj believed that the Hindus had to adapt to the ways of the Western world and so they urged the Hindus to accept new forms of education and scientific training.

"The more deeply they were imbued by English education with a humanitarian outlook, the more keenly sensitive they became when faced with missionaries' charge that Hinduism was a pagan and idolatrous religion, laden with barbarous customs. In order to defend Hinduism, therefore, they first had to reform it." 39

The Hindus were confronted with Christian Missionaries just like the First nations of Canada, but how did they successfully defend their religious and spiritual traditions? The leadership of Ram Mohan Roy instructed that the Hindu masses abandon their traditional notions of authority in all areas of life. Their rationalism meant that all ideas had to be re-tested and debated. No Hindu dogma was to be accepted through blind-faith and all tenets of Hinduism were to be re-evaluated. In religious matters, the Vedas, the Upanishads, should be re-examined to see it they relate to the changing modern world. Their main aim was to attain an interpretation of Hinduism, which could withstand the attacks and judgment on religion from the side of modern scholarship. The development of the Brahmo Samaj religious thought can be seen after their steadily increasing contact with the west. Debendranath Tagore stated:

"We base our faith on the fundamental truths of religion, attested by reason and conscience and refuse to permit man, book, or image to stand in the way of the direct communion of our soul with the Supreme Spirit." 40

No matter what the name of the higher power all is God or Cosmic Mind: God, Brahma (Hindu), Allah(Muslim), Nirvana(Buddhist), or Great Spirit (Native Spirituality) we are all connected to this reality.

"Even though their efforts primarily affected only the Western-educated (a tiny fraction of the total mass of Hindu society), this minority nevertheless possessed an influence far greater that its numbers would indicate. For they provided the leaders of the future—the Tagores and the Gandhis—whose understanding of their Hindu heritage was decisively shaped by that galaxy of religious thinkers who had preceded them in the nineteenth century."41

The impact of the Brahmo Samaj may seem small but these great thinkers would give rise to future thinkers such as Mahatma Gandhi who would later influence Martin Luther King jr. and His Holiness the 14th Dalai Lama of Tibet and countless others. So, the impact of the Brahmo Samaj is quite significant.

The Jain World

The Jain Faith Tradition is one of the oldest living traditions of the world. Jain philosophy is an Indigenous system of knowing from the sub-continent of India. Here academic administrators and, teachers of International students can learn to appreciate the ancient policy perspectives of the Jain Indigenous spiritual tradition of India.

The term Jaina means the one who follows the Jinas (Spiritual Leaders). Jinas are followed because they have won victory over the passions of attachment, and aversion and other hindrances that defile the soul. Since these spiritual teachers have this attainment they are in a state of supreme bliss and are now omnipotent. The leaders of this tradition are enlightened human teachers.

Mahatma Gandhi was a practitioner of the Jain spiritual tradition. Here he was successful in utlizing the ancient Jain doctrine of Ahimsa (non-violence) and won independence of his country India from the British Empire in 1947. What is signnificant is how the founder of this faith tradition carried this doctrine of Ahimsa not only in the physical realm but took the philosophy of Ahimsa (non-violence) into the realm of human dialogue and discourse. In order for dialogue or policy to be genuine the intent must be pure or non-violent in order to achieve true results.

Brief History of Mahavira:

Mahavira was born in 599 B.C. In a royal family in Kshatriyakunda (Modern Bihar). At the age of thirty, he began his quest to find freedom from all misery that exists in our worldly existence. After twelve years of tremendous self-discipline, physical austerities, and rigorous meditation, he finally eradicated attachment and attained the state of omniscience(Kevalajnana). The essence of Jain thought is the belief in teh innate purity of the soul or consciousness. The love for truth is innate in each living being, but one needs spirtual training for it to fully blossom into fruition. In the realm of leadership the doctrine of Ahimsa is most significant. Ahimsa is not mere human pity, it is the ability to generate genuine empathy, the sincere effort to identify oneself completely with other peoples suffering and human predicament. Mahavira said:

"If you kill someone, it is yourself you kill.
If you overpower someone, it is yourself you overpower.
If you torment some one, it is yourself you torment.
If you harm someone, it is yourself you harm." (Mahavira, 599 B.C.)

Ahimsa: Non-violence

"The Jaina claim not to be Ekantavadin, those who look at things from one point of view, but Anekantavada, those who look at things from various points of view." 42

The essence of Jainism is non-violence. In the realmof leadership it is essential to sincerely listen and emphathize with others views. In Jainism one is advised to adhere to the wisdom that there is always grain of truth in what another person says or believes. Just as one has full belief in what is truth from their point of view, so too one should respect the view-points of others. This is the doctrine created by Mahavira. He named it the Anekantavada (The Theory of Many-Sidedness). This way of thinking is practical when working in administration and when leading others for it enables one to tolerate and encompass a vast range of view-points in a spirit of co-operation even if the views are totally opposite. Therefore he took the principle of Ahimsa and extended it to the realm of human dialogue, and discourse. One is not to impose one's views on others, and one should try to blend the views of others with one's own. This ancient principle of Anekantavada focuses on respecting the views of others, the thoughs of others, and through following this method genuine discourse and policy implementation can take root. The adherence of this principle can help policy makers and educational leaders in genuinely understanding the views, philosophies, concerns, systems, ideologies, and histories of others. Therefore, the Anekantavada doctrine can be a method for promoting genuine dialogue, unityand mutual respect in our world.

The Jain logic system of Anekantavada is founded on diversity, unity; reality like truth are both definite-indefinite (anekanta). There is no ultimate reality, and there can be no ultimate truth. If there were a concept of ultimate truth it would be a many-sided truth as this the correct method to see the world.

Transcending Dualism:

Mahavira was aware of the dualistic nature of our world: discussing often the dualistic concepts of right and wrong, purity and defilement, love and hate etc. In regards to Ahimsa (Non-violence) and Himsa(Violence) there is also a duality and he took this further in his doctrine of Anekantavada (many-views) and Ekanta(one-view). Anekantavada is both Anekantavada and Ekanta. Anekantavada shows all possible sides of a topic and therefore does not make a judgement about any topic, or event in any concrete way. What is unique is that the Anekantavada view itself is also prone to become a one-sided view as well. In this way Jain scholars do not believe this contradicts Jain principles even if Anekantavada becomes one-sided because, this only strengthens the point and shows the power and relevance of the doctrine.

"Jainism came in time to see action as truly violent when accompanied by lack of care (pramada)." [43]

In the realm of policy studies having policy makers who do not genuinely want to solve existing problems, or create further obstacles perpetuated through policy can cause much violence in an indirect way. Policy makers must emphasize with the people the policy is going to effect in the short-term and long-term. Furthermore, inaction also becomes violence, in the sense that policy makers who have the power to solve an issue do not put forth the effort to produce positive meaningful change.

Conclusion:

There is a famous Indian story of the elephant and seven blind men. Here is the story told by the Jains:

"One of the men places his hands on the elephants ears, another on his legs, and so on. The first man says: ' The elephant is a big flat fan-like animal.' 'No', says the second ' I touched the animal, and it is like a thick round post all the way from the ground to as high as I could reach.' The third man shouted: 'You are both wrong'. It is a long rope-like thing with lots of hair on it and it moves up and down all the time."

Each man in turn defines one aspect of the elephant as the whole, until the animal's owner finally says:

"All of you are correct in what you have described, but all are also wrong because each of you has touched only one side of the elephant. Had you been able to examine all the sides with all your sense, you would have realised that each of you is right from your individual viewpoint, but the truth is something different altogether." 44

Blindness is a synonym for ignorance a metaphor for the obscuration of consciousness by seeing only one-side of a reality. This blindness is seen today in religious fundamentalism, in politics, conservatives against liberals, rich against the poor, policies that place economics, market capitalism and greed above human rights, self-determination and the environment. Anekantavada is non-violence of the mind, it is the intellectual aspect of non-violence. This ancient wisdom of many-sidedness of our reality will be a precious contribution to educational leaders and adminstrators today.

The Buddhist World

Buddhism is also an Indigenous system of knowing founded in the sub-continent of India. Some of our International students from India, Bhutan, Japan, China, Korea, and Tibet have traditional roots in the Buddhist tradition. Administration and teachers should have an appreciation of this traditional learning system of their students. Nalanda University was the first university in human history and it was a Buddhist academic center of learning. It was the proto-type to our academic institutions we have today.

The final phase of this research will investigate the Administration of King Ashoka. Ashoka was a leader who utilized Buddhist ideals and philosophy as the organizing principle behind his political administration. The Buddha was one of the greatest human beings, a man of noble character, penetrating vision, infinite compassion, and profound thought. Not only did he establish a remarkable new religion but his revolt against Hindu extremes such as sensual bodily pleasures (hedonism), asceticism, extreme spiritualism, and the caste system which deeply influenced Hinduism itself. Similar to Jesus Christ five hundred years later who tried to reform Judaism and thus created his own set of beliefs and teachings that today we call Christianity. This research will describe and explain how the human body is perceived is figured in early Indian Buddhism. I will examine how the body is figured in this social, historical, religious context and will also analyze how this figuring of the body delimits notions of 'same' and 'other'. The Buddha rejected the Vedic caste system. This caste system is essentially a racist system that determined a persons worth by the color of ones skin, rather than the content of ones character. The Buddha believed that all people were equal and had the same potential. This chapter will be four-fold in organization: a) a brief description of the sacred/profane dichotomy, b) the Vedic caste system, c) Buddha's response to Brahmanism, and d) examining the body from the Buddhist point of view and to see how this relates to compassion (karuna) as the essence of his teaching.

The comparisons of pure and impure, same and other, sacred and profane applies to all levels of spiritual experience. This dichotomous structure, creates order. This order is often hierarchical as the Hindu caste system. This order establishes ordering practices that assumes classes, gender, race distinctions: free/slave as if the categories are themselves natural. Society begins to value one side of the dichotomy over the other, i.e. males more important than females. Dichotomies are social categories which are then projected onto the metaphysical. Vedic offerings and sacrifices represents the establishment of Brahmans over the rest of the masses of Indian society. Since Brahmans were the priests or specialist, so a specialist/non specialist dichotomy is created. These are both organizing principles, the first acts to rank one society from another, the second orders the society itself. (We see here how Mohandas Gandhi also rejected the caste system of India and called the lowest caste of the India "Gods children" and how later his influence fuelled Martin Luther King Jr. in his civil rights movement in America.)

The Caste System, though authorized by scriptural text was, and is, more a sociological than a religious phenomenon. It is a fixed social system in which a social hierarchy is maintained generation after generation and allows little mobility out of the position to which a person is born. The origin of the caste system can be traced to the confrontation of the races: the white-skinned, blond and blue-eyed Caucasian with the dark-skinned Dravidians. The word caste is "varna", which actually means colour. (To put this in the historical context the Buddha lived roughly 2,500 years ago, 500 years ago before Lord Jesus Christ. The Buddhist teaching and perspective is highly relevant as he also dealt with many of the same issues, be it religious, social or psychological in his own time. Moreover, the four constants of the human predicament will always remain: birth, old age, sickness and death, so Gotama Buddha teaching always draws from these reflections.) All societies have caste systems of their own. Before they came to India, the Aryans had their own divisions into the Kshatriyas (nobility) and Vaishyas (commoners). When they subdued the Dravidians, sometime between 3000 and 2000 BCE, a third caste came into being. i.e. the conquered peoples, known as Dasas or slaves. This continued for centuries until the mingling of the races began to cause alarm to the "puritans" among the Aryans. Eventually the caste system slowly evolved, dividing society into four groups: the Brahmins (representing Brahman, the word for God in Hinduism is Brahma), became the scholars and priests; Kshatriyas were the warrior class, Vaishyas, the commoners became the tradesman; the Sudras were workers, artisans, farmers, and rearers of cattle. Then there were those lower than caste and society, the untouchables, whose only right was to perform the most unpleasant tasks: butchers, cleaning washrooms and making foot wear and the like. Castes represent shades of racial purity as well as functional divisions. A passage in the Mahabharata states: " Brahmins are fair-skinned, Kshatriyas are reddish, Vaishyas are yellowish, and Sudras are black."

In the earlier centuries of its development, there was considerable mobility between the castes. But eventually it came to be fixed and the sole criteria became the caste of the parents. In the Dharmashastras or Laws of Manu it clearly states: "Brahmans proceed from the Brahmas mouth, arms(Kshatriyas), thighs (Vaishyas), and feet (Shudras)." The Laws of Manu were written by Aryan priest- lawmakers created the four renowned inherited divisions of society still existent today. The Brahmans placed their own priestly class at the top of the this caste system with the title of earthly gods. Next in order in rank were the warriors, the Kshatriyas. Then came the Vaishyas, the farmers and merchants. The fourth of the original castes was the Shudras, the laborers, born to be servants to the other three castes, especially the Brahmans. Then entirely outside the social order and limited to doing the most menial of unappealing tasks, were those people of no caste, the Untouchables. These were the Dravidians, the aboriginal inhabitants of India. Therefore the Brahman priests created this caste system and made it vital part of Hindu religious law, and made secure by the claim of divine revelation. The caste system has been maintained by the strong Hindu belief in samsara (cyclic existence or reincarnation) and karma (quality of action). According to these religious beliefs, all people are reincarnated on earth, at which time they have a chance to be born into another, higher caste, but only if they have been loyal to the rules of their duty or caste in their previous life on earth. So, in this way karma discouraged Hindu people from attempting to rise to a higher caste or to cross caste boundaries for social relations of any kind. The rise of Buddhism, is itself a reaction and protest against, the unbearable bondage of the varnas system.

The Buddha and his teaching had a significant influence on the cultural pattern of the social elite and the Buddhist movement had a great effect on the course and the fiber of social life. What we will now be shown is how his leadership bettered society and to what extent did it succeed. The caste (varna) system is very important. Traditionally, as written in the Rig Veda it is stated that the Brahmans were created out of the mouth of the creator, the Kshatria (warrior) from the arms, the Vaishya from the thighs and the Shudra from the feet. As mentioned earlier, the Dharmashastras share the same theory. Vedic society was based on this caste system. The Buddha was against caste distinction, he strongly declared "actions alone count." The Buddha judged a man's greatness by his deeds and conduct, not his birth. The Buddha promoted a "casteless" society. Buddhist monks were invited to the homes of the lay people for dinner and were treated with great respect and reverence. The Buddha had a tremendous impact on the societies traditional views. Buddhism was indeed felt and indeed eased, though scarcely caste barriers. Gotama Buddha was a social reformer, and promoted liberalism. The Brahmans obviously felt threatened, by Buddhism. The Buddha's social revolution was essentially a rationalistic protest against Brahmana worship. Everything significant that was to be known about a person was known through his caste, whether for religious, mental, economic, social or political purposes. A person's physical requirements, appearance, his very essence was determined by his caste. It was if the castes were all different distinct species. In this conception there were no human beings, only Brahmans, Warriors, Farmer and Servants. The 'Awakened One' challenged this Brahmanical view, but also the two main qualities, wisdom and virtue. The Buddha believed that virtue is something anyone can have: it is not ascribed by birth, but achieved by diligence. Likewise wisdom is to be achieved and cannot be assigned at birth. What we find in early Buddhist literature is Gautama Buddha describing what the true Brahman(Hindu Priest) should aspire to be. To him the true Brahman was simply any person, born of any family lineage, who has both wisdom and virtue. He stated:

"Not by platted hair, nor by family, nor by birth does one become a Brahmana. But in whom there exist both Truth and Righteousness, pure is he, a Brahmana is he."

This view is profound, for it suggests that our very nature in essence is capable of wisdom and virtue, quite apart from one's caste. This was a revolutionary step, for until this point it was believed that Indians had no way of speaking of human life beyond the narrow local conception of castes, fixed in Indian society. Intelligence and moral honesty are the real criteria for judging a person not his birth or her birth. The Buddha, believed the Brahmans of his day had strayed from the righteous path of ancient times. The Brahmans of his day were very worldly and corrupt, so he began to preach of the ancient times when the Brahman lived a simple life, a pure life of little wants. He described the true Brahman:

"He who is not hateful but is dutiful, virtuous, free from craving, controlled, and bears his final body, him I call a Brahmana"

"He whose knowledge is deep, he who is wise, he who is skilled in the right and wrong way, he who has reached the highest goal, —him I call a Brahmana." 45

The Buddha held debates with the Brahmanas, he used their terms, and preached the basic doctrine of compassion (karuna). He utilized human kindness in his rejection of caste and ritual sacrifices as unimportant ceremonies involving wide-spread slaughter, he preached this by displaying his typical enlightened awareness. The Buddha was a religious reformer who died around 500 years before the Christian era. The following are some of the results due to the visit of this one man upon earth: a) the institution of caste was attacked, b) having more than one wife was for the first time pronounced immoral, and slavery condemned, c) Women, from being considered as property and a beast of burden, was for the first time considered a man's equal, and allowed to develop her spiritual life. The Buddhist movement was the revolt of Brahmanism. This caste, that rigid mold which India has not yet been able to extinguish, did not exist in the holy mind of the Buddha. He renounced his own caste, why should the Buddha defend the discrimination of this system? His answer was this:

"I am neither a Brahman nor prince,
Nor even a bourgeois;
I take my place with common folk
Without a penny, thoughtful I trudge.
In the monk's robe, without a home I go,
With shorn hair and soul serene,
With no truck in human affairs
My caste is no longer in season."46

Ambedkar a prominent contemporary scholar in this field stated:

"Inequality exists in every society. But it was different with Brahmanism. The inequality preached by the Brahmins was its official doctrine. Brahminism did not believe in equality. In fact, it was opposed to equality."47

All Human Life is Sacred:

Up to this point, we have examined how the Brahmans viewed the body. As mentioned before they viewed all other castes that were below them as defiled and their priestly class as intrinsically pure from birth. If we examine closely we will see how the Buddha took this even further by developing his own doctrine of Tathagata-Garbha (the innate Buddha nature in all beings). His leadership vision saw that he had to take this intrinsic purity only allotted to the Brahmins and gives it to all sentient beings. The Buddha developed his own doctrine of stipulating that this perfect nature or intrinsic purity is found in all living things not just the Brahmans. In this section we will examine how the Buddha viewed the human body. He did not believe in this dichotomy of "same" or "other", he believed all were equal and each one of us have unlimited potential, and actually believed took it even further by preaching to us that all of us are perfect at all times, but are temporarily obscured of this truth, by our past negative karma. Dr. Ambedkar stated:
"No caste, no inequality, no superiority: all are equal. That is what he (that is, the Buddha) stood for."48
The leadership of the Buddha focused on the great value of everyone's precious human existence. He realized that everyone had the right, and ability to discover their unlimited human potential. The goal or aspiration of every living being is to attain genuine happiness. As educational leader he instructed his students that there are two kinds of happiness and therefore two kinds of goal— temporary and ultimate. Temporary happiness that can be experienced by humans; is limited happiness that can be experienced while beings remain bound within samsara (cyclic existence of continual

rebirth, often called prison by devoted Buddhsits). Ultimate happiness is the pure, eternal happiness of liberation and full enlightenment, which is the goal of every single sentient being. This education was open to all, and could be accessed by all through depending on the teacher and studying the teaching for themselves. As a leader he made sure everyone realized how important and precious human life is. If we had not been born human we would not have been able to experience all the joys and pleasures of human life. Other beings such as animals cannot enjoy the happiness we enjoy because they do not possess the appropriate bodily basis. Thus, just to have this human body is very important from the point of view of experiencing human happiness in this lifetime. But he instructed that the ultimate goal was to attain the pure, eternal happiness of liberation and full enlightenment. The human form to Buddhists is said to be like a boat in which can cross the ocean of samsara and reach the distant shore of enlightenment. With this human life, each day, each hour, each minute, can be completely worthwhile. Every single moment of our precious human life has great meaning. As an educational leader he made his students realize that even if we were to lose all our money and belongings one could still borrow some, make an appeal, or find a way of making it back, but if one lost this human life without having put it to good use it will be almost impossible for us to recover our loss. This body with all the freedoms and endowments to practice spirituality is more precious than any treasure. Even if one understood the great value of our precious human life, we may still waste it if we think that it will be easy to be born human again. But in fact, to a Buddhist it is very rare to be born a human because it is rare for anyone to practice pure moral discipline, which is the cause for such a rebirth. One of the main tenets of his leadership was that women are equal to men on all levels. A woman's life is just as precious as a mans:

"Buddhism unlike Brahmanism gave equal opportunity in religious culture to women." 49

Still today many economic policies and leadership do not see the intrinsic truth of this reality. The Brahmans believed all women were inferior in every way to men, as mentioned earlier. But during the Buddhist era there was a transformation. Women came to enjoy more equality and greater respect and authority that ever previously given to them.

"Under Buddhism, more than ever before, she was an individual in command of her own life until the dissolution of the body." 50

In Hindu spiritual practice, women were considered a hindrance to the path of spiritual advancement.

"The Shudras and women—the two classes whose humanity was most mutilated by Brahmanism, had no power to rebel against the system." 51

But in time women came to enjoy more equality and greater respect and authority, as well as the Shudras since Buddhism preached equality for all. The role of women in Buddhism is of great importance. Before the leadership of the Buddha, women were seen as inferior to men and society never questioned this belief. They (women and Shudras) were denied the right to knowledge with the result that by reason of their enforced ignorance they could not realize what made their condition so degraded.

"They could not know that Brahmanism had robbed them completely of the significance of their life. Instead of rebelling against Brahmanism they had become devotees and upholders of Brahmanism." 52

This is due principally to the type of society visualized in the Arthashastra. This Brahmanical discourse was harsh towards women, and they were viewed as an inferior species. The teaching of the Buddha was much more compassionate.

"Man and women are placed by the Buddha on the same footing" 53

The resolution to allow nuns (Bhikuni's) in the Buddhist Sangha was of great importance, whereas before this, the Brahmans would not even allow women to receive an education. Buddhism allowed individuals a chance to receive education, who normally could not. The Shudras are a great example; now they could receive an education. No matter what caste one belonged to, one could receive an education. Now to move up the caste system, all one had to do was become a monk or nun, and receive an education. Through education Buddhism gave the masses who experienced discrimination for centuries the chance to break the chains of suppression.

In the last phase we will assess the example of the Buddhist King Ashoka and how he utilized Buddhist thought and principles in governing India. Ultimately we will like to make parallels with contemporary issues and show how this model can be used when governing countries today

Buddhism has many practical methods that can be utilized in the leadership field today. Essentially Buddhist strategies that can be applied to today's problems. First we must get a glimpse into the Buddhist world. From the Buddhist perspective however, these names, and ideologies should not seem so foreign and actually many who read Buddhist scripture always say something to the effect: "That is true, or I know that." This is because from the highest view-point we are all Buddha already. The only thing that is depriving us from seeing it or realizing it is our negative habitual patterns that block out our genuine true nature. The final phase of the Buddhist section will look at the benevolent rule of King Asoka. Asoka, who utilized Buddhist ideals and philosophy as the organizing principle behind his administration. Here we can compare and contrast this man and his regime with the current leaders and regimes we presently have.

The Buddha was one of the greatest leaders, a man of noble character, penetrating vision, infinite compassion, and profound thought. Not only did he establish a remarkable new religion but his revolt against Hindu extremes such as sensual bodily pleasures (hedonism), asceticism, extreme spiritualism, and the caste system which deeply influenced Hinduism itself. Similar to Jesus Christ five hundred years later who tried to reform Judaism and thus created his own set of beliefs and teachings that today we call Christianity. The main thrust of this section is how under the leadership of the Buddha the masses began to view each other as equal and racism and the caste/ class society began to be questioned on a large scale. The Buddha rejected the Vedic caste system. This caste system is essentially a racist system that determined a persons worth by the color of ones skin, rather than the content of ones character. The Buddha believed that all people were equal and had the same potential. This research will be four-fold in organization: a) a brief description of the sacred/profane dichotomy, b) the Vedic caste system, c) Buddha's response to Brahmanism, and d) examining the body from the Buddhist point of view and to see how this relates to compassion (karuna) as the essence of his leadership.

The comparisons of pure and impure, same and other, sacred and profane applies to all levels of spiritual experience. This dichotomous structure, creates order. This order is often hierarchical as the Hindu caste system. This order establishes ordering practices that assumes classes, gender, race distinctions: free/slave as if the categories are themselves natural. Society begins to value one side of the dichotomy over the other, i.e. males more important than females. Dichotomies are social categories which are then projected onto the metaphysical. Vedic offerings and sacrifices represents the establishment of Brahmans over the rest of the masses of Indian society. Since Brahmans were the priests or specialist, so a specialist/non specialist dichotomy is created. These are both organizing principles, the first acts to rank one society from another, the second orders the society itself. (We see here how Mohandas Gandhi also rejected the caste system of India and called the lowest caste of the India "Gods children" and how later his influence fuelled Martin Luther King Jr. in his civil rights movement in America.)

The Caste System, though authorized by scriptural text was, and is, more a sociological than a religious phenomenon. It is a fixed social system in which a social hierarchy is maintained generation after generation and allows little mobility out of the position to which a person is born. The origin of the caste system can be traced to the confrontation of the races: the white-skinned, blond and blue-eyed Caucasian with the dark-skinned Dravidians. The word caste is "varna", which actually means colour. (To put this in the historical context the Buddha lived roughly 2,500 years ago, 500 years ago before Lord Jesus Christ. The Buddhist teaching and perspective is highly relevant as he also dealt with many of the same issues, be it religious, social or psychological in his own time. Moreover, the four constants of the human predicament will always remain: birth, old age, sickness and death, so Gotama Buddha teaching always draws from these reflections.) All societies have caste systems of their own. Before they came to India, the Aryans had their own divisions into the Kshatriyas (nobility) and Vaishyas (commoners). When they subdued the Dravidians, sometime between 3000 and 2000 BCE, a third caste came into being. i.e. the conquered peoples, known as Dasas or slaves. This continued for centuries until the mingling of the races began to cause alarm to the "puritans" among the Aryans. Eventually the caste system slowly evolved, dividing society into four groups: the Brahmins (representing Brahman, the word for God in Hinduism is Brahma), became the scholars and priests; Kshatriyas were the warrior class, Vaishyas, the commoners became the tradesman; the Sudras were workers, artisans, farmers, and rearers of cattle. Then there were those lower than caste and society, the untouchables, whose only right was to perform the most unpleasant tasks: butchers, cleaning washrooms and making foot wear and the like. Castes represent shades of racial purity as well as functional divisions. A passage in the Mahabharata states: " Brahmins are fair-skinned, Kshatriyas are reddish, Vaishyas are yellowish, and Sudras are black."

In the earlier centuries of its development, there was considerable mobility between the castes. But eventually it came to be fixed and the sole criteria became the caste of the parents. In the Dharmashastras or Laws of Manu it clearly states: "Brahmans proceed from the Brahmas mouth, arms(Kshatriyas), thighs (Vaishyas), and feet (Shudras)." The Laws of Manu were written by Aryan priest- lawmakers created the four renowned inherited divisions of society still existent today. The Brahmans placed their own priestly class at the top of the this caste system with the title of earthly gods. Next in order in rank were the warriors, the Kshatriyas. Then came the Vaishyas, the farmers and merchants. The fourth of the original castes was the Shudras, the laborers, born to be servants to the other three castes, especially the Brahmans. Then entirely outside the social order and limited to doing the most menial of unappealing tasks, were those people of no caste, the Untouchables. These were the Dravidians, the aboriginal inhabitants of India. Therefore the Brahman priests created this caste system and made it vital part of Hindu religious law, and made secure by the claim of divine revelation. The caste system has been maintained by the strong Hindu belief in samsara (cyclic existence or reincarnation) and karma (quality of action). According to these religious beliefs, all people are reincarnated on earth, at which time they have a chance to be born into another, higher caste, but only if they have been loyal to the rules of their duty or caste in their previous life on earth. So, in this way karma discouraged Hindu people from attempting to rise to a higher caste or to cross caste boundaries for social relations of any kind. The rise of Buddhism, is itself a reaction and protest against, the unbearable bondage of the varnas system.

The Buddha and his leadership had a significant influence on the cultural pattern of the social elite and the Buddhist movement had a great effect on the course and the fiber of social life. What we will now be shown is how Buddhist leadership bettered society and to what extent did it succeed. The caste (varna) system is very important. Traditionally, as written in the Rig Veda it is stated that the Brahmans were created out of the mouth of the creator, the Kshatria (warrior) from the arms, the Vaishya from the thighs and the Shudra from the feet. As mentioned earlier, the Dharmashastras share the same theory. Vedic society was based on this caste system. The Buddha was against caste distinction, he strongly declared "actions alone count." The Buddha judged a man's greatness by his deeds and conduct, not his birth. The Buddha promoted a "casteless" society. Buddhist monks were invited to the homes of the lay people for dinner and were treated with great respect and reverence. The Buddha had a tremendous impact on the societies traditional views. Buddhism was indeed felt and indeed eased, though scarcely caste barriers. Gotama Buddha was a social reformer, and promoted liberalism. The Brahmans obviously felt threatened, by Buddhism. The Buddha's social revolution was essentially a rationalistic protest against Brahmana worship. Everything significant that was to be known about a person was known through his caste, whether for religious, mental, economic, social or political purposes. A person's physical requirements, appearance, his very essence was determined by his caste. It was if the castes were all different distinct species. In this conception there were no human beings, only Brahmans, Warriors, Farmer and Servants. The 'Awakened One' challenged this Brahmanical view, but also the two main qualities, wisdom and virtue. The Buddha believed that virtue is something anyone can have: it is not ascribed by birth, but achieved by diligence. Likewise wisdom is to be achieved and cannot be assigned at birth. What we find in early Buddhist literature is Gotama Buddha describing what the true Brahman(Hindu Priest) should aspire to be. To him the true Brahman was simply any person, born of any family lineage, who has both wisdom and virtue. He stated:

"Not by platted hair, nor by family, nor by birth does one become a Brahmana. But in whom there exist both Truth and Righteousness, pure is he, a Brahmana is he."54

This view is profound, for it suggests that our very nature in essence is capable of wisdom and virtue, quite apart from one's caste. This was a revolutionary step, for until this point it was believed that Indians had no way of speaking of human life beyond the narrow local conception of castes, fixed in Indian society. Intelligence and moral honesty are the real criteria for judging a person not his birth or her birth. The Buddha, believed the Brahmans of his day had strayed from the righteous path of ancient times. The Brahmans of his day were very worldly and corrupt, so he began to preach of the ancient times when the Brahman lived a simple life, a pure life of little wants. He described the true Brahman:

"He who is not hateful but is dutiful, virtuous, free from craving, controlled, and bears his final body, him I call a Brahmana"

"He whose knowledge is deep, he who is wise, he who is skilled in the right and wrong way, he who has reached the highest goal, —him I call a Brahmana." 55

As a leader the Buddha sought out the intellectuals and scholars of the day and held debates with them, he used their terms, and preached the basic doctrine of compassion (karuna). He utilized human kindness in his rejection of caste and ritual sacrifices as unimportant ceremonies involving wide-spread slaughter, he preached this by displaying his typical enlightened awareness. The Buddha was a brilliant leader, teacher, sociologist, psychologist, and religious reformer who died around 500 years before the Christian era. The following are some of the results of his leadership abilities: a) the institution of caste/ class hierarchical society was attacked, b) having more than one wife was for the first time pronounced immoral, and slavery condemned, c) Women, from being considered as property and a beast of burden, was for the first time considered a man's equal, and allowed to develop her spiritual life. d) poverty stricken, and homeless were welcomed into his order for educational training. The Buddhist leadership was the revolt against the injustices of the time. The caste, was a rigid mold which India has not yet been able to extinguish, did not exist in the leadership of the Buddha. He renounced his own caste, why should the Buddha defend the discrimination of this system? His answer was this:

> "I am neither a Brahman nor prince,
> Nor even a bourgeois;
> I take my place with common folk
> Without a penny, thoughtful I trudge.
> In the monk's robe, without a home I go,
> With shorn hair and soul serene,
> With no truck in human affairs
> My caste is no longer in season."[56]

Ambedkar a prominent contemporary scholar in this field stated:

"Inequality exists in every society. But it was different with Brahmanism. The inequality preached by the Brahmins was its official doctrine. Brahminism did not believe in equality. In fact, it was opposed to equality."[57]

All Human Life is Sacred:

Up to this point, we have examined how the Brahmans viewed the body. As mentioned before they viewed all other castes that were below them as defiled and their priestly class as intrinsically pure from birth. If we examine closely we will see how the Buddha took this even further by developing his own doctrine of Tathagata-Garbha (the innate Buddha nature in all beings). He takes this intrinsic purity only allotted to the Brahmins and gives it to all sentient beings. The Buddha developed his own doctrine of stipulating that this perfect nature or intrinsic purity is found in all living things not just the Brahmans. In this section we will examine how the Buddha viewed the human body. He did not believe in this dichotomy of "same" or "other", he believed all were equal and each one of us have unlimited potential, and actually believed took it even further by preaching to us that all of us are perfect at all times, but are temporarily obscured of this truth, by our past negative karma. Dr. Ambedkar stated:

"No caste, no inequality, no superiority: all are equal. That is what he (that is, the Buddha) stood for." [58]

The Buddha put a great value on everyone's precious human existence. The goal or aspiration of every living being is to attain genuine happiness Here there are two kinds of happiness and therefore two kinds of goal—temporary and ultimate. Temporary happiness that can be experienced by humans; is limited happiness that can be experienced while beings remain bound within samsara (cyclic existence of continual rebirth, often called prison by devoted Buddhsits). Ultimate happiness is the pure, eternal happiness of liberation and full enlightenment, which is the goal of every single sentient being. If we had not been born human we would not have been able to experience all the joys and pleasures of human life. Other beings such as animals cannot enjoy the happiness we enjoy because they do not possess the appropriate bodily basis. Thus, just to have this human body is very important from the point of view of experiencing human happiness in this lifetime. But our ultimate goal is to attain the pure, eternal happiness of liberation and full enlightenment. The human form to Buddhists is said to be like a boat in which can cross the ocean of samsara and reach the distant shore of enlightenment. With this human life, each day, each hour, each minute, can be completely worthwhile. Every single moment of our precious human life has great meaning. To a Buddhist, even if we were to lose all our money and belongings we could still borrow some, make an appeal, or find a way of making it back, but if we lose this human life without having put it to good use it will be almost impossible for us to recover our loss. This body with all the freedoms and endowments to practice spirituality is more precious than any treasure. Even if one understood the great value of our precious human life, we may still waste it if we think that it will be easy to be born human again. But in fact, to a Buddhist it is very rare to be born a human because it is rare for anyone to practice pure moral discipline, which is the cause for such a rebirth. To the Buddha, a woman's life is just as precious as a mans:

"Buddhism unlike Brahmanism gave equal opportunity in religious culture to women." [59]

The Brahmans believed all women were inferior in every way to men, as mentioned earlier. But during the Buddhist era there was a transformation. Women came to enjoy more equality and greater respect and authority that ever previously given to them.

"Under Buddhism, more than ever before, she was an individual in command of her own life until the dissolution of the body." [60]

In Hindu spiritual practice, women were considered a hindrance to the path of spiritual advancement.

"The Shudras and women—the two classes whose humanity was most mutilated by Brahmanism, had no power to rebel against the system." [61]

But in time women came to enjoy more equality and greater respect and authority, as well as the Shudras since Buddhism preached equality for all. The role of women in Buddhism is of great importance. Before the Buddha, women were seen as inferior to men and society never questioned this belief. They (women and Shudras) were denied the right to knowledge with the result that by reason of their enforced ignorance they could not realize what made their condition so degraded.

In the next chapter we will assess the example of the Buddhist King Ashoka and how he utilized Buddhist thought and principles in governing India. Ultimately we will like to make parallels with contemporary issues and show how this model can be used when governing countries today.

Asoka, the third Mauryan king of Magadha was the most celebrated ruler of ancient India, known for his altruistic, benevolent administration and for making Buddhism the official religion of his empire. The grandson of the great Chandragupta, founder of the Maurya dynasty, Asoka enlarged the empire that he inherited and it covered most of the subcontinent. In the process, he made war on the state of Kalinga, conquering it around the year 261 BCE. When he realized the great suffering he had caused, he was overwhelmed with regret, grief and sorrow. He had so much remorse he renounced his warfare and religion, Brahmanism, and turned to Buddhism for solace, with its doctrine of ahimsa (non-violence). He wished to apply the Buddha's principles to all aspects of everyday life. He established lighter punishments, gentler laws than the rulers before him and went among the Indian peasants, preaching and nursing to their needs. He was very much a father figure to his people. He had trees planted, wells dug, canals, bridges built, rest houses constructed, and he opened medical centers. He sent orders forbidding the brutal treatment of animals, he limited their killing, and also built hospitals for them. This provides an admirable, brief background of Asoka. Asoka spread the Dharma and made Buddhism flourish throughout the empire and Asoka used the Buddha's doctrines to revitalize Inidan society.

This research will be two-fold in organization: its main purpose is to reveal how Asoka used Buddhist leadership styles to enhance social, political, economic conditions, and education. The second phase will reveal how the universal acceptance of the nature of Dharma grew throughout his country, his views on humanity, and his fundamental belief of the need for harmony of all people and between different religious traditions.

Asoka's Buddhist influence on the cultural pattern on the social elite is very important. We can see through his Edicts the great effect of the Buddhist movement on the course and fiber of social life. Buddhism, Jainism, and Brahmanism had a great impact on the society at the time. Groups of society gathered according to religious ideals. What will be shown is how Asoka's Buddhism bettered society and to what extent did it succeed. As mentioned earlier, the Buddha was against caste distinction, he strongly declared "actions alone count." The Buddha judged a man's greatness by his deeds and conduct, not his birth. Asoka brilliantly used Buddhist leadership techniques to promote a "casteless" society. Monks were invited to the homes of the lay people for meals and were treated with great respect and reverence. Buddhism now had a greater impact, and it eased, though scarcely caste barriers. The Brahmans obviously felt threatened, by Buddhism. They must have been afraid at the social connection of the Asoka's Buddhist movement and they showed nothing but repulsion toward Buddhists. Why? This is because the Buddha rejected the Vedas (which is the sacred literature of the Hindus, which promotes the caste system).

The name of Asoka is remembered for turning Buddhism into a world religion and he is not remembered for warfare as other monarchs of India. He does not mention the idea of Nirvana, the Four Noble Truths etc. It seems highly likely, that he preached basic doctrines to society. Nirvana and the Four Noble Truths were complex for a non-Buddhist to decipher. So he taught the basics to society, such as morality. Now if Asoka was addressing the monks or nuns, then he would have certainly have strongly advised them to strive for Nirvana but as he was addressing himself to his subjects who were necessarily citizens he cannot be expected to speak of Nirvana and other highly philosophical topics. This is the only way to express Buddhism to a society who is not Buddhist or has no background in Buddhism. Asoka is responsible for the spread of Buddhism all over India and the neighboring lands. Before Asoka's conversion to Buddhism, there was much concern for worldly pleasures. There were great festivals and celebrations with much gambling, and drinking. This all changed with Asoka's conversion. In the very first Edict he inscribed:

"This record relating to Dharma has been caused to be written by King Priyadarsi, Beloved of the Gods. Here no living being should be slaughtered for sacrifice and no festive gathering should be held. For King Priyadarsi, Beloved of the Gods, sees manifold evil in festive gatherings." [62]

Asoka's Administration increased a disciplined spirit influencing greatly the social life of the people. He restricted all festivals except those with a religious significance, thus making the social life of the people more pure. For spiritual practice, women were considered a hindrance to the path of spiritual advancement. But under Asoka women came to enjoy more equality and greater respect and authority, as well as the Shudras since Buddhism preached equality for all. The role of women in the Asokan society is of great importance. Before Asoka, women were seen as inferior to men and society never questioned this belief. This is due principally to the type of society visualized by the Arthashastra. This Brahmanical discourse was harsh towards women, and they were viewed as an inferior species.

Asoka believed in the need for human understanding and harmony for a greater reason, which is simply that all his people were sentient beings. Religious, cultural and physical differences and so on are all superficial. Jainism, Hinduism and Buddhism all co-existed under his rule in peace.

The whole political organization was made secondary to moral law. Respect and tolerance reigned supreme. Asoka by his devotion and wisdom became all powerful. Since politics has always been associated to warfare and the like, Asoka's war activity was uneventful. His reign was peaceful and exceptionally serene, filled with a high level of integrity and religious spirit lasting about forty years. His Edicts give us historians a very detailed, reliable and complete picture of the dynasty of Asoka's empire. He was very much a father figure to his people, stating in one of his Edicts that "all men are my children." His Edicts reveal a sincere concern for the welfare of his people.

Agriculture has always been the centre of economic life in India. Agriculture played an important role in Asoka's empire as well. The majority of the emperors profits came from taxes on the land and its crops. Buddhist art flourished and thus, commerce and trade grew as well. Before this time the Buddha was portrayed by the use of symbols, such as Asoka's great pillar (the Lion capital at Sarnath, where the Buddha preached his first sermon at Deer park. This pillar was built where the Buddha set forth the Dharmachakra.) The lions signify Buddha himself who was considered a lion among spiritual teachers. Today, this pillar image is found on Indian currency (Rupees). Asoka's peaceful kingdom allowed economic prosperity and therefore the flourishing of culture and art. Thus, prosperous economic conditions are reflected by the diverse trades and professions.

First of all, Asoka always refers to himself as King Priyadarsi, the Beloved of the Gods. This statement displays his authenticity as well. This paragraph will deal with Dharma and how it improved India in innumerable ways. Asoka was a highly realized spiritual man. In the pillar Edict three Priyadar'in says:

"Thus saith King Priyadarsi, Beloved of the Gods. A person has an eye on his good deed only and says to himself: 'This good deed have I done.' Not in the least does he notice sin, saying to himself: 'This sinful act have I perpetrated,' or 'This indeed is what is called sin.' But this is certainly difficult to scrutinize. Nevertheless, one should verily look into the matter thus: 'These passions surely lead to sin, such as violence, cruelty, anger, vanity and jealousy. Let me not ruin myself by reason of these very passions.' One should seriously reflect on the following: 'This one is for my good only in this world and the other one is for my good also in the next world." [63]

This is significant, Asoka was informing his people that worldly materialistic pursuits are fruitless. This is because, the only 'thing' one can take with him or her at death is one's good deeds, that is all, all worldly objects are left behind with the body. The people always notice their meritorious actions thinking that they have performed meritorious deeds. But beings do not notice the sins (committed by them), the evil deed one has committed or that it is a sinful act. This is the most difficult to recognize. He is trying to explain to his people to not only remember the good things we have done for people that is a sin. But to remember what good things others have done for us that is more important. Do not do good deeds just for the sake of merit, but perform good deeds from your heart. His empire flourished because he was sincere, and the people really trusted him and believed he cared for their welfare. Through his Edicts the Buddha's doctrine prospered. Now Buddha's teaching were available to all, not just in the scriptures but now on the Edicts that were located everywhere. Even a great saying my late grandfather and father had preached to me from day one is inscribed in Rock Edict Five:

"Thus saith King Priyadarsi, Beloved of the Gods. It is difficult to do good to others. He who starts doing good to others accomplishes what is difficult indeed. Many a good deed has, however, been performed by me. And, among my sons and grandsons and the generations coming after them til the destruction of the word, those who will follow this course will don an act of merit. But whosoever amongst them will abandon even a part of it will do an act of demerit. It is indeed easy to commit sin."[64]

It is very difficult to perform a positive virtuous action. Negative action is the easiest thing to learn on this earth, but good action must be taught and needs discipline. Asoka displayed wisdom in leadership when he expressed the wrong in religious wars:

"If a person acts in this way, he not only promotes his own sect but also benefits other sects. But, if a person acts otherwise, he not only injures his own sect but also harms other sects. Truly, if a person extols his own sect and disparages other sects with a view to glorify his sect owing merely to his attachment to it, he injures his own sect very severely by acting in that way. Therefore restraint in regard to speech is commendable, because people should learn and respect the fundamentals of one another's Dharma (Religion). [65]

This is the kind of leader we so urgently need today. Someone who understands and respects all peoples and their beliefs. This quote from Asoka is truly an eternal truth or law. One who reverences one's own religion and belittles that of another from devotion to one's own religion and to praise it over all other religions does injure one's own religion more certainly. This world leader was a teacher, a teacher of religious tolerance and mutual understanding. From interpreting his Edicts, Asoka sums his teaching in the word "Dharma". It is clear that he envisioned his mission to consist in outlining, publishing, and spreading of the Dharma. He regards Dharma as the order of the universe. His Edicts show tolerance to all faiths, he regards all as his children, and stressed communication, since wars begin when there is a lack of communication. Great communication allowed the regime of Asoka to reign supreme. Through poets, holy men, monks and nuns genuine communication thrived. The world today faces many of the same problems as the past and Asoka faced many of the same problems of today. He experienced tension in the social classes, and religions. He dodged war at all costs by pushing human well-being and happiness as most meaningful. He concentrated on the Dharma(truth), rather than military victories; his concern was the elevation of the practice of morality.

Respect For All Religious Traditions:

"All religious sects should live harmoniously in all parts of my dominions"

He was able to see the true purpose of religion, the main aim, not on the secondary things that are involved, and if focuses in the correct direction looking at the main aim, then all religions are aiming towards the same lofty goal.

"People should learn and respect the fundamentals of one another's Dharma... There should be a growth of the essentials of Dharma among men of all sects." [66]

The leadership of Asoka believed we should analyze all philosophies and despite the differences in the names and forms used by various religions, the ultimate truth to which they point out is the same. For over forty years, the great reign of Asoka enjoyed peace, tranquility and freedom. His Dharma was the backbone of his regime and he sincerely believed in it. As long as he followed that goodness that sincerity in everything he did, then he knew his empire would enjoy peace. The focus on moral responsibility rather than favoring one ideology over another. His inscriptions are shining reminders of a utopian time and his spirit is captured within his rock edicts. These Edicts serve as guidance to future generations and Asoka has shown that one pious leader can certainly make a difference. Through utilizing Buddhist leadership styles he enhanced the: social, political, economical, education and spread kind-heartedness throughout ancient India.

Emotional Intelligence in the Digital Classroom:

Here we are searching for solutions. In order to look for solutions we must first understand what needs to be improved. Here we needed to look at our school systems and view all the issues that have hindered quality educational outcomes throughout history and see if we can understand what works in school improvement strategies.

First, we need to look at all the issues in education. The reader may ask: why are we looking at all the negative aspects of education ? We are looking at all the issues in education so we can arrive at a solution. The solution must also find its way back to the student. How do we educate the whole child, enlighten, reach and make sure every child reaches their unlimited potential. This is the goal of this text and research. Here we are looking at education management, curriculum, school systems and teaching and learning from a holistic approach. Throughout the text we will look at specific experiences that have had to adapt the curriculum to the needs of Indigenous students and low economic communities specifically. Why was there a need to adapt the curriculum to a more Indigenous curriculum? Was our curriculum and education management system founded on the capitalistic model of creating highly skilled workers for our growing economy? This is very well and good but what of Indigenous communities or low socio-economic areas of inner-cities. Communities battling severe poverty would this curriculum work there as well? Every city or town has a poorer area of town, how do these students perform in our schools? Why are our schools failing low income families and communities? Communities where there is an absence of an economy? Communities where it is more than a recession but, an economic depression in their families history.

School systems have failed these members of our community. Families and, communities have been struck with poverty for generations in their family history. This is how we find solutions to Education Management and curriculum. How do we in the Education Management field really communicate with our staff, and begin to seriously look at the students we are responsible for each day.

This research looks at real cases and can be equated with inner-cities, or cities or communities with very high levels of unemployment, and no existing economy at all and this is why this Indigenous research is compelling. It clearly displays how education and education management is linked with our economies. If our curriculum or management teams are disconnected from the student and their communities then we will fail in our lofty goal of truly educating the child. We need to help, educate, and reach every child. Education management needs to make sure this happens. This is how we build student success.

This is why we will look at solutions-based policy that focuses on the student, and the writings of

Bowles and Gintis(1976) who clearly professed that our school system is linked with capitalism and if the student does not conform or 'fit' with the system they will fall off the assembly line of the school system. If this is indeed, the case we in the field of education management, curriculum and school leaders need to pay close attention to the research of this text. Focusing on the low socio-economic status communities and Indigenous students are important not only because it is a morally right, but these numbers and experiences really stand out to why and how the process hinders our Indigenous and lower socio-economic students. This research in education management clearly shows why these marginalized students struggle in our school systems. This is why their grandparents struggled, parents struggled, and why this generation of low-socio economic students struggle. This research helps us be more aware and makes sure we do not neglect these students and in this way create a more inclusive school community. We argue this is the true lofty goal of education.

Reflections Questions:

1. How can Intercultural Communication assist you in your teaching and communication with your students of color and lower socio-economic students?
2. Students of color and lower-socio economic students rely on the teacher to be compassionate and adept in intercultural communication in what ways can we improve as teachers and academic administrators in this important field of teaching and reaching our students each day?

CHAPTER SIX

Emotional Intelligence in a Robotic System

First Published in Education Management, Chukdong, 2016 (Revised).

⌘

Introduction:

"This common core of ethical values transcends human differences and is based instead on human similarities." Campbell (2003) The Ethical Teacher pg.5

What we share is that we all belong to the same human family and we all by our very nature want to find solace. Humanity is the supreme focus of all ethical and philosophical ideology. Genuine joy or contentment is synonymous with ethical behavior. We can all agree that once the mind is not disturbed by external events, emotional hindrances, selfish motives, the mind naturally becomes peaceful. The more peaceful our mind, the clearer it becomes. The more peaceful it becomes, the more it gains in wisdom and clarity. Therefore this is how ethics and morality ties in to the attainment of genuine peace and solace. If we engage in negative actions of body, speech and mind these negative actions will way on our minds, thus not letting us achieve a peaceful existence. In order to discover the right or suitable solutions to ethical issues we need peace of mind so we can achieve clarity of thought. Therefore we also must engage in an ethical lifestyle in order to arrive at ethical solutions.

As human beings we are given a conscience a higher self that constantly judges our behavior and we must listen to our inner teacher. As human beings trying to find our truest selves ironically arrive at the realization that the problems and the very answers to difficulties confronted in this life are both found within us. The answers to these ethical issues dwell within the individual and this is why constant awareness, the cultivation of moral practices and the development of wisdom remain the fundamental practices of practitioners of ethical inquiry. However, this innate conflict or duality between the individual, society, and community or society will be the judge of the person or the act is positive, negative, or neutral. In the realm of conscience the intention will let our minds find peace but this may lead to the eventual suspension of our morality. Campbell (1992). Our goal may become to find relative mental peace over doing what is right in a given situation. If we suspend our morality once, then who is to say we will not eventually suspend it all together. If we are able to lie to ourselves then why would it be difficult to lie to others? This further extends to the issues of complying, and conforming to events in order keep ourselves out of harms way. The writings of Bowles and Gintis (1976), Hamberger and Moore(1997) individuals and educators are likened to factory workers who conform and become just another part of the assembly line of life. They actually state that schools are special kinds of factories, so is conflict, conformity and compliance to be expected in the teaching profession?

In the case study below we are introduced to Mr. James who is put into an awkward position and confronted with the hierarchical structure of school systems very early in his young teaching career.

Case Study: Professional Ethics of Teaching and Schooling

Mr. James is a novice full-time teacher. He teaches grade 8 and is in his third month of teaching; everything is going smoothly. One day it comes to the attention of Mr. James that two of his students have been bullying each other in the community, and one of the parents wants to meet with the Principal and Mr. James after school. At the conclusion of the school day, Mr. James reports to the Principal's office for the meeting. When Mr. James arrives the parent, his student and the Principal Mr. Jinnah are there already engaged in conversation. Mr. Jinnah introduces Mr. James to the parent and Mr. James greets both his student and parent.

Mr. Jinnah explains that a student, Mary has been bullied in the school and away from school by Teresa both Mary and Teresa are students in Mr. James's class. Mr. James explains that he had no idea and stated that Mary and Teresa seem to behave properly in class and also sit across from each other every day in class. Mr. James says that he will keep an open eye for bullying behavior and asks the parent if anything is of further concern?

Mrs. Jones, the mother of Mary, says: I want Teresa disciplined immediately; if she is not disciplined I will take my child out of this school!

Mr. Jinnah: This is not the best action for your child. You are acting foolishly!

Mrs. Jones takes her child by the hand and storms out of the office. Mr. James runs after them and repeats again: "Please Mrs.Jones if you want to talk about this matter further please contact me."

Mr. Jinnah: Get in here right now and close the door!

Mr. James was puzzled and tried to understand what has just happened but was shocked by the way the Principal yelled at the student's parents.

Two Days Later:

Mrs. Jenny explained that there would be an investigation of the Principal and asked him to write a detailed report of what he noticed in the meeting that day with the student, parent and the Principal. Also, Mr. James was given a note written by his student, Mary, as Mrs. Jones could not write properly in English. The note stated that the Principal said or made inappropriate comments to the mother and tried to touch her foot from under the desk with his.

The Director says: What do you think Mr.James?

Analysis: What to Do?

"Responsibility for the relationship lies with the professional, who must ensure that it benefits the other person, that power is not abused and that the relationship is not exploited." Colnerud(2006). Pg.372

Colnerud stresses the importance of professional ethics and moral education in regards to collegial relationships in school systems. The belief that conduct toward others is a critical part of viewing their competence and an example of how one achieves the moral obligations embedded in the complex professional relationship. This power dynamic needs to be understood by teachers as they may be needed to make decisions as the one above in a quick and haste manner and must be given a fair chance to respond in a thoughtful and ethical way.

"The need to act on the spot, lack of time and performing in public are characteristics of teaching which give few opportunities for contemporary reflections of ethical choices." Colnerud, (1997), pg.627.

The power dynamics can be abused and how this is linked to morality is a critical one. Do authority figures who naturally hold more power get to exercise this power whenever and however they like?

Mrs. Jenny is asking Mr. James to document a report stipulating the events that occurred during the meeting. Also, Mr. James is not to tell the Principal. Should Mr. James cooperate in this investigation or not and should he keep this investigation a secret from the Principal? There are many aspects that come into play in this critical case study. At the micro level of the classroom nothing was stated about the bullying issue of his two students Mary and Teresa. The Director of Education never even mentioned the reason why all parties were there in Mr. Jinnahs office that day.

"Teachers sometimes seem to be ready to abandon the value of caring for children due to the respect of adults. This aim can be achieved by exploring the ethical conflicts in a teacher's relations to pupils, parents and colleagues." Pg.627 Colnerud

Second, could there already be an investigation against Mr. Jinnah and the testimony of Mr. James will only add more fuel to the fire against Mr. Jinnah as acting Principal of the school? Personally, Mr. James must know how important it is to have the Principal on your side especially when needing more resources and special activities for your classroom so having good relations with the Principal is paramount in the school environment. But according to the hierarchical structure of the school system the Director of Education is at the top of the organizational chart and one does not want to anger the person who is responsible for renewing your contract. However it is normal for people to listen to those who they know hold an authoritative position, but it is a mistake to describe authority based only in hierarchical terms. Campbell (1992). Thirdly, Mr. James as a novice full-time teacher will need to rely on Mr. Jinnah for a teaching evaluation and reference by the end of the school year, so good relations are of great importance once again. This is just an ethical dilemma as Freeman(1998) warns us about when actions take place that will surely benefit one party at some expense or inconvenience to another.

Is it right to keep this investigation a secret from the Principal? Campbell(1992) discusses this exact issue when discussing:

"….secrecy, 'whistleblowing, loyalty, and covert subversion by an individual of the organizational ethics. These issues, so central to the research problem itself, will reveal the potential for social disapproval and sanctions against individuals who take moral stands in opposition to the majority ethic." Campbell (1992) p.33

Student Centered Pedagogy:

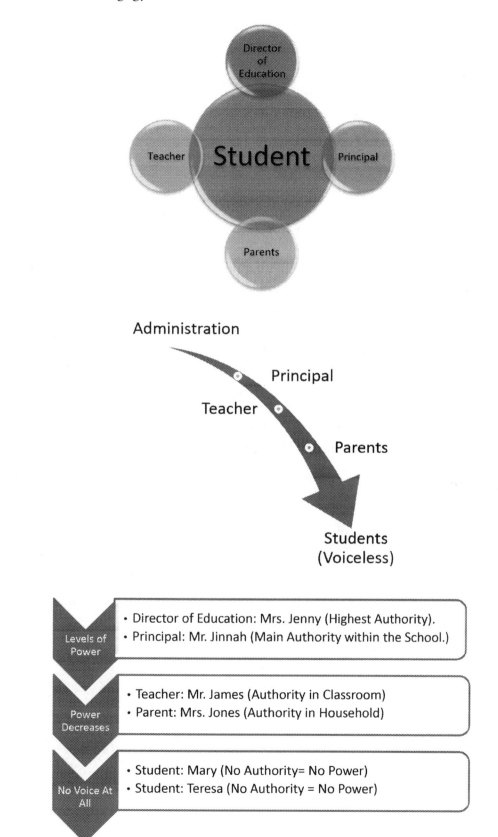

The questions of following orders and being obedient to your superiors plus having the added awkward hindrance of secrecy within these power dynamics is a stressful position for Mr. James to be put in. As a new teacher Mr. James is no doubt thinking about his students first Mary and Teresa who have a problem with bullying. But is lost and forgets about the real issue when he is mixed up in this game of power, control and deception. Is Mr. Jinnah threatening Mrs. Jenny's power in some way? Has Mrs. Jenny been bullying Mr. Jinnah throughout the school year thus far? But what of Mrs. Jones is she a victim of bullying behavior from Mr. Jinnah? This bullying phenomenon can be seen in the hierarchical structure itself and no wonder why our children are engaging in similar bullying on their individual levels. But what is the root cause of this bullying behavior?

Conformity:

Why is the Director of Education putting Mr. James in such an awkward position? How alone he must feel and is she testing his loyalty to the school board and the community over the Principal? Does the Principal already have a troubled past and this is the last piece of evidence to remove our Principal for the school year? How awkward for Mr. James, not to be able to tell his colleagues of what has transpired in the last couple of days. Does right and wrong come after maintaining secrecy and loyalty to your employer?

"Conformity to organizational values for the sole purpose of conformity is not, in itself, a moral pursuit, whether that pursuit is considered either personally or within an objective context." Campbell, (1992).pg. 46.

More often than not obedience and conformity become the main ethic of the teaching profession, the mantra of going with flow can be heard far too often. Campbell (1992). This suspended morality and how the individual must compromise moral beliefs for the betterment of the organization is a reality. However, if one is aware of the structures and forces that are arrayed against us we can not only teach our students, but teach our peers, colleagues and supervisors. The more one is involved in teaching the similar patterns repeat themselves. In order to create positive change in the school system we must see the urgency of unity. However, the powers of division and competition are what one sees and experiences. These patterns of divide and rule of staff in schools and in our larger society of dividing our society into classes could be the aim of our political policies. So, it is not surprising to see our schools also divided, full of conflict and the practice of immoral behavior in its building. But schools have the power to change this by seeing the power of unity. Seeing the power of unity we are no longer a powerless victim pushed around in this bureaucratic cycle because this invisible force of division and conflict has now been finally recognized. Unity can be achieved by all parties to focus on the betterment and welfare of the students. The well-being of the students to be in a safe and healthy environment can break down these barriers to division, selfishness, and competition between individual in this hierarchical system.

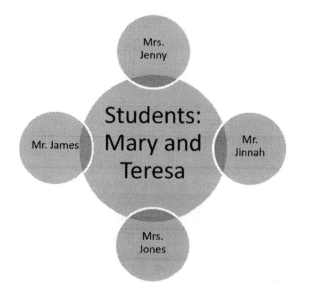

Framework: Nancy Freeman- Systemic/ Reflective Case De-briefing Method in 5 Steps

1) **Write down your first reaction. How do you instinctively resolve this dilemma? What is your first answer to the question "What should the good teacher do?" Answer:** Mr. James needs to listen to the Director of Education. Mrs. Jenny has the highest authority in the school board.

2) **Identify the stakeholders. Who cares what happens?** Director of Education: Mrs. Jenny wants the investigation to take place and needs the report from Mr. James. However, Mrs. Jenny may be looking for a solution from Mr.James? Principal: The investigation of Mr. Jinnah will be conducted against him in secret. Teacher: Mr. James needs to be obedient or share his thoughts. Parent: Mrs. Jones wants the Principal disciplined? But ultimately wants her child to feel safe while in the school and in the community. Students: Want to feel safe at school and in the community.

3) **Identify the issues that make each stakeholder care about this dilemma being resolved.** Two quotes that directly relate to this section of the case study are by Colnerud (1997) and Campbell (1992). "Accusing one of your own colleagues and violating the code of loyalty is a complicated matter." Colnerud (1997) pg. 634 and "Much of this internal conflict develops from tension between individuals' personal moral convictions and their perceived expectations of the roles they occupy." Campbell (1992) pg.80. As we have seen each stakeholder has a distinct role, responsibility and obligation.

4) **Brainstorm Solutions.** Mr. James should request to have all parties involved to have a meeting so they can voice their concerns in an open forum. Transparency in a respectful way can eradicate most of the conflicting issues that have arisen in this case. Even if Mr. Jinnah is being investigated on incidents outside the present one, this should be known as well. All parties will be notified and given ample time to get their main points prepared and all will meet in a caring, respectful environment headed by Mrs. Jenny. Of course Mr. James has stepped way outside his role as a mere teacher and a novice one at that but in this way he can share a solution and know he did everything he could do in a professional, respectful,

and caring way. Everyone needs to be on the same page and secrets, gossip, defamation of character, and lack of trust are dysfunctions that can cripple a school, its staff, a society and community.

5) **Apply your code of ethics.** Respect for Students, Respect for Families, Respect for Colleagues, Respect for Community. In every one of these codes the virtue of honesty, transparency, equality, respect, compassion, and loyalty will be paramount in securing the best learning environments for our students and this will create a unified teaching staff.

Summary:

So, what is right and what is wrong? Whether looking at this case study from the Relativist and Subjectivist view where rightness and truth cannot be known because of too many variables or the Objectivist view that an eternal truth exists, or the Feminist Ethic where one tries to understand the others point of view. What box or label does one want to be put in? Right and wrong in this case study aimed at combining justice and care together. Callan (1992). Consequentialism looks at an action and its consequences which are very important but it often falls into the utilitarianism trap of putting the comfort of one group over another lesser group of smaller representation.

Right and wrong must be seen from the wider societal issues at play. In our society there exists an intense feeling of competition, and ethics is needed not only to punish wrongdoers but to quench the fire that these divisions create. Why do we constantly look down on each other, have selfish motives, and are in constant competition with each other? This competitive nature can be seen between countries, states, family members, siblings, and even between spouses in the realm of individual salaries. What is the reason behind all of this? From one perspective our world is simple and natural but we humans have made this life more problematic and more confusing. This is why as members of the human family who see the urgency of our unity will work together to solve these ethical problems. In the end all human problems can be rectified because all problems are human created from the beginning. The goal of our study was to find the antidote to the constant conflict and divisiveness that permeates our school culture. In order to achieve morality and ethics in the school system we must put staff unity, our students and the community above all conflicts. In this way we can eradicate the divisions and the manipulation that we encounter in school systems that Colnerud (1997), Campbell(1992), Emile Durkheim, Rothstein, Pierre Bourdieu, Hamberger and Moore (1997) warn us about.

Reflections:

1. This theme of hierarchy and the robotic nature of relationships of school systems and work place relationships, makes one ask questions of: " So what?" Can we change this hierarchical system that most likely places students and parents at the bottom of the system?

_____

_____

_____

_____

_____

_____

_____

2. From the Business model the student would be the customer and the parent would be the shareholder. Are we looking after them what is going to happen to the future of education?

_____

_____

_____

_____

_____

_____

CHAPTER SEVEN

Self-Care Age and Education

First Published in Education Management, Chukdong 2016(Revised).

⌘

Academic Administration Today:

    Academic Administration is both a field of study and a group of highly trained educational professionals. Those working in academic administration are researchers, curriculum teams, and policy-makers that work to develop and evaluate new methods to improve our educational system at all levels.

    There is no defining definition of educational management since its essence encompasses many diverse disciplines like: sociology, political science, and economics. As this text has clearly shown the purpose of educational management is to bring students and teachers under positive conditions so high academic achievement can take place. This research looked at our education system and its origins. We looked carefully at the sociological, historical, and economic sides of our education system. When school systems are modelled after the business model or 'factory model' the student and the teacher ultimately will be left out of the equation. This is because, a factory which focuses on the assembly line, the workers and the product are always at the bottom of the production line. In this analogy the teacher and student are linked to the assembly line in our education system. As educational leaders and administrators we must be mindful of these studies, and make sure we combat this trend to treat schools as just another business. Since the dawn of the Industrial Revolution our education system was patterned after this 'factory model' of conforming students as a unified 'product' passed through an assembly line if you will guided down the halls grade by grade until graduation. This revelation has shocked many of us professionals in education management. How can we improve this model so we can better educate the entire child and compassionately help students? This business model is inherent in our educational system. So, where is the child left in this complicated system of education? The solutions found in this text have made education seem less complex and it has helped to make a positive contribution to the vast amount of research already existing in the area of school improvement strategies for today.

    Most experienced teachers arrive at the realization that our curriculum is a generic one, but, an essential one that gives us a measuring stick a standard that gives us results. What really stands out is that our students are not generic they are all unique, and gifted in the real sense in so many ways. This is the crux of this text: how do we educate the whole child and how can we help administrators understand that the student must always be first in education systems? Through the monumental work of Bowles and Gintis(1976) "Schooling in Capitalistic America" states without hesitation that our school systems is founded on the business model, in fact they state our schools are based on the Factory-Model meaning our students are uniform products, and their parents are shareholders. If there groundbreaking thesis is correct we the educator, the police maker, the curriculum designer, the administrator really need to re-think education.

Education Management and educational leadership have been discussed quite a bit over the years in Doctor of Education programs throughout the world and especially in Canada. The work of Kenneth Leithwood in the realm of educational leadership is unparalleled. Having had the tremendous good fortune to discuss these matters and be his student in graduate work I was shown all the diverse leadership styles that exist in education. Education Management, School Culture, and Leadership are all intertwined. Throughout this research there were three main themes: Power, Control and Organizations. As all educators taking the Doctor of Education and Master of Education programs in higher education we were all optimistic about the field of education. What our master professors taught us in the program was for us to look seriously at all the issues in education, so much so the professor would ask us: "Now why would you want to pursue a career in education at all?" They were convincing, schools as factories, conflict, power struggles, control, just another organization. They convinced many a graduate student to re-think this whole profession. But, as an optimistic learner I noticed a lot of the literature, or papers left out the student. In their terms what about the product? And labelling the student a product was one of the main issues of our education system.

How can all these diverse levels of educational leadership have a productive conversation about education and how to improve our schools. Parents, teachers, supervisors, principals, deans, and presidents of schools systems all can have a productive conversation without conflict if we begin to talk about the student first.

Some believe our education system is fine, and one of the best in the world in fact. That is true, especially in terms of educational resources. But, as research and experience clearly displays, the marginalized student, the student of low-economic status, and most importantly the Aboriginal student are not being cared for by our education system. The results and status of the fastest growing demographic of our population the Indigenous and their educational results must be taken seriously by all members of our academic community. In this way we can see how education management must incorporate and care for all levels of the educational system.

Kenneth Leithwood has clearly stated that educational leadership alone cannot improve our schools. Participative Leadership is the new wave of leadership that strays from the Authoritative Leadership of traditional school systems. Participative leadership divides the responsibilities of the Dean, Principal, or Vice-principal to other departments and levelling out the power to other groups within the school system. The only serious draw-back of this style is that there lies a danger of the educational leader at the top of the hierarchy may distribute the responsibility so well, that the leaders below her or him may feel they are doing more work than the boss.

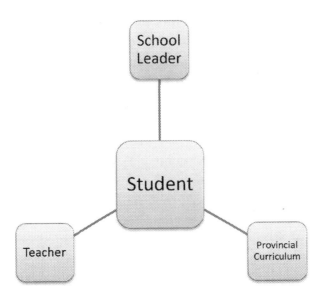

The invention of Henry Ford and the assembly line was the analogy that Bowles and Gintis (1976) had of producing a consistent product to be sold to the masses of our society. These researchers forced us look at our school buildings, our students and why do certain students always seem to fall off the assembly line, never to get back on the assembly line, and therefore fail to become a suitable 'product' for our society. This is the main issue this text will take on, why are we still viewing our children as products to be sold to customers future employers in our society.

What are we to think about the students that fall off the assembly line in schools? The students that end up in the hall, end up in the Principals office, kicked out of school, or drop out of school all together? This text will show that we are failing these students and when we begin to see the student as more than a product that needs to be conformed or molded into a specific product model then we can reach the student who is about to fall off the assembly line and make sure all students have an equal opportunity at life, and to be a productive member of our communities and society.

Next we will look at the curriculum the life blood of school systems and how the curriculum mixed with the leadership of the Principal and teacher really determine if the marginalized, low-economic, or Aboriginal student will succeed, or continue to be invisible in our school systems today. This is the core principal that all levels of education tries to live up to this inclusive curriculum that includes everyone.

Finally, the reason this research focused a great deal on the Indigenous student, is because it is highly necessary that these students receive a quality education. Secondly, understanding and educating policy makers, curriculum designers, and teachers of the obstacles facing Indigenous students is equally important. Lastly, focusing on the Indigenous student clearly shows how our current curriculum is not serving these communities or students. Therefore, our curriculum and system is not as inclusive as we could be. Then we can see why there is a correlation between large number of drop-outs or why attendance levels are in steady decline throughout our country from certain members of our community.

Furthermore, in terms of education management we clearly see why putting the student first is highly necessary as a moral principle. Even if you still view our education system from the business model perspective then: if the curriculum is not meeting the standards or expectations of the customer or shareholder the products (students) will stop coming to the factory (school). As a compassionate student-centered educator it is not suitable to look at the child in this way but our education management according to Bowles and Gintis and other scholars believe this is and was the blue-print of our school systems. This text is giving a solution on how to truly improve our school systems.

This text is written for policy-makers, curriculum designers, principals, heads of departments, and deans of colleges who can provide professional development to their staff. Staff will be empowered with this compassionate student-centered pedagogy that can enhance their teaching and student performance. Ideally, this text is written in way that can be easily accessible to parents. Parents who care so deeply about their child but do not know where to start, with long work days, and overtime not having time to truly understand complex systems like education. I hope that the dedicated and passionate parent can read these findings and gain confidence in student-teacher interviews no longer intimidated by teachers, vice-principals and principals but can see how true change can happen for their child. The hope is this text can help them plan properly and to avoid as many obstacles as possible in education for their child so they may soar throughout their high school journey, post-secondary, graduate school and in their career of choice in the future. This is the intent of the research herein and with hope and certainty this research will achieve all these lofty aims.

CHAPTER EIGHT

Post-Colonial Lens for Educators

⌘

Introduction: Unity in Our Diversity

This paper investigates the ways we can unite our students, with diversity and literature in an effective way. Teachers must find ways to empower our students and create safe environments for our students to excel and perform at their highest potential. Specifically, this paper will see Children's literature as a tool to investigate discrimination, and stereotypes. Multicultural children's stories are a great method for seeking and finding solutions to social problems and injustice. This research will prove that when educators use Multi-Cultural Children's books, role-plays, double-tracked books, and poetry in skillful and well intentioned ways tremendous positive change can occur in our schools and this will eventually filter out to our communities and thus making our world a better place for all peoples.

<u>Critical Reflection:</u>

Part I) Stumbling Blocks

Children's Literature: A Special Book From Your Childhood

My grandfather gave me a book while I was visiting him in India in 1990. This book was wrapped in an orange cloth as it was a very esoteric Tibetan Buddhist Scripture. This Buddhist scripture is called the Tib: Bardo Thodol, in English it is called the Tibetan Book of the Dead. This religious scripture outlines the process of living and dying well. Most importantly it gives us a road map of what path to follow when the process of life after death commences. Bardo literally means the intermediate state between this life and the next. This text is important to every Tibetan Buddhist as it helps one secure an appropriate rebirth to continue our practice of benefiting sentient beings and helping them on their path of compassion and happiness. Over the centuries the Tibetan language has been the main medium both for scriptures, sutras, and the practice instructions of Buddhism. Still at this day and age, the Tibetan language is the only language in our world that can fully express the entire canon of Buddhist scripture that are found in the Theravada, Mahayana, and Vajrayana Buddhist Schools. Ironically, this religious text is written in Tibetan script and I cannot read it. My grandfather knew I could not read, write or speak Tibetan but he gave this holy religious book to me anyways. Perhaps to him being able to read this text culminating in true education? As an academic now I see the role of globalization creeping in once again. I still treasure this text and have it in my possession and I have print of the introduction prayers with English phonetics with pictures of my grandfather giving me this text(see appendix). I have many university degrees but I still cannot read a text in my own language. With more and more Tibetan Buddhist texts being translated into the English language in an alarming rate, one may ask will there be a reason to learn Tibetan if all the esoteric texts are now available in English?

The Indigenous, Modernization, Globalization, School Buildings, School Improvement and the Industrial Age:

The general pattern throughout our CTL program and our course were: identity versus modernity, and the Industrial Revolution. However, the Indigenous populations hold that their knowledge, wisdom, and tradition as important and there is an innate resistance to modernity and Industrialization happening in their own countries. Indigenous peoples may not be aware of what they are resisting but their world-view or identity may be in strike contrast to our view of education, knowledge and modernity. Identity is linked with their native language and the globalization of the English and French languages. These are the major languages one requires for high employment and to rise up the corporate ladder.

Globalization:

"This is a strange moment in history, but we as teachers will endure. In our own way we will not despair nor be defeated. We will soldier on because we are in it for love and for the long haul.

And in the final analysis there is no greater gift- and no greater weapon- than love and compassion." Feuerverger p.142.

Globalization makes it necessary not to retain your own traditional language because one cannot make any money or your job does not require you to know how to read, write or speak your native language so eventually you and your children will lose your native language and thus you will lose your identity. In order break free from your poor economic situation you must put your identity and native language on hold and pursue English and be a part of the Capitalistic system.

The compatibility of science and Indigenous knowledge this is another level of understanding. Science and Indigenous knowledge are both on the same path and are often seen as having more in common than not. The field of science is on a quest for truth, and Indigenous knowledge was and is also on a quest for truth. Both fields are trying to understand and discover the nature of reality. Indigenous knowledge naturally has much truth as it has endured as knowledge for centuries and peoples have found some intrinsic value and worth in these teachings and beliefs. Again, the best definition that sums up what was stated above on Globalization was given by Noam Chomsky when he stated in a lecture:

"The poor complain as they always do but that is just idle chatter, our system brings rewards to all at least to those who matter." - Noam Chomsky-

Modernization:

Modernity on the other hand has more to do with market capitalism, technology and the Industrial Age. The question that this program and course asks us are: who are the colonized? Once we recognize who were colonized how do we de-colonize the world? Can we de-colonize our curriculum and schools? Do the Indigenous populations assimilate, or resist or are they even aware they are assimilating or resisting? It seems one needs to be aware firstly and then one can blend both worlds together. Assimilate should be termed as integrate and then not resist but retain your cultural and traditional identity. On the other hand, one must admit this focus on modernization and the Industrial Revolution has made us emotion-less, and robotic in our daily lives. It seems we have lost something, are we more happier than our ancestors? Where are the important virtues of love and the compassion in our world today? Are our families as close knitted, loving and stable? Or have we lost the intrigue, the magic and mystery of life? As human beings we need to believe in something more magical something beyond and above us. Humanity has labeled everything, and have made this world dualistic, boring and ordinary. Must we know everything? Must we own everything? Maybe that is what we have lost, the humbleness of not knowing, we have stopped looking at the skies in wonder and to be in awe of our existence. This mystery that binds us all as sentient beings on this magical small blue planet.

I have been trying to get away from the history of colonialism and just focus on individual countries and their economic and educational development. After living on a First Nation reservation for two years I have been thinking very negatively about colonization and other injustices as I have experienced it first hand on the reservation. Having my stomach heart because the water is not up to standard and hearing that there is a boiled water advisory for the community way after the fact that we have been drinking the water for months. Not having roads, sidewalks, street lights, houses that are heated, schools with mildew and fungus growing in its walls. But I am trying to reconcile this with the argument of scholarship that says that higher more complex societies were seen as the end-points toward which the primitive (less-developed) societies would eventually reach. However, all societies, even the advanced ones, were seen as evolving in the direction of great progress. Fagerlind and Saha (1989).

This is true from the modern scientific model but there is a cultural side that is not seen. For some societies for example Indigenous, First Nation, Aboriginal, Muslim and even Buddhist cultures look to a Golden Age and in fact see our world as declining not getting better or progressing. For example, the Muslim world-view would view the time of Prophet Muhammad as the ideal society and world, the same can be true of Buddhists at the time of Siddhartha Gotama that was a Golden Age. The process of Fagerlind and Sha undermine these views and convictions of the traditional society. Their process of Modernization is:

Modernizing Institutions> Modern Values> Modern Behaviour> Modern Society> Economic Development.

That is the first goal of the process of Modernization as proclaimed by Fagerlind and Sha is Modernizing Institutions. The developing world does not have modern institutions so this is the phenomenon we will investigate next.

School Buildings:

From my own experience visiting my relatives in South India, Mysore I saw first hand their schools and living conditions. These factors in my opinion out weigh all other factors.

Their houses were made of mud and their schools were also made of mud. They did not have washrooms, just holes in the ground, nor toilet paper nor running water and lizards all over the ceilings of their houses and schools. These factors need to be considered first. As well myself working in a First Nations community in Northern Ontario, the school building was the main obstacle I feel for drop-outs and low-attendance.

Our school was essentially a very large portable, it was not a building. The children did not have running toilets, even the staff did not have running toilets we had to use the janitors office for washroom use. We did not have working fountains, there was no clean drinkable water, all water must be boiled before drinking.

The building had mildew and fungus within its walls, we had poor air quality, windows were broken, and our classrooms were too small for the large growing population of this community.

Essentially, I believe we must send architects and build suitable structures and school buildings first before we talk about literacy and other high educational aims. This does not only stop at education, but the hospitals in India are well below standard.

These hospitals in the village are also made of mud and we must help these developing countries build infrastructure first before sending doctors, nurses, teachers, and researchers.

On the reservation the hospital is also a large portable with a few nurses, no doctors or dentists on call. So, if one is dedicated and serious about helping developing countries, nations and peoples with their well-being, education and health we should be sending architects and resources to help them build their communities and nations.

As we all know when we have infrastructure one can feel pride and work toward progress but if one has nothing but despair and poverty then the situation becomes hopeless and the fires of resistance are ignited.

"Issues of resistance, reaction, compliance, and accommodation at the national, local, and individual levels." Mundy(1993) p.390

School Improvement:

How can we fix all societal ills and issues of society in schools? I also recall a class presentation we had with four group members all of different professional background one from the middle-east who was a college instructor, one was a principal in the Catholic District School Board, one a new mother who was taking time off from teaching elementary, and myself a high-school teacher who is studying full-time.

Our presentation was to take what we have learned in the TPS course and apply the theories and lessons and implement it into a school improvement action plan. It was horrible we still could not comply and see each other's point of view.

So, in retrospect the power and control aspect maybe an underlying factor in decision making and also showing how complex school improvement is. It is a basic human right for everyone to be able to have access to primary education and literacy but how does it fit with a given country? If we are wanting all countries to be able to compete with all other G8 and G20 nations then we need to build infrastructure, world-class hospitals, schools, and colleges first.

Then we can send the researchers and scholars in the assess the situation, its like sending scholars in to research an natural disaster of course there is nothing there- the same can be said of colonized lands that we are sending our scholars to research.

Colonized lands are behind not innately but because of colonization that left their countries barren, and infertile. This something K. Mundy points to when the article points to Martin Carnoy and his writings no doubt leading to his influential text: Education as Cultural Imperialism.

Resnick (1987) equates schooling with economic participation. As I was reflecting in class that week was that when education and capitalism mix it ceases to be a moral activity.

The Industrial Age:

We can learn a lot from France and Britain in terms of the Industrial Revolution. The main aspects of Industrialization that I can gather from this age are many and I do not think the developing countries we are studying nor the First Nations or Tibet have entered this stage in development as of yet, since they are lacking many of these key aspects:

1) Roads
2) Waterways
3) Fuel and Power
4) The Iron Industry
5) Textile Raw Materials, wool, linen, cotton and silk
6) Labor-wages, a positive attitude toward labour.

7) Capitalistic mind-set
8) Technology and machinery.
9) Railroads

What are the signs of colonization? Well in the realm of education one will begin to doubt your traditions, lose your identity and look down on your Elders. When you look down on your own Elders then the doctrine of the colonizers prevail.

It seems if you still adhere to your identity, culture, spirituality, and still hold your mother tongue as supreme you will be alienated and isolated from this capitalistic society. People of conscience must stand up against this colonization rooted in globalization and market capitalism.

The goal of our course was to slow down and recharge our batteries. Our class lead by our Professor Grace Feuerverger had us engage in the ancient practice of meditation. This practice seemed so fitting because this curriculum of life based on the Industrial Revolution our lives every day is so fast paced it is almost like our life is likened to an existence in a factory.

"We teachers are increasingly de-skilled and hammered into interchangeable cogs in a bureaucracy, pressured to reduce teaching to a set of manageable and easily supervisible tasks, and to sum up all our efforts on the basis of a single and simple minded metric, to strip teaching of any moral purpose or intellectual engagement or creative action whatsoever." William Ayers P.xi

What is Education?

In Indigenous societies such as Tibet education was for self-betterment, knowledge of self and spiritual liberation. Education in capitalistic countries tends to be for self-gain, intense competition, and more capital and profit ideology. Curriculum, pedagogies and assessment tools help achieve its goal. How did modern educational systems originate?

"Education was less than ever linked to learning alone. At its center were the correction and reformation of the immigrants child's language, culture, moral outlook and inner self. The alien nature of such youth could be transformed only by severe discipline and a rejection of their parental heritage and values." Rothstein (1991). Pg.29

A teacher with this knowledge can see how this plays out as a negative pattern of failure, a trend that surrounds many generations of urban poor, minority, and Indigenous children. The minority or marginalized child who lacks the cultural and social capital will blame herself or himself for their failure in school and society.

Symbolic Violence: The mission of Bourdieu was to uncover the primary principles underlying the inequalities in academic achievement of children of different social origins and sexes.

Cultural Capital: The education system gives an unfair advantage to those who already possess a substantial advantage, by valuing highly the culture and language of dominant classes and seeking to reproduce these beliefs, values, and norms in our society and work settings. This cultural capital and symbolic violence as Bourdieu describes is inherently linked because we teachers are forced to look negatively, label, alienate, and ignore the students who do not have enough of this cultural capital. Our students who are from the dominant discourse or culture are naturally viewed more highly than those students who do not, and the issues of symbolic violence and injustice are carried on from one generation to the next.

Part II) Solutions

Meaningful and Culturally Relevant Curriculum:

"The construction of curriculum is in fact a relational act, and therefore a discourse of empowerment needs to be created out of the historical, social, linguistic and cultural realities that are the bedrock of the forms of knowledge and meaning that teachers and students bring to the school. Reciprocity is important. These activities, however are in themselves not enough; they need to be positioned within a larger social and intellectual perspective. A curriculum infused with egalitarianism and mutual understanding must be located within formal and informal school activities." Feuerverger, pg. 144.

Education From a Traditional Perspective: Schooling is a process that helps our students integrate smoothly into our given society. Classroom management and the focus on discipline, rules, and proper school conduct is seen as paramount in the classroom setting. Testing, standardized tests, punching the clock, stratification into streams and tracks is the main focus of administrators and teaching staff. Character education is linked with helping our students in becoming better citizens. The role of conforming and teaching proper behavior is one of the main tasks of administrators and staff.

Education For Today's Multi-Cultural Reality: Education should be aimed at helping our students see morality in terms of the larger societal issues. We must be skilled at addressing larger societal issues in our classrooms. Introducing important topics such as: assimilation, control, systematic oppression, power, resistance, identity, globalization, religion, culture and diversity must be done in a meaningful and in an intelligent way. The amount of work attributed to bringing up these critical issues properly will take a huge amount of time and trying to raise these important issues in a hastily manner will not bring it justice and might cause problems for you with parents, and the administration. Since this preparation and critical reflection takes much energy and time some teachers may just stay with the standard curriculum and not address the hidden curriculum. Or some teachers may not even be aware of anything else besides the dominant discourse and who can blame them as the dominant discourse permeates our current system.

Role Play To Engage Critical Reflection: Grade 8 History Lesson on Confederation

We get a glimpse into a Grade 8 History Lesson entitled: Confederation. Mrs. Martin is giving a short over-view of the history lesson on Confederation before a major test on the unit. Take a look at the classroom picture and see some of the negative outcomes of such a lesson.

Mrs. Martin: Okay class as we all know we have a major test coming up next week so I want to go over some important issues of this test on Confederation. We have discussed in great length the factors and important events that lead to the creation of the Dominion of Canada. When was the Dominion of Canada created?

Joseph: Miss what does Dominion mean again?

Mrs. Martin: Does anyone else know the answer?

Mary: Dominion means to control or to seize control over something.

Mrs. Martin: That is correct it is normally associated with sovereignty.

Joseph: Doesn't sovereignty mean to have supreme control over territory?

Mrs. Martin: That is right!

Joseph: So, who was in control of the territory before the Confederation of 1867 then?

Mrs. Martin: The main point for the test Joseph, is that yes Confederation was created in 1867.

Joseph: Was Canada called 'Canada' before 1867 and who named our country Canada? What does Canada mean anyways?

Mary: I heard that Canada was pronounced 'Kanata' and was meant to mean village in an Iroquoian language of Eastern Canada.

Mrs. Martin: I think we are getting off topic here for the purposes of the test that is next class we must know the dates of 1867, the definition of Confederation and that Sir John A. MacDonald was the father of Confederation and the first Prime Minister of Canada.

Mary: So, Canada is only 153 years old then?

Mrs. Martin: Remember the dates and the major historical persons for the test next week.

Bell Rings and students leave for recess.

From the above role play that I created we can see the structural factors that come into play. The teacher, the tests, the standardization of the tests, the cultural capital and social capital of the teacher and curriculum planners all come into play in when symbolic violence happens in our schools. Whose voice is missing? Who is absent in the curriculum? Who is invisible in the classroom? Who is silenced and who is empowered? All these crucial factors must be assessed before one can even discuss a multi-cultural curriculum and a multi-cultural society that is promoted and actualized. How can we promote a multi-cultural curriculum until we truly raise and let the First Nation, Metis and Inuit voices be heard in our classrooms, schools and society.

Critical Multi-Cultural Analysis:

"Violence is initiated by those who oppress, who exploit, who fail to recognize others as persons- not by those who are oppressed, exploited, and unrecognized." Freire, pg.41

The reason why I felt compelled to see Children's literature from the Critical Multi-Cultural Framework was because of the field trip our class took to the Toronto Public Library. The librarian chose to discuss children's books which focused on Multi-Culturalism and that could be shared in our classrooms. However, two of the children's books that were shared by the librarian made me feel very uncomfortable and I usually stay silent I had to raise my hand and speak my thoughts. I was really fatigued that day, no energy and I just had a three-hour lecture before this one and finished two presentations in the two other courses- but was able to say express these few thoughts:

"It seems there is a slippery slope in regards to multi-cultural literature. I felt very uncomfortable with two of the books that were shared today."

The librarian stated:

"Which ones made you feel uncomfortable?"

"The book entitled: 'The Visit' which gives a very poor image of black men and black fathers and the book entitled: 'Coolies' which is a degrading term given to Indians and Chinese during the days of British Colonization." I stated.

Most stayed quiet but "The Visit" a book which discusses how a jailed black man was expecting a visit from his daughter while in prison. Interesting enough it was the only African/Canadian/American book shared to the class. The "Coolies" book was equally if not more offensive as Coolie essentially means slave. Indians and Chinese people were indentured slaves that were shipped from India and China to other parts of the Dominion of the British Empire to work in the fields or build rail-roads.

I wanted the librarian to expand on these books but when she stated that her presentation was over and asked if we had any questions then I had to speak my mind. Especially in our class we learned about the Critical Multi-Cultural Analysis Framework. This framework shows us how to assess and make informed decisions about which books are shared in your classroom. This framework is excellent as it helps teachers investigate the issues of gender, culture, power, race, politics, history, and class structures in the books. The two questionable books: "The Visit" and "Coolies" can help students use their critical thinking skills however, I would not have these two specific books in my classroom or in my school library.

Classification:

The three main classifications of suitable books for students are: a) Social Conscience Books, b) Melting Pot/ Culturally Generic Books, and c) Culturally Conscious/ Culturally Specific Books.

a) Social Conscience Books: These types of books foster social conscience, help the dominate group empathize and educate them about other ethnic and diverse cultures and world-views.
b) Melting Pot/ Culturally Generic Neutral Books: Universal themes and the goal or theme is an integrated society and world.
c) Culturally Conscious/ Culturally Specific Books: Focus on unique experiences of ethnic groups, language emphasis, and world-views. Book takes place in important settings of the specific culture.

The three books that I highly recommend and are excellent resources to foster social conscience are: "The Golden Rule" by Ilene Cooper, "It's Okay To Be Different" by: Todd Parr, and "The Peace Book" also by Todd Parr. All three of these books foster the important virtue of inclusiveness. The books that are seen as problems are the ones that exclude the student population that the book was meant to help. The "Golden Rule" book is so important as it innately unifies all our students into one vision and one quest of human unity. These are the books we need, books that do not focus on difference solely but on the myriad of factors that unite us. The Christian, Jewish, Taoist, Confucian, Native, Buddhist and Muslim traditions have the Golden Rule in all of their religious scripture. What a marvelous and important discovery for a student to recognize and appreciate. "The Visit" however, will give negative stereotypes to the black students in your class and make them feel excluded from their peers, and the book entitled: "Coolies" will make your Chinese students feel negatively about themselves and further subjugate them as the "other". Again presenting a multi-cultural children's books is a slippery slope as books that have multi-cultural happy faces on them does not automatically make them socially acceptable.

Summary:

"We have turned schools into knowledge factories. This is not the way. Every person is a kind of artist. Real education is when we are walking together on a journey of self-realization: the teacher, the student, the parent. The universe is a communion of subjects not a collection of objects. We are all capable of a great energy which sows the seeds of Divine inspiration." Feuerverger, pg. 147.

If teachers are aware of the inherent conflict of the power and control dynamics we can better prepare ourselves for a long and rewarding career in teaching. If we are aware of the structures and forces that are arrayed against us we can not only teach our students but our peers, colleagues and supervisors.

Here the curriculum can be viewed as a computer chip or the program and in a robotic fashion we recite the curriculum (the program) to our students who is then also programmed and the knowledge is further deposited into the mind streams of the students. From my experience and my studies in the TPS program at OISE I have been given ample readings and research showing the negative side and not so positive origins of education and schools. But from the courses I am taking in CTL with Prof. Feuerverger I have seen the many positive sides of teaching and schools when the educator is truly empowered and becomes a genuine educator. An educator is not one holds knowledge, an educator is one who holds wisdom to be shared in our everyday real experience. The great enthusiasm and passion my professor has for teaching and the education system was very inspiring. I needed to see my professor every week as she gave me hope and inspiration. The TPS and other CTL courses were so depressing for me as a minority student, I think it was because all of the readings of the negative side of education I could directly identify with. The constant theme in my courses were the minorities were the survivors if they made it to university and received a degree. I felt uncomfortable again, my peers and colleagues looking at me like how did he get here, according to the readings he should not have made it this far, maybe he is a token minority in the class? I had to prove myself and show I belonged, I have worked so hard in my life to make a difference. This is my second Masters Degree from the University of Toronto and I can only find employment as a security guard at Robarts library, why should minorities have to work so hard, why must we be survivors just to get a university degree? I will not give up not only for my Tibetan people I want to be a positive role model, but the reason I entered OISE Graduate studies was to be a voice for the First Nations that I served and taught on reservation #209 and reservation #210 in Northern Ontario, Canada. One weekend after a very trying week of school I reflected alone in the school gymnasium that I find it very hard to believe that anyone of my students will make it out of here to get a college or university education. I must use my privilege and opportunity to be more for them and give them a voice in academia. Maybe I will be able to make the change in our education system so they can make it to college and university. But once I got here, I realized how difficult it was to bring up the First Nation issues in my courses here, and how most did not want to hear about it. I was frustrated initially but after listening to Prof. Feuerverger and her optimism and mantra of change and hope for a brighter tomorrow I now realize education and curriculum is not declining but it is just getting started! When more teachers and administrators see and understand what I know the education system will change rapidly and move to a more just form of education. This course has empowered me and has given me the strength, wisdom, compassion and the love to truly make the change our education system needs. As soon as I stand in front of the students in my future classroom the change is there, the future is there, and then the future generations will also naturally see our world differently and more holistically than the past.

Humanity is the supreme focus of all religious and philosophical ideologies. The religious ideologies that have endured in this world of ours, have as their supreme focus, the human being as their focal point in scripture. The goal of scripture was to assist human beings attain a state of peace, this has been the aim of all religious founders and teachers. Even though, the very conception of contentment, perfection or an idealized state does clash from one religion to another, but the main goal which all religious leaders have striven was to guide humanity towards a higher goal in life, to give us purpose and to uplift us. This research will reveal the unity in our diversity. As educators and administrators we often seem to look into the classroom to solve apparent problems and issues with our students. However, through more experience we find that family, historic events, environment and society shape our children before they ever enter the classroom. This research takes on the lofty goal of educating not only students but the masses of the interconnectedness of all of us to the Human Family. By implementing this philosophy the issues we as educators strive to eradicate: discrimination, racism, bigotry, social inequality, poverty, and pollution will be solved. This research will propel the reader to change one's conventional thinking and one will see that our world is truly interdependent, there is only one race: The Human Race. The divisions, war, deception, injustice, pollution, poverty, racism, bigotry, human slavery, discrimination, and bullying we see from person to person, and nation to nation is totally human created. Looking at the world in a holistic way, our globe has no divisions, no lines separating one country from another. Nor is there an intrinsic label dividing one country from another; we have created these divisions and labels. All the problems we are facing as a people, can be solved, because we are the creator of these problems. This research will give the educator sound methodology to implement into his or her classroom and beyond. It looks into the origins of these problems, finds the source or root of the problem and tries to propel us in the 21st century with a more enlightened outlook in the field of academic administration.

The Topic

Objective: Analyze interview data to identify and describe Educational Leaders responses to obstacles facing First Nations attaining leadership roles in education.

Setting the context.

What is the problem?
Significant absence of First Nation Leadership in Education.
What is known about the problem?
Residential School System (First Nation)
Confederation of 1867
Assembly of First Nations (Composed their own separate Education Policy from the Ministry of Education of Ontario)

10 major themes discovered through interview process of Minority Leadership:

1) Obstacles
2) Dysfunction
3) Colonization/Imperialism
4) Racism
5) Religion
6) Addiction
7) Government Policy
8) Poverty
9) Lack of Role-Models
10) Lack of Resources

What evidence do you have to support your claim that this is a problem?

First Nation Focused Curriculum

After discussing with my colleagues at Aglace Chapman Education Centre (Big Trout Lake, Ontario) I was told that my current students all failed but one the year before and that many have become depressed and none thought they could successful complete grade 8. I was completing my long-range plans for the grade 8 academic year and realized that most of the objectives in the curriculum guidelines did not mesh well with the reality of these children. However, I understood that my goal was to catch these students up to the rest of the standards of Ontario and that I must cover all the curriculum objectives of the province. However, I started off every class: geography, history, English, Language Arts, and science from a First Nation perspective. As my goal was to keep attendance high, as if the students attended school regularly this increased their chances of graduating. Everything was from the First Nation perspective focusing on First Nation stories, legends, history, achievement, invention, and special contributions they have had to the country of Canada. The staff, principal and community were amazed at the high attendance levels and achievement of the students. Many variables may have came into play as in math and other areas themes and objectives were repeated from last year, but the attendance was strikingly higher than the year before and thus all 25 students passed their examinations in Literacy and Math that year.

Big Trout Lake: Grade 8 Results 2004-2005 (First Nation Focused Curriculum)

Standard Ontario Curriculum 2003-2004	# of Students in Grade 8	# of Students Failed Grade 8	# of students passed onto Grade 9
Teacher taught standard Ontario Curriculum	24	23	1
Teacher taught from a First Nations World-View Focus	26	1	25

What is First Nation Leadership?

First Nation lineages are passed down orally through the generations. The belief that the Great Spirit created the Earth and is the Mother of all creation. Plants and animals have spirits that must be venerated, honoured, and cared for. It is a holistic system that centers not only on human life but also the life of the world and all things in it. The medicine wheel symbolizes how all life is interconnected and embarked on in a circular journey. The four cardinal directions, each of which as a guiding spirit and special attributes, reflects the stages of the life journey.

When I talked to Elders, one can see the change in the children and see the many negative aspects effecting their children. Children involved in gangs, loss of identity, drug use, and being sent to mental health centres is an aspect of everyday life in these communities.

"What is needed is funding that encourages and supports comprehensive long-term planning and action. Such funding must address both healing as recovery (crisis intervention) and community health and a healthy community and nation." (Aboriginals Peoples Collection, pg.52)

Their loss of identity, hopelessness, and loss of language has had serious negative effects on their confidence and self value. Families trying to understand and cope with the injustices and confusion of the past resorted to drugs and alcohol to deal the pain, suffering and confusion. Not knowing that these negative habits would be passed onto their children who are now affected with many disorders of Attention Deficit Disorder (ADD), Attention Deficit Hyperactivity Disorder(ADHD) and Fetal Alcohol Syndrome (FAS).

"If the goal is to heal the nation, it is critical to invest heavily in healing the nations children." (Aboriginal Peoples Collection, pg53).

These alternative policies out-lined in this paper will truly help First Nations get back on their feet and help them heal their past and move them forward into the future.

Assembly of First Nation Educational Plan Document (A Separate Policy Plan created by First Nation Leaders).

The growing rate of suicides in First Nation communities and large amounts of Black and First Nation representation in Jail systems throughout our country.

What is the relationship of your study to the problem you outline?

Major theme is power and control. First Nations want full jurisdiction over their issues, and education.

What research to date has been carried out on your study topic?

Policies on success for student success: Ministry of Education 2007 Document. First Nation voice is not heard in this policy document.

Assembly of First Nations created their own Policy document entitled: Assembly of First nation Education Document. Its focus is on full jurisdiction over First Nation Education.

Paulo Freire: Pedagogy of the Oppressed, but I have yet to find researchers who have lived amongst First Nations communities for 2 years, most research is for a very small period of time.

How does this research inform us?

I will utilize the five interviews describing the obstacles facing minority leadership. These findings will help my research in understanding the reasons for lack of First Nation Leadership in education. Essentially minorities still have an identity and religious background that sustains them and gives them solace. However, the First Nations in Canada has lost this identity because of the implementation of the Residential School System. Other groups of people still have their histories, heritage and religion to give them comfort, solace and confidence in trying times. But our First Nation brothers and sisters have lost this part of their lives.

This may explain why other minorities are doing better economically than most First Nations of this country.

What is wrong with this research?

I have a very strong background in First Nation issues, and educational systems. However, I still need more research in trying to link their issues to other peoples and groups like students of low-economic backgrounds, South Asian Canadians, African Canadians, Tibetan Canadians, and other ethnic groups.

What is missing in this research?

My strength: The First Nation world-view is absent, many policy documents and research claim to represent the minority view of leadership and view but do not articulately describe what it is or how this can contribute greatly to the leadership role in education.

What is missing: Field research in other communities for instance: Tibetan Communities, African Canadian Communities and other ethnic communities. I want to see if these 4 main aspects of: 1) Spiritual Leadership, 2) Educational Leadership, 3) School Building/Infrastructure and 4) Poverty are important in all cultural settings pertaining to the attainment of educational leadership roles.

What effect will this study have on the problem? Why is this study important? (Significance)

This study can strengthen Canada as a nation. This study will give the silenced a voice and educate Canadians on the whole of the great importance First Nation Leaders can have a unique contribution in the realm of educational leadership. Presently we only look down on First Nation leaders as not having enough, and that they are not up to our 'standards', but if we appreciate the unique abilities they bring to the educational leadership role plus the added training, this can strengthen Canada in the Global level.

Focus:

What do you intend to study?

The obstacles First Nations face in attaining leadership positions in education.

What are the obstacles facing First Nations in attaining leadership positions in education?

I would like to use a genealogical lens focusing on the history of imperialism and colonization. I would like to then focus on solutions to propel our country into the future, and to make us truly powerful nation where all voices are heard.

Karma M. Chukdong B.Ed, M.A., M.Ed

Perspective Lens

What is the phenomenon you are studying?

Policy Genealogical Approach

The Webster's Dictionary definition of imperialism is: the state policy, practice, or advocacy of extending the power and dominion of a nation, especially the direct territorial acquisition or by gaining indirect control over the political or economical life of other areas. The impoverished lands of Africa, Latin America, and Asia are today called Third World Nations—to distinguish them from First World Nations of North America and Europe. In our society Third World poverty is treated by contemporary western society as a timeless condition. Society is made to believe that this has always been the case. Impoverished countries are poor because their lands have always been infertile or their people unproductive and lazy. This is incorrect. In reality the lands of Africa, Middle-East, Asia and Latin America have long produced rich natural resources of minerals, oil, foods, and precious stones. This is the reason why Western Imperialism went through all the trouble to control and seize them. The Third World is not underdeveloped but over exploited. Western colonization and investments have created a lower rather than higher standard of living. Case and point the extreme poverty that we find on First Nation reservations in Northern Ontario, Canada. The historical injustices of the past cannot be overlooked or forgotten as there resides the root cause of many of the obstacles of genuine self-determination, and democracy in our country. Once we address the root causes as Gillborn suggests then we can move forward and remedy the problems and stumbling blocks to true understanding. Being students of history of imperialism and colonialism we can see how many of these same practices utilized by the British Empire, were utilized to subjugate the First Nations of Canada.

"Schooling is a hierarchical structure is therefore a colonizing device. Schooling was primarily for 'civilizing' and governing conquered people." (Carnoy, 1971, pg.349)

This was directly reflected in the Residential School system of Canada. This was a method employed to assimilate, destroy an identity, and a way of erasing language, even changing the names of children, and making them ashamed of being of Native descent.

"More importantly it instilled in them a respect and awe for the aristocratic virtues of the majestic English language, culture and corresponding contempt and disdain for their own background." (Carnoy, 1971, pg.101)

In the realm of language we see the same internal struggle. First Nations children and parents stress the importance of their Native language classes as more important than other subjects taught at school. They force their children to attend Native language class but are not as strict with attending other courses. Most ethnic peoples love and cherish their language, as language is the essence of one's culture, history and identity.

"Possession of two languages is not merely a matter of having two tools, but actually means participation in two physical and cultural realms. Here, the two worlds symbolized and conveyed by the two tongues are in conflict; they are those of the colonizer and the colonized." (Carnoy, 1971, pg.70)

The two schools that draw upon first-hand experience are reservation number 209 (Big Trout Lake, Ontario) and reservation number 210 (Kasabonika Lake, Ontario).

Why is there an absence of First Nation Leadership in Education?

One of the first things one notices upon entering a First Nation school in the north is the absence of First Nation teachers. If there is a First Nation teacher he or she would be assigned to teach Native language courses. This responsibility is usually given to a highly respected Elder of the community to teach the next generation of their peoples. Therefore, Native language is seen as far more vital than other school subjects because it is their education and it is taught by a First Nation teacher and Elder. Many students skip the majority of classes and just attend the Native language courses and physical education that is usually after Native language class everyday. This is a very important point recognized by the research of the Aboriginal Policy documents as well. They recognize that attendance is almost 95% in their Native Language Classes in contrast to their other subject classes at their schools. There maybe many variables to the reason for this, but their research concludes that it has to do with the children learning their culture, tradition and language. Also this Native language class is always taught by a Native Elder from the community, and that the importance of this class is always stressed by their parents.

Age- appropriate students by extent of First Nation Language Instruction, 2000-01 (Aboriginal Policy Research, 2006)

Native Language Attendance	Age-appropriate
None	82.9
½ Time	88.8
<1/2 Time	83.2
Subject	81.7
Subject P/T	82.8
Subject F/T	94.0

When traditional language is offered as a subject and full-time medium instruction, is significantly higher than all of the other categories. These researchers conclude:

"The striking point about Canadian assessments of First Nations and Aboriginal education is the lack of any real modeling of reasons for the particular patterns of educational attainment." (Aboriginal Policy Research, Pg.143)

Native teachers cannot teach in the elementary end of the school because the school board is funded by the Federal government and must abide by the policies of teachers having an Ontario teaching degree. The reason being is that schools on reservations only go to grade eleven, and if a student wants to get their high school diploma they must leave their community. They will have to live and attend a school outside their community in order to earn their high school diploma:

"The community has an elementary and a junior high school. In order to complete school, students have to board in Sioux Lookout." (Denied Too Long, pg.29)

The road block is further compounded in the realm of leadership of schools and community. The communities of Big Trout Lake and Kasabonika Lake have never had a First Nation Principal because of this system. For most children and families just making it to Grade 8 is seen as finishing high school in their communities. The grade 8 graduation is far more elaborate and celebrated in these communities. Grade 8 graduation is given as much applause and recognition as high school graduation here in central Ontario. When one looks down the hall at the high school end of the school the halls are empty and classes having one or two students enrolled in high school classes where they attend sporadically throughout the semester.

This study will focus on the First Nation leadership today, and will focus on the obstacles they face in securing leadership roles in education.

Consider:

What are the various elements/ dimensions/ processes associated with it?

The historical implications will be assessed in great detail, the sociological and psychological implications will be investigated as well.

What has been written about these things?

At the moment because of this Capitalistic agenda of our world certain voices are being ignored and are no longer seen as significant. Communist China is oppressing the Tibetan voice in Tibet, Black people world-wide are still facing much injustice, the First Nations in Canada and America are still resisting the colonization of the west. In order for us all to move forward we need to see what obstacles these peoples are facing in order for them and their peoples to have a voice in today's world. Education is the main reason for social and mental happiness and all peoples should have an equal chance at securing academic success and ultimately leadership roles in the educational field.

What is right with these sources?

Many journals discuss the issue and bring up the issue, but not enough studies try to pin point the root of the issue.

What is wrong with them?

There is a lack of urgency in many articles and policy documents. Everyday great potential is being lost because of socio-economic, poverty and lack of resources and education. We must educate the public and people in positions of power to the reasons why First Nations are not attaining the success in the leadership roles in education.

What is the best way to arrange/ describe these elements/dimensions/ processes so that you can answer your research question?

My field research: I lived and taught in a First Nation Community in Canada for two years. I have interviewed First Nation teachers, non-native teachers employed there, Native Administrators, minority leaders in Ontario.

Essentially in policy discourse, one voice is heard, but some may be given an opportunity to enter the dialogue but still not be represented in the policy directives and document. For instance the Ministry of Education Policy document on First Nation, Metis, and Inuit Students. In this document the Ontario government plainly says on page 23 that the Provincial government has full jurisdiction over First Nation education. Naturally the First Nations have a separate policy document discussing the right they have over the education over their people and children.

Method

How are you going to answer your research questions?

Through interviews and using my experience as a case study while teaching in First Nation community for two years, and witnessing a lack of First Nation teachers in their own school systems. This is because teachers still must have an Ontario College of Teachers Degree, and First Nations have so many obstacles that even finishing grade eight is a major accomplishment in these communities.

I will answer this by utilizing a Qualitative study and Quantitative analysis.

Why are you choosing these methods/ this approach?

I will use qualitative approach to assess the thoughts and perspectives of the leaders in the field. Quotes and responses will give us a glimpse of the their beliefs, concerns and thoughts. It allows us to experience their world.

Case Study: Gives this study more credibility because of the long duration I was there(2 years) so I have a clear understanding of what really goes on in a First Nation community, and the societal obstacles these peoples face.)

Quantitative: When I code these responses of the interviews many clear themes emerge to why these obstacles are and have occurred over time. Also when I taught the Ontario curriculum from the First Nation Perspective the success of the students improved drastically. This is correlated to the Black focused schools in Toronto, where when their voice or perspective is given prominence their community believes success is inevitable. Ultimately I would like to cross-reference these findings with other Minority groups in their struggles to attain Leadership Positions within school systems.

How and why are you choosing participants/sites?

I chose a First Nation community because as an outsider I felt their people should be doing quite well, but once I got there I realized the third world poverty they are living in. Also I would like to investigate the TCV (Tibetans Children Village) in India where the Tibetan community in exile have the same resources and facilities but their children are having tremendous success in academics. I would like to investigate the leadership impact of His Holiness the 14th Dalai Lama in establishing this confidence in success of his people.

How are you going to analyze your data?

Coding of interviews and statistical information of drop-outs, and failures amongst students. I would like to investigate how the Tibetan Buddhist university system administers doctorate degrees in Buddhist philosophy and how this corresponds to confidence and respect amongst the Tibetan community. Therefore they have sustainable leadership, and academic success in their refugee communities. However, here in Canada First Nations have lost their leadership roles(Elders) because of colonization and residential schools and this has lead to lack of leadership, and much dysfunction in these communities. I have 5 interview transcripts: 3 from a First Nation teaching perspective, and 2 from a minority teachers perspective. I can utilize these findings and see what is important to each of these leaders in education.

I also have data on success rates of teaching from a First Nation focused curriculum in contrast to teaching the standard Ontario curriculum to First Nation students. These finding will be put in chart form.

The Educational Leaders Interviewed:

A) First Nation Administrator (Female) Big Trout Lake First Nation Reservation #209
B) Non-Native Teacher (Female) Elementary: Taught One-year at Big Trout Lake First Nation.
C) Non-Native Teacher (Male) Special Education: Taught One-Year at Big Trout Lake First Nation. Currently teaches in an Inuit Community in Quebec.
D) Canadian Chinese Administrator: Vice-Principal in Toronto, Ontario.
E) Canadian Tibetan Teacher (Male) Taught English Language in India, and Tibetan Language in Canada. Currently is a Safety Coordinator in a Factory in Belleville, Ontario.

Inductive Coding (Grounded Theory Approach)

Objective: Analyze interview data to identify and describe educational leaders responses to obstacles facing minority leaders attaining leadership roles in education.

Obs = obstacle
Dys = Dysfunction
Col= Colonization
Rac= Racism
Rel= Religion
Add= Addiction
Gov= Government
Pov= Poverty
LML= Lack of Minority Role- Models
LOR= Lack of Resources

Obstacles = Innate and systemic obstacles these leaders faced. Focus on assimilation and Integration obstacles.

Dysfunction = Past research dictates when colonization occurs, dysfunction occurs at the family level, community level, and nation-hood level. (Work of Paulo Freire, 1970.)

Colonization/Imperialism = The policy of extending a nations authority by territorial acquisition or by the establishment of economic and political hegemony over other nations.

Racism = Racism as a cause of the absence of minority leadership in education.

Religion = Religious discrimination as a cause of absence in minority leadership in education.

Addiction = as an obstacle to securing leadership roles in education.

Government = Government and government policy as blocking the path to securing leadership roles for minorities in education.

Poverty = Minorities living at or below the poverty line as the cause of lack of opportunity and attainment of leadership roles in education for minorities.

Quantitative Data Retrieved From Inductive Coding

Educational Leader	Number of Times the Word Obstacle Was Used.	Number of Times the Theme of Dysfunction Was Addressed.	Number of Times the Word Colonization Was Used.	Number of Times the Word Race Was Used.	Number of Times the Word Religion Was Used	The Number of Time the Word Minority Was Used.	The Number of Times the Word Government or Government Policy Was Addressed.	
First Nation Administrator (Female)	2	3	0	2	2	0	1	
Non-Native Teacher Female (Elementary)	1	1	4	0	1	1	2	
Non-Native Teacher Male (Special Education)	0	3	0	1	0	0	0	
Canadian Chinese Administrator (Male)	1 * term 'structural barrier' was utilized	0	0	1	0	2	0	
Canadian Tibetan Teacher (Male)	0	0	0	4	8	6	0	

Educational Leader	Number of Times the Word Poverty Was Used	Number of Times the theme of Lack of Minority Leadership Was Stated.	Number of Times Lack of Resources Were Mentioned.
First Nation Administrator (Female)	3	2	2
Non-Native Teacher Female (Elementary)	0	3	0
Non-Native Teacher Male (Special Education)	1	2	0
Canadian Chinese Administrator (Male)	0	3	1
Canadian Tibetan Teacher (Male)	0	2	2

These themes continue to be mentioned throughout the interview of both First Nations, Minority Leaders, and Educators in Ontario. Lack of minority leadership was stressed by all interviewees during our interview. Religion was a key component to the Tibetan teachers success but was noticeably absent in other interviewees, this has much to do with the Residential School system and assimilation practices that are presently happening in our world today. Lack of Resources is a major issue as the First Nation Administrator at Big Trout Lake, Ontario stated:

"I see a lack of vision. What are we doing if we do not know where we are going? The other is sometimes there is a lack of resources, misuse of resources or they don't know how to use them. The latter is the sad part."

Here what is being displayed is our government policy of allocating monies to the First Nation schools is not the solution as their leaders do not know how to utilize these monies in an effective way. We must assist First Nation communities in organizing their school systems and their funding in this way First Nations will become strong academically and strengthen Canada as a nation. This First Nation administrator also discussed poverty in great detail when she stated:

"These are some of the reasons why I think we are covered in poverty.

a) apathy or lack of interest. So many opportunities in education that are not taken or completed.
b) Lack of teaching from parents and Elders.
c) Welfare and Government housing creates lack of responsibility.
d) Sometimes lack of resources or opportunities
e) Nepotism
f) Community members oppressing eachother.
g) Distorted family values especially discipline.

I think that these are some of the reasons for poverty. I believe that as long as one is young, healthy and intelligent, anyone is capable of at least some form of achievement. I was shocked to see the number of people at the Band office to go claim their welfare cheques."

These findings are outlined in Paulo Freire's: <u>Pedagogy of the Oppressed</u>, the lack of teaching from the parents and Elders occurred because of colonization, nepotism is a form of bullying that can be found in many of this remote communities. Community members oppressing each other is a serious effect of colonization, the divide and rule concept employed intentionally or unintentionally when colonization takes place. Another offspring of these happenings are the harm it has on individual families where a sense of love and warmth is replaced with dysfunction, bitterness and distortion. The last point emphasizes that even if leaders have employment they still will collect their welfare checks; therefore the government policy of financial compensation is not helping the First Nations people. As the Elementary Non-Native Teacher stated:

"In your opinion what has attributed to First Nation poverty on reservations in Northern Ontario? Answer: The Indian Act."

The Indian Act was enacted in 1876 by the Parliament of Canada under the provisions of Section 91(24) of the Constitution Act of 1867, which provides Canada's federal government exclusive authority to legislate in relation to "Indians and Lands Reserved for Indians". As well in regards to educational policy the Ministry of Education stipulates that they have full jurisdiction to govern all aspects of First Nation Education:

On page 23 of the Ministry of Ontario document created to help First Nation, Metis and Inuit students it states:

"Aboriginal and treaty rights of the Aboriginal peoples of Canada are recognized and affirmed in the Constitution Acts, 1867 and 1982 (section 35). Section 35 (2) indicates that Aboriginals peoples of Canada include Indian, Inuit, and Metis people. Section 91 (24) gives the Parliament of Canada exclusive jurisdiction over the creation of laws relating to " Indians and lands reserved for the Indians", and section 93 gives provincial legislatures exclusive jurisdiction over the creation of laws related to education." Pg.23

Naturally the First Nations are against this policy and have created their own educational policy document counteracting this policy. This becomes transparently clear not only in regards to First Nations education, self-determination the Canadian government has all the power and control in concerns and issues related to the future of First Nations in the province of Ontario and Canada as a country. Therefore, one can say that genuine dialogue or policy discourse cannot take place until First Nations are given the power, freedom and voice to help their communities in meaningful ways. As only peoples who actually live in these communities and live the daily life as a First Nations in Canada will truly know what solutions will work for their plight and struggle. This is the perspective and discourse of what the First Nation chiefs and Elders believe when they state in their Assembly of First Nations Educational Policy Document:

"The Assembly of First Nations (AFN) has long advocated for First Nation control over First Nation education. In 1972, the AFN released its first comprehensive, policy statement on education with the publication of Indian Control of Indian Education. The themes that this document embodied remain relevant today, having been further developed and refined over the three decades, culminating in the themes advocated by First Nation leaders at the Canadian-Aboriginal Peoples Roundtable sessions in 2004. the central thrust of these initiatives has consistently called for the recognition of First Nations jurisdiction over education." Pg.1

The policy created by the Ministry of Education fails to voice the First Nation perspective in the document. The First Nation discourse clearly shows that they want full jurisdiction over their peoples education and not addressing this view-point leaves the Ministries document obsolete and pointless.

The Native voice is further expounded in when it states:

"There is a need to recognize First Nations jurisdiction as a central tenet of education reform. Since before the last century, formal education has been used by colonizing governments as a tool for the assimilation of First Nations Peoples." Pg.1

The Elementary Non-Native Teacher further articulates her findings of the obstacles facing First Nations attaining teaching positions:

"There is most likely a disinterest in working within an education system due to volatile history of residential schools. Perhaps, there is also a recognized affiliation of Western-framed education curriculum to historical assimilation policies targeting First Nations."

The erasing of the First Nation spiritual traditions has had an impact that needs more research. As the Tibetan traditions and First Nation religious traditions are very similar and the Tibetan Teacher states how important his spirituality is in his life:

"I think religion plays a great role in everyone's life. Religion plays a great role in every aspect of my life."

Some Tibetan Buddhists were able to escape religious persecution from Communist China and escape to India in exile. The First Nations are still searching for their lost identity and spiritual ways that were lost during the Residential School era.

A further example of dysfunction is discovered when the Special Education Non-Native Teacher who now teaches in an Inuit community stated:

"From what I have heard, local Inuit do not respect their Inuit peers--- outsiders are respected more. Locally, the mayor (an Inuit elected solely among an Inuit and mixed blood electorate) frequently hires whites for major positions."

The Inuit community has lost trust and respect in their own peoples judgment to govern and lead their people. I asked him as a teacher in a remote Inuit community what was your greatest shock upon arriving and teaching in this community? He stated:

"None. I enjoy living here and pre-anticipated the problems

What we must be cognizant about here, is that these are not separate incidents or happenings. Wherever colonization took or is taking place these types of dysfunctions are going to happen.

Four major aspects were most crucial in understanding First Nations obstacles in attaining educational leadership roles: i) Spiritual Leadership, ii) Educational Leadership, iii) School Building and iv) Poverty.

Spiritual Leadership:

Elders are the leaders of these communities. The Elders look down on their own Traditional ways and are now inherently disconnected from the youth, by loss of language and world-view. The First Nation youth of today have much pride in their traditional ways, beliefs and religion. The youth look to the Elders for guidance and wisdom but they have become empty vessels of past history, heritage, Native wisdom and story-telling as this was the generation that was lost to Residential Schools. What we discover through assessing all these diverse leadership styles is that religion plays a powerful role. Therefore, we see very clearly why the First Nations are struggling in so many areas as their identity and spirituality has been erased by colonization. Specifically this research will show how Hindu and Muslim leadership successfully combated Western Imperialism and how this suppression of their self-determination actually made their faith and leadership stronger. Today, the Tibetans are fighting a similar struggle for over 57 years against Communist China.

Educational Leadership:

There is an absence of First Nation Principals and teachers in their own communities. All the teachers and Principals come from southern and central Ontario to teach at these schools. Why? Schools abide by the Ontario educational policy that teachers and Principals must have an Ontario College of Teachers Certificate to teach.

Effect: Teachers of non-native background appear smarter by this community because the teachers have the position and power in the community.

Societal Effect: Foreign teachers(which is us) have the best jobs in their communities. Having their children begging the non-native teachers for food and money on the way to school and all day is not something the community members feel very good about.

Ontario College of Teachers: How can these children get to University or Teachers College?

The Ontario curriculum does not correspond to their everyday reality, or world-view. (Reading of Shakespeare, English curriculum for example is very difficult).

Lack of Resources: Staff must continually create photocopies because of lack of text books, teachers are burnt out after one year and this leads to high amounts of teacher turn over (effect: students feel insecure about their community, lose connection to teachers, and begin to feel hopeless.)

School Buildings:

I believe this attributes to high levels of drop outs. From K-Gr.11 all these children are in the same building for their entire school career. 12 years in the same building, using the same computers, library and gymnasium is not fair. They need a change and something to look forward to. Here in the rest of Canada, after grade 8 have the excitement of meeting new students and going to high school which is usually a new building and in a new area.

Monies need to be allocated to the creation of Colleges and Universities that are in close proximity to these First Nation Communities in Ontario. Creating a college system or higher education facility on these reserve communities would bring hope, and much excitement to these communities. Plus it would create jobs for college and university professors in the field. Library facilities, and gymnasiums or recreation centers are desperately needed to keep First Nation youth out of trouble and mischief. Most petty crimes concerning First Nation youth are labeled "Mischief" because is boredom essentially.

Poverty:

First Nations of Northern Ontario are living in third world nation poverty.

The first aim of this study is to help give the First Nations a voice, to let Canada and Canadian understand their struggle, oppression, and plight, the second aim is to find solutions to the underlying problems facing First Nations Peoples, and the third is to make an impact on the Canadian pysche ; to prove that this is not only a problem for First Nations, it is an urgent concern that effects all Canadians living in Canada.

Compared and contrast two policies the Ontario First Nation, Metis, and Inuit Education Policy (2007) and the Assembly of First Nations Education Action Plan Policy (2005). I will do so using a Critical Policy Genealogy Framework. The two main questions I address are as follows: 1.) Who made these policies? 2.) Whose voices are being heard in the policy process? I am particularly interested in analyzing how truth and knowledge are relative to the historical context. My, analysis is Critical as I propose to uncover how policy decisions are made and how power is exerted in the process. The purpose of this work is to determine how including voices who are traditionally the objects of policy influences policy. My goal ist to see how the two policies differently address the educational road blocks that First Nation students face on a daily basis living in Ontario, Canada and if it would make a difference depending on who was included in the policy process. My paper is organized in the following way: I) Introduction, II) Context or Background, III) Framework, IV) Scholar and Personal Reflections and IV) Discussion of Implications and Significance of the Topic.

Underlying Assumptions: In order for Canada to be a strong and unified country we must work to help and heal First Nation Communities. This can only derive from genuine understanding, dialogue and compassion. We must understand and respect our First Nation brothers and sisters view in regards to history, self-determination, values and education.

"This process is largely unconscious, as discourse and discursive webs make invisible the exercise of power. Multiple discourses from different sources work together as mechanisms of power to create a truth and structure power/ knowledge relations." (Goldberg, 2006.)[1]

Introduction:

All Canadians must work together to heal the First Nations Peoples, and ultimately we will be healing our entire nation. On any level one wants to look at it, we cannot have Canadians living in third world conditions. The situation is getting worse, with higher rates of suicide, and culture of hopelessness. Other third world nations living conditions are improving, but the First Nations of Canada's predicament is actually getting worse. The first aim of this study is to help give the First Nations a voice, to let Canada know their struggle, pain, and predicament, the second aim is to give solutions to the underlying problems facing First Nations Peoples, and the third is to make an impact on the Canadian heart and minds to show that this problem is not just a First Nation issue, it is an issue that effects every Canadian living in Canada. After teaching in two remote First Nation Communities in Northern Ontario, and talking with many other leaders there, I believe these are the outlining issues facing the educational success for the First Nations.

Monies need to be allocated to the creation of Colleges and Universities that are in close proximity to these First Nation Communities in Ontario. Creating a college system or higher education facility on these reserve communities would bring hope, and much excitement to these communities. Plus it would create jobs for college and university professors in the field. Library facilities, and gymnasiums or recreation centers are desperately needed to keep First Nation youth out of trouble and mischief. Most petty crimes concerning First Nation youth are labeled "Mischief" because is boredom essentially.

These findings and solutions are discussed and mapped o t in the Assembly of First Nations: First Nation Education Plan Document (2005). Yet they do not appear in the Ontario Ministry of Education Policy. In this paper, I will compare and contrast the two policies and examine reasons for and the implications of their differences. The First Nations having their own separate Education Plan Document speaks volumes of the lack of dialogue and cooperation in the policy discourse. There exists a major disconnect to the reality the First Nations are living with daily and the Ministry of Education policy makers who are creating policy for a people they have little understanding of. This policy created by the Ministry of Education is an activity that gives the appearance of addressing the issues but which, manifestly fails to tackle the real problem. (Gillborn, 2006).[2]

II) Context or Background:

The Ontario Ministry of Education released this policy in 2007. Our Prime Minister apologized to the First Nations for the implementation of the Residential School System publicly in 2008. Possibly, predicting possible disruptions of the First Nations during the 2010 Winter Olympics in Vancouver, seeing similar protests of the Tibetans during the 2008 Beijing Olympics in China. Section of this paper will use a policy genealogy approach and explore the impact and innate obstacles

First Nations face because of the Residential School System. A school system which practiced cultural, and religious genocide on our First Nation brothers and sisters.

Policy Genealogical Approach

"We do not deconstruct discourse to reveal the 'truth', but to reveal how something has become known as the truth at a given point in time or how certain discourses operate as truthful and further demonstrating the bases of power that underpin, motivate and benefit from the truth-claims of the discourse in question." (Goldberg, 2006.)

The Webster's Dictionary definition of imperialism is: the state policy, practice, or advocacy of extending the power and dominion of a nation, especially the direct territorial acquisition or by gaining indirect control over the political or economical life of other areas. The impoverished lands of Africa, Latin America, and Asia are today called Third World Nations—to distinguish them from First World Nations of North America and Europe. In our society Third World poverty is treated by contemporary western society as a timeless condition. Society is made to believe that this has always been the case. Impoverished countries are poor because their lands have always been infertile or their people unproductive and lazy. This is incorrect. In reality the lands of Africa, Middle-East, Asia and Latin America have long produced rich natural resources of minerals, oil, foods, and precious stones. This is the reason why Western Imperialism went through all the trouble to control and seize them. The Third World is not underdeveloped but over exploited. Western colonization and investments have created a lower rather than higher standard of living. Case and point the extreme poverty that we find on First Nation reservations in Northern Ontario, Canada. The historical injustices of the past cannot be overlooked or forgotten as there resides the root cause of many of the obstacles of genuine self-determination, and democracy in our country. Once we address the root causes as Gillborn suggests then we can move forward and remedy the problems and stumbling blocks to true understanding. Being students of history of imperialism and colonialism we can see how many of these same practices utilized by the British Empire, were utilized to subjugate the First Nations of Canada. Therefore, some important questions come to mind when researching First Nations Educational Policy. Who made this policy? Whose voices are being heard? How are these policies challenged or resisted? After one has some experience researching First Nations policy and discourse one becomes well aware of an innate duality in these studies. There is an 'insider' versus 'outsider' dichotomy especially made lucid after visiting and teaching in these First Nation communities. Who made the policy? The Ministry of Education created this policy, depending where you stand, or direct experience one can question or not question the intent of the policy makers. We know the Ministry of Education created this policy then how many of the policy makers were First Nation? If the policy is to genuinely help First Nations how many First Nations were consulted with its creation? Why does the Assembly of First Nations feel the need to create their own First Nation Education Action Plan, if the Ministry has already consulted the First Nation leaders? As Gillborn states:

"an activity that gives the appearance of addressing the issues but which, in reality, manifestly fails to tackle the real problem." (Gillborn, pg.85)7

The above quotation is the definition of what a placebo is. Now we are beginning to see how certain policies are being challenged and resisted, because the First Nation Leaders know they were not consulted in these important matters concerning their children's future and future of their people.

III) Framework: Policy Genealogy: when describing the history of First Nations and the Critical Policy approach when analyzing current and future policies of First Nations in Canada.

Methodology:

Although various approaches to policy analysis exist, three general approaches can be distinguished: the policy process, and the meta-policy approach.

This approach focuses on individual problems and its solutions; its base is the micro-scale and its problem interpretation is usually of a technical nature. The primary goal of this approach is to identify the most effective and efficient solution in technical and economic terms (e.g. most efficient and distribution of resources). Looking at First Nation educational goals from this perspective one would look at the building of colleges and universities that would be in close proximity or one located in one central reserve, that would be easily accessible to all First Nation communities. This would also give many employment opportunities to Canadian teachers and professors who would now have new job openings here. Long-term benefits eventually First Nations will be teaching at these colleges and universities and in turn more graduates will help the Canadian labor market.

The policy process: this approach puts its focus onto political processes and investigates who the stakeholders are; its scope is the meso-scale and its problem interpretation is usually of a political nature. What are the aims at determining what processes and means are used to explain the role and influence of stakeholders with the policy process? Here the study looks at policy genealogy when looking at the history of First Nations in Canada, and investigate policy as discourse as their voice is absent in important issues pertaining to them. This analysis looks at power struggles and influence of these peoples in discourse and consultation, solutions to problems are identified.

The meta-policy approach: This approach investigates the role of First Nation educational leadership from the macro-scale and it is viewed from a structural stance. Here the analysis investigates the contextual factors of the policy process; the political, economic, and socio-cultural factors influencing it.

I will compare this policy document on First Nation Educational Objectives with the First Nations, Metis, and Inuit Education Policy Framework of Ontario that was released in 2007. Ultimately seeing how these policy objectives compare with the First Nations Education Action Plan that was created by the Assembly of First Nation Chiefs. I will also code and use Interviews from colleagues who taught in these communities, use myself as a case study and develop qualitative and quantitative evidence to show how this policy will not truly solve the innate issues facing First Nations in the realm of education. I will utilize the Policy Analysis of Carl V. Patton (1986). as my organizational framework. It has six stages: 1. Verify, define and detail the problem, 2) Establish evaluation criteria, 3) Identify alternative policies, 4) Evaluate alternative policies, 5) Display and distinguish among alternative policies, and 6) Monitor the implementation policy. Carl V. Patton's Stages of Policy Analysis:

1. **Verify, Define and detail the problem**: The problem is that this policy document is not addressing the root cause of the issue. The real issue is rooted in lack of First Nation Leadership in the realm of education. Interviews of: Non-native and First Nation Teachers.

Mr. Darren Luck over 6 years teaching experience in First Nation Communities. Mrs. Jeannie Beardy Director of Education at Big Trout Lake, Ontario.

2. **Establish evaluation criteria:** I will analyze the two policies based on these criteria, identified as critical to First Nations educationin the background section above.

Leadership:

One of the main aspects not addressed in the Ontario Ministry of Education Policy concerning First Nations, Metis and Inuit Peoples is a solution for the absence of First Nation Leadership. Elders are the leaders of First Nation communities. They hold spiritual and educational authority. They have lost their power and influence in their communities. In order to teach and lead in educational settings in Ontario one needs a teaching degree from the Ontario College of Teachers. Even if one invites Elders into the school and teach their knowledge know seems 'other' or irrelevant to the modern world.

Throughout the entire First Nation Education Action Plan (2005)(created by First Nation Chiefs and Elders) it constantly stresses the importance of the Elders in their community, learning, wisdom, education, leadership, knowledge and schools. The word Elders is mentioned only once in the Ministry of Education document on pg.20 describing policy to help First Nation students in Ontario.

The two schools that draw upon first-hand experience are reservation number 209 (Big Trout Lake, Ontario) and reservation number 210 (Kasabonika Lake, Ontario).

Why is there an absence of First Nation Leadership in Education?

One of the first things one notices upon entering a First Nation school in the north is the absence of First Nation teachers. If there is a First Nation teacher he or she would be assigned to teach Native language courses. This responsibility is usually given to a highly respected Elder of the community to teach the next generation of their peoples. Therefore, Native language is seen as far more vital than other school subjects because it is their education and it is taught by a First Nation teacher and Elder. Many students skip the majority of classes and just attend the Native language courses and physical education that is usually after Native language class everyday. This is a very important point recognized by the research of the Aboriginal Policy documents as well. They recognize that attendance is almost 95% in their Native Language Classes in contrast to their other subject classes at their schools. There maybe many variables to the reason for this, but their research concludes that it has to do with the children learning their culture, tradition and language. Also this Native language class is always taught by a Native Elder from the community, and that the importance of this class is always stressed by their parents.

As mentioned earlier Native teachers cannot teach in the elementary end of the school because the school board is funded by the Provincial government and must abide by the policies of teachers having an Ontario teaching degree. The reason being is that schools on reservations only go to grade eleven, and if a student wants to get their high school diploma they must leave their community. They will have to live and attend a school outside their community in order to earn their high school diploma:

"The community has an elementary and a junior high school. In order to complete school, students have to board in Sioux Lookout." (Denied Too Long, pg.29)[10]

The road block is further compounded in the realm of leadership of schools and community. The communities of Big Trout Lake and Kasabonika Lake have never had a First Nation Principal because of this system. For most children and families just making it to Grade 8 is seen as finishing high school in their communities. The grade 8 graduation is far more elaborate and celebrated in these communities. Grade 8 graduation is given as much applause and recognition as high school graduation here in central Ontario. When one looks down the hall at the high school end of the school the halls are empty and classes having one or two students enrolled in high school classes where they attend sporadically throughout the semester.

3. **Identify alternative policies**: Policy makers must be cognizant of First Nation educational policy aims and objectives to truly achieve the result they want. Unfortunately, similar to the implementation of the African Canadian School Board in Toronto; First Nation leaders want to implement a college and university system created for and by First Nation Peoples. The reason why these types of solutions are happening is because peoples are not feeling the system is genuinely fair and democratic. Black teachers and principals are absent in most Ontario schools, black history is not given enough importance. So, the correlation is very similar for the First Nation peoples in Canada. The proof of these systems not working for these groups is the strikingly high rates of African Canadian and First Nation in the Canadian Jail systems today. As mentioned earlier, we will compare and contrast the Ontario Ministry of Education Policy for First Nations, Metis, and Inuit Peoples versus the First Nation Educational Policy composed by the Assembly of First Nation Leaders. On page 23 of the Ministry of Ontario document it states:

"Aboriginal and treaty rights of the Aboriginal peoples of Canada are recognized and affirmed in the Constitution Acts, 1867 and 1982 (section 35). Section 35 (2) indicates that Aboriginals peoples of Canada include Indian, Inuit, and Metis people. Section 91 (24) gives the Parliament of Canada exclusive jurisdiction over the creation of laws relating to " Indians and lands reserved for the Indians", and section 93 gives provincial legislatures exclusive jurisdiction over the creation of laws related to education."[11]

This becomes transparently clear not only in regards to First Nations education, self-determination the Canadian government has all the power and control in concerns and issues related to the future of First Nations in the province of Ontario and Canada as a country. Therefore, one can say that genuine dialogue or policy discourse can not take place until First Nations are given the power, freedom and voice to help their communities in meaningful ways. As only peoples who actually live in these communities and live the daily life as a First Nations in Canada will truly know what solutions will work for their plight and struggle. This is the perspective and discourse of what the First Nation chiefs and Elders believe when they state in their Assembly of First Nations Educational Policy Document:

"The Assembly of First Nations (AFN) has long advocated for First Nation control over First Nation education. In 1972, the AFN released its first comprehensive, policy statement on education with the publication of Indian Control of Indian Education. The themes that this document embodied remain relevant today, having been further developed and refined over the three decades, culminating in the themes advocated by First Nation leaders at the Canadian-Aboriginal Peoples Roundtable sessions in 2004. the central thrust of these initiatives has consistently called for the recognition of First Nations jurisdiction over education."[12]

The policy created by the Ministry of Education fails to voice the First Nation perspective in the document. The First Nation discourse clearly shows that they want full jurisdiction over their peoples education and not addressing this view-point leaves the Ministries document obsolete and pointless.

The Native voice is further expounded in when it states:

"There is a need to recognize First Nations jurisdiction as a central tenet of education reform. Since before the last century, formal education has been used by colonizing governments as a tool for the assimilation of First Nations Peoples."[13]

This statement and view is well documented especially by the scholarly research by Paulo Freire and Martin Carnoy who espouse the thesis that education is a tool utilized to assimilate and control a conquered people.

In the policy document on page 15 section Strategy 2.2: Provide additional support in a variety of areas to reduce gaps in student outcomes. The policy needs to address the reasons for the gaps, otherwise educators or society at large my look down on First Nation children in school systems. The 'gap' is not because of intelligence but because of the colonization, loss of identity, confidence, and history. Specifically on reservations the school policy is that from grade K-5 all course instruction will be in their native language. This so that the children will reclaim and see the importance of their identity. However, from our standards we would say:

"The Native children of these schools are five years behind the rest of Ontario."

This is the belief that the non-native staff at our schools view the children. As we must teach the Ontario curriculum at the grade level the children are in. However, we would have to use grade one, or grade two text books to teach to the children as their English skills were at the grade one and grade two level. Again when I was at Kasabonika Lake, Ontario First Nation Reservation #210 we as a staff had the responsibility to make up for the is 'gap'. But, again I focused on the First Nation perspective in regards to curriculum and found success.

Kasabonika Lake, Ontario First Nation: 2006-2007

Grade Level: 6	# of Students	# of years behind according to Special Ed. Assessment 3-4 years behind In terms of comprehension, literacy and math	# of students at Grade 6 level at the end of school year assessments
	23	23	21

Having a focus on First Nations perspective and world-view is a must for academic success of these children throughout the academic year. However, as the Special Education teachers advised me that over the long summer months of no schooling retention rates of these children are low and also account to some of the gaps in their learning from year to year. So, therefore more funding to these boards are necessary so they can hire staff to teach summer courses to the students so they can maintain their learning throughout the summer months and to keep them out of mischief. This is true in regards of giving a test after an fractions unit the students for example, they would do very well, however giving a culminating exam at the end of the year one would have to give two or three exemplars of the question on the board to refresh there understanding of the topic.

Also, on page 15 the policy discusses the prevention of Fetal Alcohol Syndrome. If one truly understands the cycle and damage colonization has created one will understand the rise of FAS in First Nation communities. The sexual abuse, genocide, and loss of life that existed in Residential school has left deep scars in their collective psyche. Many resorted to alcohol to numb the pain, not knowing the further damage they were having on their offspring who were born with this syndrome. Therefore you cannot prevent Fetal Alcohol Syndrome without seeing the reason why this is happening. On page 17 the policy addresses Strategy 3.1: Build educational leadership capacity and coordination. The policy objective suggests to offer assistance to First Nations by strengthening educational leadership in areas as training principals, with sensitivity to First Nation traditions and practices. But what are these traditions and practices? Why are they not mentioned in detail if they are so critical to the success of this policy? The Assembly of First Nations Education Action Plan gives detailed description and definition of what is their world-view, culture, history and beliefs are. Also, constantly marginalizing this as a First Nation issue undermines the severity and great importance this has in strengthening the entire nation of Canada. The question arises if Principals who have no current students who are First Nation would they still implement these policies focusing on First Nation equality and importance? Again, this is an issue of a strong and united Canada. On page 18 policy c) aims at fostering Aboriginal student's leadership skills. How does one achieve this aim? When he or she has never seen a First Nation person in any significant role of leadership and influence? On page 18 Strategy 3.2 the policy aims at building capacity to support identity building, including the appreciation of Aboriginal perspectives, values, and cultures by all students, school board staff, and elected trustees. If this is a genuine policy directive one would think that one mention of what the First Nation world-view was, or what values they hold dear would be described in some detail. The current education system in Ontario, is marginalizing all these policy directives they seek to improve. First Nation history is not even mentioned in Canadian History textbooks throughout our province, as these texts begin Canadian history in the year of 1867 during Confederation when Canada became a nation. However, from the First Nation perspective Canada had an important history and was thus a nation before this date. Essentially Canada Day, formerly known as Dominion Day, is disrespecting First Nation importance and history. Perhaps this was the reason for implementing the special day dedicated to First Nations on June 21st of every year(Aboriginal Day).

4. **Evaluate alternative policies**: The alternate policies are: a) Focus on Leadership, b) Having their own college and university system, c) having courses based on a First Nation perspective, d) Make sure there is adequate funding for summer school programs in First Nation communities. All these interdependent policy alternatives focus on one thing: Success for the First Nation Student. a) First Nation leadership is critical when understanding how this relates to power, confidence, and success for these peoples. After establishing what First Nation Leadership is, we will implement the Participative Leadership style of Dr. Kenneth Leithwood to remedy these issues. b.) Establishing colleges and universities based on First Nation world-view and teaching styles is very important. This will bring them hope, excitement and a vision of a better tomorrow for their peoples. This policy directive is located in the Assembly of First Nation Education Action Plan as well. The result will be, that First Nations will be able to help Canada in the labor market, and to richly contribute to the over all identity of Canada as a nation. c.) Having courses from a First Nations perspective has shown great results from my case study in Big Trout Lake, Ontario, and Kasabonika Lake, Ontario. What was the key factor was the

rise in attendance because of curriculum focused on their world-view, and naturally success was inevitable when students attended school on a consistent basis. and d.) Provide funding for summer school courses for First Nation youth. There is critical issue of retention in these communities. In these communities there is a greater obstacle to maintaining and sustaining academic success from the previous year because of lack of educational, academic and mental stimulation for these students. Parents are generally have low literacy skills, who speak their mother tongue, Oji-Cree and do not read to the children in English, do not create study room for the children to study,(housing is very small and cramped, many living under one roof), so they need a positive place to maintain their knowledge base throughout the summer months. There is the added obstacle of FAS, ADD, and ADHD so having programs to help the children retain knowledge, skills and to make sure they are constantly improving like the rest of the students in Ontario, Canada.

5. **Display and distinguish among alternative policies:**

First Nation Focused Curriculum

After discussing with my colleagues at Aglace Chapman Education Centre (Big Trout Lake, Ontario) I was told that my current students all failed but one the year before and that many have become depressed and none thought they could successful complete grade 8. I was completing my long-range plans for the grade 8 academic year and realized that most of the objectives in the curriculum guidelines did not mesh well with the reality of these children. However, I understood that my goal was to catch these students up to the rest of the standards of Ontario and that I must cover all the curriculum objectives of the province. However, I started off every class: geography, history, English, Language Arts, and science from a First Nation perspective. As my goal was to keep attendance high, as if the students attended school regularly this increased their chances of graduating. Everything was from the First Nation perspective focusing on First Nation stories, legends, history, achievement, invention, and special contributions they have had to the country of Canada. The staff, principal and community were amazed at the high attendance levels and achievement of the students. Many variables may have came into play as in math and other areas themes and objectives were repeated from last year, but the attendance was strikingly higher than the year before and thus all 25 students passed their examinations in Literacy and Math that year.

Big Trout Lake: Grade 8 Results 2004-2005 (First Nation Focused Curriculum)

Standard Ontario Curriculum 2003-2004	# of Students in Grade 8	# of Students Failed Grade 8	# of students passed onto Grade 9
Teacher taught standard Ontario Curriculum	24	23	1
Teacher taught from a First Nations World-View Focus	26	1	25

These types of findings are critical in understanding the mind-set of First Nation Leaders. As we will see the Assembly of First Nations Education Policy Document reiterates these types of objectives and expectations throughout their education documents. If the Ministry, teachers and Ontario College of Teachers are cognizant of the importance of this we can make many positive change for these peoples, and ultimately Canada will benefit.

Why all this emphasis on leadership in educational policy? Is it really this important?

"Leadership is second only to teaching in its impact on student outcomes." (Putting Ontario's Leadership Framework Into Action, pg. 5)14

Leadership has a critical role to play when discussing change and policy development in school systems. Leadership is directly linked to administration, community, power, authority, change, diversity, and value systems. The stumbling block encountered while teaching at these two separate First Nation schools is the lack of leadership and specifically the absence of First Nation leadership. Policy makers who want to improve the education of these communities should research the leadership styles described by Dr. Kenneth Leithwood and Daniel Duke. The six types of leadership are: Instructional, Transformational, Moral, Participative, Mangerial, and Contingent forms of school leadership. Therefore what of the six styles fit within the First Nation world-view? What type of leadership is congruent with the environment and culture of your school? When first assessing these two First Nation schools one thought that the Transformational Leadership style was best suited for these schools. This type of leadership has seven vital dimensions for genuine change in school systems:

"building school vision, establishing school goals, providing intellectual stimulation, offering individual support, modeling best practices, and important organizational values, demonstrating high performance expectations, creating a productive school culture, and developing structures to foster participation in school systems." (Leithwood, 1994). 15

This type of leadership eventually becomes a moral force in maintaining and sustaining these very high standards.

"Transformational leadership eventually becomes moral leadership in that it raises the standards of human conduct and ethical grounding to both the leaders and the lead, and thus a true culture of change can occur." (Burns, 1978)16

Fundamentally it is important to be mindful of these diverse types of leadership when creating policy to improve school systems. Also, what is more important is to genuinely understand the school culture and community that these schools exist in. Specifically the field of First Nation leadership is quite complicated. Not only is there a systematic way in which First Nation leaders have obstacles in securing power, and authority in school systems but once they do they are brought down by their very own community and members. Having studied Paulo Freire's monumental book: The Pedagogy of the Oppressed one should not be surprised of these happenings. Most colonized peoples he explained have difficulty securing power in their own communities because they already begin to doubt each other and leadership amongst their own peoples. We will return to this theme later. But the Aboriginal Peoples Collections findings were:

Aboriginal communities that have been traumatized display a fairly predictable pattern of collective dysfunction in the form of rampant backbiting and gossip, perpetual social and political conflict and in-fighting, a tendency to pull down the good work of anyone who arises to serve the community, political corruption, lack of accountability and transparency in governance, widespread suspicion and mistrust between people, chronic inability to unite and work together to solve critical human problems, competition and turf wars between programs, a general sense of alienation and disengagement from community affairs by most people (what's the use?), a climate of fear and intimidation surrounding those who hold power and a general lack of progress and success in community initiatives and enterprises (which often seem to self-destruct)." (Aboriginal Peoples Collection, pg.4)

Change and policy implementation must be intimately linked with their community, resources, beliefs and needs. The policy objectives must be linked with the Elders and other cultural leaders. Viewing these events and realities from a macrocosmic level we can see a relationship between the colonized and colonizer directly when investigating leadership, policy discourse, and divide and rule ideologies of imperialism.

"Those members of the communities who show sufficient leadership capacities to be chosen for these courses necessarily reflect and express the aspirations of the individuals of their community. They are in harmony with the way of living and thinking about reality which characterize their comrades, even though they reveal special abilities which give them the status of 'leaders'. As soon as they complete the course and return to the community with resources to control and submerge and dominate consciousness of their comrades, or they become strangers in their own communities and their former leadership position is thus threatened. In order not to lose their leadership status, they will probably tend to continue manipulating the community, but in a more efficient manner." (Paulo Freire, (1970.)Pg.138-139)[18]

Policy makers who comprehend all these hindrances and issues in First Nation communities it is wise to incorporate the Participative Leadership Style of Dr. Kenneth Leithwood. Since, there is a tendency to attack and ridicule leadership that arises and that community has more weight and power than individual leaders this is the most suitable type of leadership style to apply to educational policy. Leadership in First Nation and other non-western cultures is a bottom-up trajectory. Meaning the society or community will raise the leader who best serves the community. The community members choose the leader in contrast to the individual deciding he or she should be a leader and authority figure. According to First Nation legend the greatest leader would be the hunter. The hunter was not seen as a leader because he could catch the most prey or because of his athletic ability, or intelligence. He was seen as a leader of the community because after hunting for weeks he would return to the community and share all his prey with the community equally. This is why he was seen as a leader because of his altruism and his sharing nature.

Another obstacle mentioned earlier facing teachers who teach on in these communities is that the Ontario curriculum does not relate to the community, people, world-view, or day to day life of people living in third world conditions. Therefore, the Participative Leadership is best suited for First Nation communities.

"Is that curriculum of the school ought to directly reflect the values and preferences of parents and the local community." (Leithwood, year, pg.52)[19]

This type of leadership focuses on the school professionals need to be responsive to local beliefs, concerns and values and preferences(Leithwood). This type of leadership involves all members of the community and this is critical in a community still battling the negative effects of colonization. This type of leadership distributes leadership:

"Community-control SBM aims to increase the authority and influence of parents and community members." (Leithwood, pg.52). Parents and community members who already question and doubt the intention of schools because of indoctrination, genocide, and assimilation practices of the past need to be given some power and control. The Participatory Leadership style will give parents and the community the power and authority to make decisions for their future generations.

"That professionals are willing to be quite responsive to the values and preferences of parents and the local community under conditions in which parents are in a position to act as partners with schools in the education of their children." (Leithwood,1999, pg. 52)

Current Situation:

What is First Nation Leadership?

If the policy document created by the Ministry of Education was clear and genuine, we would know what First Nation leadership is. As the Education document created by the Assembly of First Nations discussed First Nation leadership in education throughout their document. First Nation lineages are passed down orally through the generations. The belief that the Great Spirit created the Earth and is the Mother of all creation. Plants and animals have spirits that must be venerated, honoured, and cared for. It is a holistic system that centers not only on human life but also the life of the world and all things in it. The medicine wheel symbolizes how all life is interconnected and embarked on in a circular journey. The four cardinal directions, each of which as a guiding spirit and special attributes, reflects the stages of the life journey.

From listening to Elders, one can see the change in the children and see the many negative aspects effecting their children. Children involved in gangs, loss of identity, drug use, and being sent to mental health centres is an aspect of everyday life in these communities.

"What is needed is funding that encourages and supports comprehensive long-term planning and action. Such funding must address both healing as recovery (crisis intervention) and community health and a healthy community and nation." (Aboriginals Peoples Collection, pg.52)[21]

Policy makers should have these aspects in mind when creating policy documents concerning First Nations. The future of a people depends on their children. Their children are raised in dysfunction where alcoholism, drug abuse, smoking in elementary grades, are daily occurrences. Their loss of identity, hopelessness, and loss of language has had serious negative effects on their confidence and self-value. Families trying to understand and cope with the injustices and confusion of the past resorted to drugs and alcohol to deal the pain, suffering and confusion. Not knowing that these negative habits would be passed onto their children who are now affected with many disorders of Attention Deficit Disorder (ADD), Attention Deficit Hyperactivity Disorder(ADHD) and Fetal Alcohol Syndrome (FAS).

"If the goal is to heal the nation, it is critical to invest heavily in healing the nations children." (Aboriginal Peoples Collection, pg53).[22]

These alternative policies out-lined in this paper will truly help First Nations get back on their feet and help them heal their past and move them forward into the future.

6. **Monitor the implementation policy**: One key aspect that this study is trying to convey is the sense of urgency of this issue. This is also vital in monitoring and implementing this alternative policy. If there is no sense of urgency or importance of this alternative policy then nothing substantial will result for the First Nations Peoples of Ontario, Canada. Policy

makers and Canadians must see the inherent value of creating policy that gives First Nation students a successful path to educational aims and goals. Furthermore, Canadians must see the value this will have on making us more competitive in the labor market, provincially, nationally, and internationally. The benefits are higher still, when seeing that our countries ancient soul will be reborn and revitalized to bring a much needed balance to our current fast paced capitalistic world.

The important thing is that these schools will be given as much importance and respect as other colleges and universities in Canada. This will not be an easy solution, but these peoples will have genuine hope and excitement of going to college and university in the future. As for right now they view their future as hopeless. As evident by the rising rates of youth suicide in First Nation Communities. Suicide is not a failure of the individual, ultimately it is a failure of the society.

IV) Scholarly Research: Works cited are: Assembly of First Nations Education Action Plan Policy, First Nation, Metis, and Inuit Education Policy Framework by the Ministry of Ontario, First Nation, Metis and Inuit Eduacation Policy Framework from the Ministry of Alberta, Dr. Michelle Goldberg (Forming, Reforming, and Performing Education: Using Foucault to Rethink Canadian Schooling.), Martin Carnoy (Education as Cultural Imperialism), Sue Winton, (2007). (Rhetorical Analysis and of Character Education Policy), Kenneth Leithwood: Studies in Leadership Styles, Paulo Freire (Pedagogy of the Oppressed), Aboriginal Policy Research, Thomas Educational Publishing, Inc., and Carl V. Patton, David S. Sawicki (Basic Methods of Policy Analysis and Planning).

V) Independent Critical Discussion and Analysis:

Reflections, personal responses, interview analysis, case-study of my teaching experience on two separate First Nation Communities in Ontario, Canada: Big Trout Lake, Ontario and Kasabonika Lake, Ontario.

VI) Discussion of Implications and Significance of the Topic:

This was a policy analysis of the Ontario First Nation, Metis, and Inuit Education Policy Framework. The policy framework employed was the Policy Genealogy Framework when discussing: Who makes the policy? Whose voices are being heard? Especially when analyzing how truth and knowledge are relative to the historical context. Finally, the analysis was from the Critical Policy approach when displaying how the policy decisions are made and how power is exerted in the process. Does this educational policy really address the educational road blocks that First Nation students face on a daily basis living in Ontario, Canada?

This policy analysis has successfully proven that this policy created by the Ministry of Education in Ontario does not provide a genuine remedy of solving the inequality and absence of voice of the First Nations peoples and leaders in the realm of education. This policy analysis was six-fold in organization: I) Introduction, II) Context or Background, III) Framework, IV) Scholarly Research, V) Independent Critical Discussion and Analysis and VI) Discussion of Implications and Significance of the Topic.

Karma M. Chukdong B.Ed, M.A., M.Ed

Summary:

This study compared and contrasted these two policy documents on First Nation education, and have formulated four critical alternative policies that will truly achieve the aims of the Ministry of Education document.

The Ontario Ministry of Education Mission Statement:

"First Nation, Metis, and Inuit students in Ontario will have the knowledge, skills, and confidence they need to successfully complete their elementary and secondary education in order to pursue postsecondary education or training and/or enter the workforce."23

After this study we are well aware of the obstacles to this statement are. We are also aware that the Ministry of Education document does not address any of these obstacles facing First Nation students in Ontario. The four policy alternatives outlined in this vital study were: 1) Establishing Leadership, specifically empowering First Nation Leadership in schools, and school systems, 2) Create their own First Nation College and University school system, 3.) Modify Ontario Curriculum to have a First Nation perspective option, and 4) Implement a Summer School System in these communities so students can maintain, sustain, retain, and build on knowledge bases acquired the year before.

Canadians of conscience and our government must see that in order for Canada to be a strong and respected nation we must heal and reconcile First Nation communities and issues. This can only derive from genuine understanding, dialogue and compassion. We must understand and respect our First Nation brothers and sisters view in regards to history, self-determination, values and education. We must make sure our policies are just, genuine and fair to all peoples who belong to the great nation of Canada.

It is only the oppressed who, by freeing themselves, can free their oppressors." Freire, (1981)

<u>Teacher Development:</u> Many of themes of: Language, Identity, Two-World Dichotomy, Culture, Spirituality and Capitalism and interconnect throughout my life.

One reason I will discuss later in the academic piece of this paper will be the Streaming or Tracking system that our public school boards implement. Myself almost being a victim of streaming in my grade 8 year, did not realize how important my decision was at the time until I started reading about the studies of Bowles and Gintis, Paul Willis and others. Naturally while reading these studies on Schooling in Capitalist America by Bowles and Gintis(1976) one thinks of one's own situation. Not even realizing it I recall that I had two intense meetings with my grade 8 teacher who was trying to convince me that the general (non-academic) stream would suit me better. Saying like many studies say" It would be easier for me." Thinking back as a 14 year old who always respected and was compliant with my teachers, I could not believe that I stood up to this authority figure. I told him that I believe I can go to university and my family believes in me. In my mind I knew that I had not given my all to school, because basketball took up almost 60% of my time. Now reading about the research of streaming and the detrimental effects it is having on minority and students of low-economic status I feel it is important that I make it known.

"The schools stream kids according to background and neighborhood. If you're in a public housing area, schools stream to non-university programs and stress punctuality, etc. The educational system is set up to do this." Curtis (1992) pg.23

I have already talked and spoke to Tibetan leaders about the fact of this streaming system and to make sure our students get into the academic stream as once one is in the non-academic stream it become almost impossible to get into the academic once placed there.

All my life I wanted to be a role model for the Tibetan people. I am so disheartened to hear our youth and elders say "His Holiness the Dalai Lama is all we really have." In my formative years I also had no role models, and had to search for them. My closest role model while growing up was Michael Jordan, and did I ever emulate him. I wore the number 23 just like him and I became the best basketball player in grade 6 year playing for the grade 8 team, and when I got to high school I played for the Junior team and in my senior year I was selected to play for OBA (Ontario Basketball Association) representing Kingston, Ontario. My point is, if I had an educational role-model or a Tibetan teacher or minority teacher I could have advanced quite far in the academic realm as well. Reflecting on current NBA players they had the similar response when asked about election of President Obama:

"Now we really believe that we can be anything, when I was growing up all I thought I could be was a basketball player or make a living as a sports player." (Lebron James, Cleveland Cavaliers).

This is how important role models are for our students today. So, what happen to my basketball career? Well I received an offer to come out and try-out with the Windsor University team. The coach could not travel to see my games in Belleville Ontario, but heard of me and invited me to come and play. However, once I realized how much money was required to pay for tuition, and how important my GPA was in getting in to graduate school I had to make the difficult decision: Do I play basketball and risk my GPA or sacrifice basketball and make sure my GPA stays high? I had to quit basketball and focus on school 100%. I earn such a high GPA at the University of Windsor that I was able to transfer to the University of Toronto and from there my academic career soared and achieved much success in the academic world. During those years as a Tibetan my only role model was His Holiness the Dalai Lama, and Mohandas K. Gandhi. I would work on my assignments and essays while having their lectures, videos, or movies playing in the background. This gave me a sense of purpose, inspiration, and self-discipline that helped me rise above the obstacles that could have hindered my path. I wanted to be just like them, I had found my role models and in my papers, assignments, and lectures I saw things through their perspective lens. After my Honours B.A. I enter into the Masters of History: South Asian Studies Program at the University of Toronto. Here I really got to study under world-renowned scholars of History of South Asia, Jain Studies, Buddhist Studies and Philosophy. I realize now why I went in this direction. Of course it is a search for identity, search of what is truly valuable, a sense of having something substantial to share to our future generations; but what is more this identity I was searching for was absent for so long.

Our curriculum in the public school does not address the identity of the "other". If one is not totally self-aware one may easily be assimilated and not value your own tradition, but I found myself especially in university after my 3-hour lectures going to the library to find books on Tibetan Buddhism, Buddhism and Buddhist scripture. I was thirsty to compare what I learned in class with these texts, I wanted to see how similar the findings where of western and Tibetan scholars. I wanted to see what Tibetan masters have to say about the issues discussed in class. After awhile I would be reading 80% Tibetan Buddhist knowledge and 20% my course work. But it did not matter the more I understood my own tradition the more confident and the better my grades where in my academic courses. So, this why when I went to teach at a First Nations School I emphasized First Nation knowledge and principles before the standard Ministry of Ontario Curriculum guidelines. Again

I want to close this section with the importance of role-models. If I did not have His Holiness the Dalai Lama as an example I really do not know where I would be. His life and example fascinated me, my parents said I would stare and watch his videos for hours, most likely not knowing what he was saying, but I do recall saying to myself: " Is he Tibetan? I want to be just like this guy."

Living in Two- Worlds:

"Every child is waiting for a teacher who seeks to make a genuine difference in the world by giving students permission to acknowledge their inner capacity for greatness. And when such students and teachers come together, miracles happen, and the classroom becomes a nurturing, creative, and safe place that we can call home." (Grace Feuerverger).

This two-world dichotomy never really hit home for me until I started teaching on a First Nation reserve. Reservation #209 to be exact Kitchenmahya Koosib Innuwig (Big Trout Lake, Ontario). At a staff meeting we had a mini professional development day with First Nation admin from Winnipeg. We kept discussing this two-world dichotomy. And when the teachers had a chance to share I kept reflecting on a Tibetan Buddhist analogy of needing two wings to fly. I realized that it sounded like it could have come from the First Nation spirituality tradition so I wanted to share. The Tibetan Buddhist analogy is that of the importance of combining Compassion and Emptiness. Emptiness represents one wing of a bird and the Compassion aspect represents the other wing of a bird. In order for a healthy bird to fly it needs to healthy wings. So, if a bird only has one healthy wing it will only fly in circles and not really get anywhere, and not reach its destination. Having the knowledge of Emptiness(Shunyata) is good but does not mean much if you have not cultivated the Compassion to see others who have not realized the Emptiness of all things. So, for your practice to soar and to be truly able to benefit others one needs both to achieve the goal.

Likewise, in the First Nation predicament I stated: "Our First Nation Children can be likened to birds, in order to fly they need two healthy wings to fly. One wing must be rooted in their Traditional knowledge and the other must be rooted in Modern knowledge of the rest of Ontario. If they embrace both forms of knowledge our children will soar and the community will prosper."

The staff and the presenter really liked the analogy, and I would not have been able to share this without a knowledge of my own tradition and identity. The presenter said:

"Where are you from?" Most likely wanting to know where is my heritage from, but I said I am from Toronto. And then he said: " Oh Toronto, that is a one big reserve down there." Everyone laughed and we continued to give our insights and reflections.

After meeting with my Director of Education many times throughout the year, I did express that my classroom was likened to a home and wanted my students feel like their at home. The year before the drop-out rate was the highest the school had seen in some time, and after my year with my grade eights the attendance was almost 100% for the entire school year. After sometime I would say 2 months, late October the students started to open up and trust the staff. They shared the problems of their homes, communities and people. My grade eight students would say to me: "Your not coming back here are you? You think our reservation is a disgrace."

After awhile I realized the dysfunction of the community and the hopelessness of the people. I knew when the parents received their government checks because this is when the students would be late, absent for half the day or come to school intoxicated. This is because this is when the parents would be able to afford to make "homebrew" a alcohol drink made up mouth wash, hair spary and other liquids with alcohol in it." I learned this because I wanted to buy AXE a popular body deodorant but I was asked to sign after I bought this. I inquired why, and the store owner said that everyone can only buy one of these per month. I asked a senior staff member what the problem was, and he said they maybe worried that if you buy a lot you may sell it. Why would I sell it, when it can be bought here in the store? He said, some people with these ingredients make homebrew to get intoxicated.

At any rate after awhile the students would come over to my house and ask me to open the gym and play hockey or basketball with them. Parents would drop off moose meat to my house as a gift and this made me feel that I was making small miracles in the classroom. No doubt the students had good things to say about my teaching and most importantly about school and that is what is most important.

The issue also going back to the research findings of Bowles and Gintis and others about teacher burn-out is very accurate. Especially on a First Nation reserve where students know where you live and you really have no personal time, you actually become like a second parent and they spend more time with you than their own parents many times. So, this is an issue of the school institution itself coupled with the dysfunction of the reservation itself poses many negative side-effects for teachers, and administrators in the school setting.

"Each soul is a sacred entity, and as a teacher I tried to the best of my ability to communicate this to my students." Feuerverger(2007), pg. 3

This is the goal and true aspiration of teachers. This is why we teachers are so frustrated and burn out because I believe the educational system is against our altruistic objectives and selfless duty for our students, and children.

"The teacher who comes to teaching 'to help children must use the approved curriculum guides and linguistic practices to retain a position. But these materials generate ideological insights that cause students to accept institutional definitions of themselves, their families, and their potential in schools and in the labor market." Rothstein, (1991),pg.111

From this perspective schools are likened to a factory: lunch breaks, recess, punctuality reflected in attendance that get them ready for the work in factories and the labor market once they enter the adult world. The primary function of schooling is to function as a major factor in the reproduction of society. The teacher can be likened to working on an assembly line in a factory molding our product (students) to be all the same product and to be allocated out into our society. This explains many of the problems of our school and that our current curriculum is founded during the Industrial Revolution, and also explains the streaming/tracking system that is found within our schools today.

"The Afro-American student, among others, suffers from these ideological stereotypes and practices of schooling and society. Afro-Americans, with some exceptions, have attempted to integrate themselves into wider American culture for more than 400 years. In this respect, they are like other newcomer groups that have migrated during the past from other parts of Europe, Asia, and South America. However, their separate world has endured, because the dominate ruling class in the United States have opposed their assimilation." Rothstein, (1991) pg. 115

"Bourdieu's teachers and students are persons with no free will." Rothstein (1991), pg.56

Improving Our Education System:

"Now individuals do not make their own histories. Rather, the histories of significant others and mimetic structures compel individuals to march down a predetermined path." Rothstein (1991), pg.64

<u>Sociology of Education</u>: a student's future was predetermined to a great extent by his or her class position in society. From this Structural Perspective perspective teachers, students, and parents are trapped into a caste like status and our school systems reproduce their status in our schools. What is most important according to this perspective was 'cultural capital'. Depending on one's cultural capital will have the greatest influence on the success of the student in his or her future life.

Emile Durkheim and Pierre Bourdieu both agreed that those individuals who were from the dominant group who shared the same language and culture of the educational system had the best prospects of doing well in our schools. They agreed that this was a structure where the school system sustained its structures and culture that it was meant to re-create.

"Educational production also refers to the specific ways youth learn to accept the purpose and moral understandings of classroom life. This happens when students accept the teacher's right to decide everything that happens in the learning situation and to evaluate students' work on a continuous and arbitrary basis: a docile worker and unquestioning citizen, who accepts the status quo without question." Rothstein, (1991). pg.142.

"A classroom is both a dangerous and a wondorous place. It can destroy students or it can save them." Feuerverger (2007), pg.16

Post- Colonial Lens:

This is important in our society we are made to believe that Third World nation poverty as a timeless condition. Third World nations have always been poor, poverty stricken and the people of those lands unproductive, backward and lazy. This is incorrect, the Third World people and lands are over exploited and now underdeveloped. Looking at the great histories of India, Africa, Middle-East and Latin-America they have long produced great material wealth, abundant natural resources, and precious stones. This is the reason why European Imperialist invaded and stole and plundered the land, people and natural resources. Furthermore, G8, and G20 nations are powerful now because of their colonial conquests of the past, the developing world is not behind innately it is because they are trying to pick up the pieces of being left with nothing and less nothing after colonization took place.

Look at the example of the country of Tibet. Tibet was country with the an abundant source of natural resources, water, minerals, stones, lumber, gold, and diamonds. Today Tibet and its people are poor and poverty stricken because China has stripped Tibet of all its natural resources.

"Schooling is a hierarchical structure is therefore a colonizing device. Schooling was primarily for 'civilizing' and governing conquered people." Carnoy, (1974) pg.349.

The focus in on the cultural identity after colonization has taken place. The process of nations trying to create a national identity and the complex issues of trying to severe their history with the colonizer and the colonization that has taken place. The example of British India when the British left and India had to recreate its identity. Before the British invasion of India it was able to exist with many diverse identities, world-views and religions. This diversity and rich cultural pluralism was the identity of India before colonization, however after the British Empire the divisions were magnified, by a divide and rule strategy that left India divided which lead to the partition of India.

Teacher Professional Development:

The main aim of post-colonialism for educators is for us to see the side-effects of imperialism on people, countries and cultures. We are not only concerned with history, but how we can reconcile what has happened and create a world of mutual respect.

The marginalized world-view, voice or people that have been invisible, need to be made visible and not only seen but understood. This is what it means to be an educator, the ability to really understand our students, our society and our world.

"And in the final analysis there is no greater gift- and no greater weapon-than love and compassion." Feuerverger (2007).pg.142

It takes much effort, love and compassion to research and try to find these solutions to the problems of our schools, society and global world. But arming yourself as teachers, educators, administrators, and policy makers of the history, events and happenings of our world we can better educate our future generations that are in our classrooms, schools, and education systems. Looking from the multicultural perspective helps the educator to recognize the truth based in science and in our common understanding; we are one race: the human race. There is only one human family. Post-colonialism fights to decolonize our future and to recognize that we are all members of the human family and all problems are workable because we human beings are the creator of these problems.

The two main questions I address are as follows: 1.)Who made these policies? 2.)Whose voices are being heard in the policy process? I am particularly interested in analyzing how truth and knowledge are relative to the historical context. My, analysis is Critical as I propose to uncover how policy decisions are made and how power is exerted in the process. The purpose of this work is to determine how including voices who are traditionally the objects of policy influences policy. My goal is to see how the two policies differently address the educational road blocks that First Nation students face on a daily basis living in Ontario, Canada and if it would make a difference depending on who was included in the policy process. My paper is organized in the following way: I) Introduction, II) Context or Background, III) Framework, IV) Scholar and Personal Reflections and IV) Discussion of Implications and Significance of the Topic.

Underlying Assumptions: In order for Canada to be a strong and unified country we must work to help and heal First Nation Communities. This can only derive from genuine understanding, dialogue and compassion. We must understand and respect our First Nation brothers and sisters view in regards to history, self-determination, values and education

"This process is largely unconscious, as discourse and discursive webs make invisible the exercise of power. Multiple discourses from different sources work together as mechanisms of power to create a truth and structure power/ knowledge relations." (Goldberg, 2006.)1

Karma M. Chukdong B.Ed, M.A., M.Ed

Introduction:

Current Situation of First Nation School Boards in Ontario:

I am a certified teacher affiliated with the Ontario College of Teachers. I am a Canadian Tibetan who also holds Masters Degree from the University of Toronto. I recently published a book outlining Tibetan Buddhist Leadership in the Modern World. The book title is <u>The Human Family: A Modern Tibetan Buddhist Perspective(2008)</u>, published by AuthorHouse Publications. Tibet was occupied by Communist China in 1959, and every since I was young I wanted to be able to give a voice to the Tibetan people and to raise awareness of what has happened in Tibet. After completing my Teachers College at OISE, I wanted to teach in a First Nations Community. Why? As most Canadians I thought First Nations were doing quite well with their own school system, Native school boards, Education and Self-Government. So I thought this could be an invaluable experience and I could share these findings with my Tibetan people and establish our own school boards, school systems in Southern, and Central Ontario.

The First Nations of Northern Ontario are living in third world nation poverty. Prior to going there, my understanding and perception was totally opposite. Our Tibetan tradition in terms of schooling, school board, and educational leadership is doing better than the First Nations. So I went there with the motivation to learn from them to help our Refugee

Tibetan School systems in the future, but ultimately realized I was there to serve them as much as possible—this was my duty as a Canadian and human being of conscience.

All Canadians must work together to heal the First Nations Peoples, and ultimately we will be healing our entire nation. On any level one wants to look at it, we cannot have Canadians living in third world conditions. The situation is getting worse, with higher rates of suicide, and culture of hopelessness. Other third world nations living conditions are improving, but the First Nations of Canada's predicament is actually getting worse. The first aim of this study is to help give the First Nations a voice, to let Canada know their struggle, pain, and predicament, the second aim is to give solutions to the underlying problems facing First Nations Peoples, and the third is to make an impact on the Canadian pysche to show that this problem is not just a First Nation issue, it is an issue that effects every Canadian living in Canada. After teaching in two remote First Nation Communities in Northern Ontario, and talking wiht many other leaders there, I believe these are the outlining issues facing the educational success for the First Nations.

Leadership: Elders are the leaders of these communities. The Elders look down on their own Traditional ways and are now inherently disconnected from the youth, by loss of language and world-view. The First Nation youth of today have much pride in their traditional ways, beliefs and religion. The youth look to the Elders for guidance and wisdom but they have become empty vessels of past history, heritage, Native wisdom and story-telling as this was the generation that was lost to Residential Schools.

Educational Leadership: There is an absence of First Nation Principals and teachers in their own communities. All the teachers and Principals come from southern and central Ontario to teach at these schools. Why? Schools abide by the Ontario educational policy that teachers and Principals must have an Ontario College of Teachers Certificate to teach.

Effect: Teachers of non-native background appear smarter by this community because the teachers have the position and power in the community.

Societal Effect: Foreign teachers(which is us) have the best jobs in their communities. Having their children begging the non-native teachers for food and money on the way to school and all day is not something the community members feel very good about.

Ontario College of Teachers: How can these children get to University or Teachers College? The Ontario curriculum does not correspond to their everyday reality, or world-view. (Reading of Shakespeare, English curriculum for example is very difficult).

Lack of Resources: Staff must continually create photocopies because of lack of text books, teachers are burnt out after one year and this leads to high amounts of teacher turn over (effect: students feel insecure about their community, lose connection to teachers, and begin to feel hopeless.)

School Buildings: I believe this attributes to high levels of drop outs. From K-Gr.11 all these children are in the same building for their entire school career. 12 years in the same building, using the same computers, library and gymnasium is not fair. They need a change and something to look forward to. Here in the rest of Canada, after grade 8 students have the excitement of meeting new students and going to high school which is usually a new building and in a new area.

Monies need to be allocated to the creation of Colleges and Universities that are in close proximity to these First Nation Communities in Ontario. Creating a college system or higher education facility on these reserve communities would bring hope, and much excitement to these communities. Plus it would create jobs for college and university professors in the field. Library facilities, and gymnasiums or recreation centers are desperately needed to keep First Nation youth out of trouble and mischief. Most petty crimes concerning First Nation youth are labeled "Mischief" because is boredom essentially.

These findings and solutions are discussed and mapped o t in the Assembly of First Nations: First Nation Education Plan Document (2005). Yet they do not appear in the Ontario Ministry of Education Policy. In this paper, I will compare and contrast the two policies and examine reasons for and the implications of their differences. The First Nations having their own separate Education Plan Document speaks volumes of the lack of dialogue and cooperation in the policy discourse. There exists a major disconnect to the reality the First Nations are living with daily and the Ministry of Education policy makers who are creating policy for a people they have little understanding of. This policy created by the Ministry of Education is an activity that gives the appearance of addressing the issues but which, manifestly fails to tackle the real problem. (Gillborn, 2006).2

II) Context or Background:

The Ontario Ministry of Education released this policy in 2007. Our Prime Minister apologized to the First Nations for the implementation of the Residential School System publicly in 2008. Possibly, predicting possible disruptions of the First Nations during the 2010 Winter Olympics in Vancouver, seeing similar protests of the Tibetans during the 2008 Beijing Olympics in China. Section of this paper will use a policy genealogy approach and explore the impact and innate obstacles First Nations face because of the Residential School System. A school system which practiced cultural, and religious genocide on our First Nation brothers and sisters.

Karma M. Chukdong B.Ed, M.A., M.Ed

Policy Genealogical Approach

"We do not deconstruct discourse to reveal the 'truth', but to reveal how something has become known as the truth at a given point in time or how certain discourses operate as truthful and further demonstrating the bases of power that underpin, motivate and benefit from the truth-claims of the discourse in question." (Goldberg, 2006.)[3]

The Webster's Dictionary definition of imperialism is: the state policy, practice, or advocacy of extending the power and dominion of a nation, especially the direct territorial acquisition or by gaining indirect control over the political or economical life of other areas. The impoverished lands of Africa, Latin America, and Asia are today called Third World Nations—to distinguish them from First World Nations of North America and Europe. In our society Third World poverty is treated by contemporary western society as a timeless condition. Society is made to believe that this has always been the case. Impoverished countries are poor because their lands have always been infertile or their people unproductive and lazy. This is incorrect. In reality the lands of Africa, Middle-East, Asia and Latin America have long produced rich natural resources of minerals, oil, foods, and precious stones. This is the reason why Western Imperialism went through all the trouble to control and seize them. The Third World is not underdeveloped but over exploited. Western colonization and investments have created a lower rather than higher standard of living. Case and point the extreme poverty that we find on First Nation reservations in Northern Ontario, Canada. The historical injustices of the past cannot be overlooked or forgotten as there resides the root cause of many of the obstacles of genuine self-determination, and democracy in our country

"Schooling is a hierarchical structure is therefore a colonizing device. Schooling was primarily for 'civilizing' and governing conquered people." (Carnoy, 1971, pg.349)[4]

This was directly reflected in the Residential School system of Canada. This was a method employed to assimilate, destroy an identity, and a way of erasing language, even changing the names of children, and making them ashamed of being of Native descent.

"More importantly it instilled in them a respect and awe for the aristocratic virtues of the majestic English language, culture and corresponding contempt and disdain for their own background." (Carnoy, 1971, pg.101)[5]

In the realm of language we see the same internal struggle. First Nations children and parents stress the importance of their Native language classes as more important than other subjects taught at school. They force their children to attend Native language class but are not as strict with attending other courses. Most ethnic peoples love and cherish their language, as language is the essence of ones culture, history and identity.

"Possession of two languages is not merely a matter of having two tools, but actually means participation in two physical and cultural realms. Here, the two worlds symbolized and conveyed by the two tongues are in conflict; they are those of the colonizer and the colonized." (Carnoy, 1971, pg.70)[6]

Therefore some important questions come to mind when researching First Nations Educational Policy. Who made this policy? Whose voices are being heard? How are these policies challenged or resisted? After one has some experience researching First Nations policy and discourse one becomes well aware of an innate duality in these studies. There is an 'insider' versus 'outsider' dichotomy especially made lucid after visiting and teaching in these First Nation communities. Who made the policy? The Ministry of Education created this policy, depending where you stand, or direct experience one can question or not question the intent of the policy makers. We know the Ministry of Education created this policy then how many of the policy makers were First Nation? If the policy is to genuinely help First Nations how many First Nations were consulted with its creation? Why does the Assembly of First Nations feel the need to create their own First Nation Education Action Plan, if the Ministry has already consulted the First Nation leaders? As Gillborn states:

"an activity that gives the appearance of addressing the issues but which, in reality, manifestly fails to tackle the real problem." (Gillborn, pg.85)[7]

The above quotation is the definition of what a placebo is. Now we are beginning to see how certain policies are being challenged and resisted, because the First Nation Leaders know they were not consulted in these important matters concerning their children's future and future of their people.

III) Framework: Policy Genealogy: when describing the history of First Nations and the Critical Policy approach when analyzing current and future policies of First Nations in Canada.

Methodology:

Although various approaches to policy analysis exist, three general approaches can be distinguished: the analycentric, the policy process, and the meta-policy approach.

The approach focuses on individual problems and its solutions; its base is the micro-scale and its problem interpretation is usually of a technical nature. The primary goal of this approach is to identify the most effective and efficient solution in technical and economic terms (e.g. most efficient and distribution of resources). Looking at First Nation educational goals from this perspective one would look at the building of colleges and universities that would be in close proximation or one located in one central reserve, that would be easily accessible to all First Nation communities. This would also give many employment opportunities to Canadian teachers and professors who would now have new job openings here. Long-term benefits eventually First Nations will be teaching at these colleges and universities and in turn more graduates will help the Canadian labor market.

The policy process: this approach puts its focus onto political processes and investigates who the stakeholders are; its scope is the meso-scale and its problem interpretation is usually of a political nature. What are the aims at determining what processes and means are used to explain the role and influence of stakeholders with the policy process? Here the study looks at policy genealogy when looking at the history of First Nations in Canada, and investigate policy as discourse as their voice is absent in important issues pertaining to them. This analysis looks at power struggles and influence of these peoples in discourse and consultation, solutions to problems are identified.

The meta-policy approach: This approach investigates the role of First Nation educational leadership from the macro-scale and it is viewed from a structural stance. Here the analysis investigates the contextual factors of the policy process; the political, economic, and socio-cultural factors influencing it.

I will compare this policy document on First Nation Educational Objectives with the First Nations, Metis, and Inuit Education Policy Framework of Ontario that was released in 2007. Ultimately seeing how these policy objectives compare with the First Nations Education Action Plan that was created by the Assembly of First Nation Chiefs. I will also code and use Interviews from colleagues who taught in these communities, use myself as a case study and develop qualitative and quantitative evidence to show how this policy will not truly solve the innate issues facing First Nations in the realm of education. I will utilize the Policy Analysis of Carl V. Patton (1986). as my organizational framework. It has six stages: 1. Verify, define and detail the problem, 2) Establish evaluation criteria, 3) Identify alternative policies, 4) Evaluate alternative policies, 5) Display and distinguish among alternative policies, and 6) Monitor the implementation policy. Carl V. Patton's Stages of Policy Analysis:

1. **Verify, Define and detail the problem**: The problem is that this policy document is not addressing the root cause of the issue. The real issue is rooted in lack of First Nation Leadership in the realm of education. Interviews of: Non-native and First Nation Teachers. Mr. Darren Luck over 6 years teaching experience in First Nation Communities. Mrs. Jeannie Beardy Director of Education at Big Trout Lake, Ontario.

2. **Establish evaluation criteria:** I will analyze the two policies based on these criteria, identified as critical to First Nations educationin the background section above.

LEADERSHIP:

One of the main aspects not addressed in the Ontario Ministry of Education Policy concerning First Nations, Metis and Inuit Peoples is a solution for the absence of First Nation Leadership. Elders are the leaders of First Nation communities. They hold spiritual and educational authority. They have lost their power and influence in their communities. In order to teach and lead in educational settings in Ontario one needs a teaching degree from the Ontario College of Teachers. Even if one invites Elders into the school and teach their knowledge know seems 'other' or irrelevant to the modern world.

Throughout the entire First Nation Education Action Plan (2005)(created by First Nation Chiefs and Elders) it constantly stresses the importance of the Elders in their community, learning, wisdom, education, leadership, knowledge and schools. The word Elders is mentioned only once in the Ministry of Education document on pg.20 describing policy to help First Nation students in Ontario.

The two schools that draw upon first-hand experience are reservation number 209 (Big Trout Lake, Ontario) and reservation number 210 (Kasabonika Lake, Ontario).

Why is there an absence of First Nation Leadership in Education?

One of the first things one notices upon entering a First Nation school in the north is the absence of First Nation teachers. If there is a First Nation teacher he or she would be assigned to teach Native language courses. This responsibility is usually given to a highly respected Elder of the community to teach the next generation of their peoples. Therefore, Native language is seen as far more vital than other school subjects because it is their education and it is taught by a First Nation teacher and Elder. Many students skip the majority of classes and just attend the Native language courses and physical education that is usually after Native language class everyday. This is a very important point recognized by the research of the Aboriginal Policy documents as well. They recognize that attendance is almost 95% in their Native Language Classes in contrast to their other subject classes at their schools. There maybe many variables to the reason for this, but their research concludes that it has to do with the children learning their culture, tradition and language. Also this Native language class is always taught by a Native Elder from the community, and that the importance of this class is always stressed by their parents.

Age- appropriate students by extent of First Nation Language Instruction, 2000-01 (Aboriginal Policy Research, 2006) [8]

Native Language Attendance	Age-appropriate
None	82.9
½ Time	88.8
<1/2 Time	83.2
Subject	81.7
Subject P/T	82.8
Subject F/T	94.0

When traditional language is offered as a subject and full-time medium instruction, is significantly higher than all of the other categories. These researchers conclude:

"The striking point about Canadian assessments of First Nations and Aboriginal education is the lack of any real modeling of reasons for the particular patterns of educational attainment." (Aboriginal Policy Research, Pg.143)[9]

Native teachers cannot teach in the elementary end of the school because the school board is funded by the Provincial government and must abide by the policies of teachers having an Ontario teaching degree. The reason being is that schools on reservations only go to grade eleven, and if a student wants to get their high school diploma they must leave their community. They will have to live and attend a school outside their community in order to earn their high school diploma:

"The community has an elementary and a junior high school. In order to complete school, students have to board in Sioux Lookout." (Denied Too Long, pg.29)[10]

The road block is further compounded in the realm of leadership of schools and community. The communities of Big Trout Lake and Kasabonika Lake have never had a First Nation Principal because of this system. For most children and families just making it to Grade 8 is seen as finishing high school in their communities. The grade 8 graduation is far more elaborate and celebrated in these communities. Grade 8 graduation is given as much applause and recognition as high school graduation here in central Ontario. When one looks down the hall at the high school end of the school the halls are empty and classes having one or two students enrolled in high school classes where they attend sporadically throughout the semester.

3. **Identify alternative policies**: Policy makers must be cognizant of First Nation educational policy aims and objectives to truly achieve the result they want. Unfortunately, similar to the implementation of the African Canadian School Board in Toronto; First Nation leaders want to implement a college and university system created for and by First Nation Peoples. The reason why these types of solutions are happening is because peoples are not feeling the system is genuinely fair and democratic. Black teachers and principals are absent in most Ontario schools, black history is not given enough importance. So, the correlation is very similar for the First Nation peoples in Canada. The proof of these systems not working for these groups is the strikingly high rates of African Canadian and First Nation in the Canadian Jail systems today. Here we will compare and contrast the Ontario Ministry of Education Policy for First

Nations, Metis, and Inuit Peoples versus the First Nation Educational Policy composed by the Assembly of First Nation Leaders. On page 23 of the Ministry of Ontario document it states:

"Aboriginal and treaty rights of the Aboriginal peoples of Canada are recognized and affirmed in the Constitution Acts, 1867 and 1982 (section 35). Section 35 (2) indicates that Aboriginals peoples of Canada include Indian, Inuit, and Metis people. Section 91 (24) gives the Parliament of Canada exclusive jurisdiction over the creation of laws relating to " Indians and lands reserved for the Indians", and section 93 gives provincial legislatures exclusive jurisdiction over the creation of laws related to education."[11]

This becomes transparently clear not only in regards to First Nations education, self-determination the Canadian government has all the power and control in concerns and issues related to the future of First Nations in the province of Ontario and Canada as a country. Therefore, one can say that genuine dialogue or policy discourse can not take place until First Nations are given the power, freedom and voice to help their communities in meaningful ways. As only peoples who actually live in these communities and live the daily life as a First Nations in Canada will truly know what solutions will work for their plight and struggle. This is the perspective and discourse of what the First Nation chiefs and Elders believe when they state in their Assembly of First Nations Educational Policy Document:

"The Assembly of First Nations (AFN) has long advocated for First Nation control over First Nation education. In 1972, the AFN released its first comprehensive, policy statement on education with the publication of Indian Control of Indian Education. The themes that this document embodied remain relevant today, having been further developed and refined over the three decades, culminating in the themes advocated by First Nation leaders at the Canadian-Aboriginal Peoples Roundtable sessions in 2004. the central thrust of these initiatives has consistently called for the recognition of First Nations jurisdiction over education."[12]

The policy created by the Ministry of Education fails to voice the First Nation perspective in the document. The First Nation discourse clearly shows that they want full jurisdiction over their peoples education and not addressing this view-point leaves the Ministries document obsolete and pointless.

The Native voice is further expounded in when it states:

"There is a need to recognize First Nations jurisdiction as a central tenet of education reform. Since before the last century, formal education has been used by colonizing governments as a tool for the assimilation of First Nations Peoples."[13]

This statement and view is well documented especially by the scholarly research by Paulo Freire and Martin Carnoy who espouse the thesis that education is a tool utilized to assimilate and control a conquered people.

In the policy document on page 15 section Strategy 2.2: Provide additional support in a variety of areas to reduce gaps in student outcomes. The policy needs to address the reasons for the gaps, otherwise educators or society at large my look down on First Nation children in school systems. The 'gap' is not because of intelligence but because of the colonization, loss of identity, confidence, and history. Specifically on reservations the school policy is that from grade K-5 all course instruction will be in their native language. This so that the children will reclaim and see the importance of their identity. However, from our standards we would say:

"The Native children of these schools are five years behind the rest of Ontario."

This is the belief that the non-native staff at our schools view the children. As we must teach the Ontario curriculum at the grade level the children are in. However, we would have to use grade one, or grade two text books to teach to the children as their English skills were at the grade one and grade two level. Again when I was at Kasabonika Lake, Ontario First Nation Reservation #210 we as a staff had the responsibility to make up for the is 'gap'. But, again I focused on the First Nation perspective in regards to curriculum and found success.

Kasabonika Lake, Ontario First Nation: 2006-2007

Grade Level: 6	# of Students	# of years behind according to Special Ed. Assessment 3-4 years behind In terms of comprehension, literacy and math	# of students at Grade 6 level at the end of school year assessments
	23	23	21

Having a focus on First Nations perspective and world-view is a must for academic success of these children throughout the academic year. However, as the Special Education teachers advised me that over the long summer months of no schooling retention rates of these children are low and also account to some of the gaps in their learning from year to year. So, therefore more funding to these boards are necessary so they can hire staff to teach summer courses to the students so they can maintain their learning throughout the summer months and to keep them out of mischief. This is true in regards of giving a test after an fractions unit the students for example, they would do very well, however giving a culminating exam at the end of the year one would have to give two or three exemplars of the question on the board to refresh there understanding of the topic.

Also, on page 15 the policy discusses the prevention of Fetal Alcohol Syndrome. If one truly understands the cycle and damage colonization has created one will understand the rise of FAS in First Nation communities. The sexual abuse, genocide, and loss of life that existed in Residential school has left deep scars in their collective psyche. Many resorted to alcohol to numb the pain, not knowing the further damage they were having on their offspring who were born with this syndrome. Therefore you cannot prevent Fetal Alcohol Syndrome without seeing the reason why this is happening. On page 17 the policy addresses Strategy 3.1: Build educational leadership capacity and coordination. The policy objective suggests to offer assistance to First Nations by strengthening educational leadership in areas as training principals, with sensitivity to First Nation traditions and practices. But what are these traditions and practices? Why are they not mentioned in detail if they are so critical to the success of this policy? The Assembly of First Nations Education Action Plan gives detailed description and definition of what is their world-view, culture, history and beliefs are. Also, constantly marginalizing this as a First Nation issue undermines the severity and great importance this has in strengthening the entire nation of Canada. The question arises if Principals who have no current students who are First Nation would they still implement these policies focusing on First Nation equality and importance? Again, this is an issue of a strong and united Canada. On page 18 policy c) aims at fostering Aboriginal student's leadership skills. How does one achieve this aim? When he or she has never seen a First Nation person in any significant role of leadership and influence? On page 18 Strategy 3.2 the policy aims at building capacity to support identity building, including the appreciation of Aboriginal perspectives, values, and cultures by all students, school board staff, and elected trustees. If this is a genuine policy directive one would think that one mention of what the First Nation world-view was, or what values they hold dear would be described in some detail. The current education system in Ontario, is marginalizing all these policy directives they seek to improve. First Nation history is not even mentioned in Canadian History textbooks throughout our province, as these texts begin Canadian history in the year of 1867 during Confederation when Canada became a nation. However, from the First Nation perspective Canada had an important history and was thus a nation before this date. Essentially Canada Day, formerly known as Dominion Day, is disrespecting First Nation importance and history. Perhaps this was the reason for implementing the special day dedicated to First Nations on June 21st of every year(Aboriginal Day).

4. **Evaluate alternative policies**: The alternate policies are: a) Focus on Leadership, b) Having their own college and university system, c) having courses basedon a First Nation perspective, d) Make sure there is adequate funding for summer school programs in First Nation communities. All these interdependent policy alternatives focus on one thing: Success for the First Nation Student. a) First Nation leadership is critical when understanding how this relates to power, confidence, and success for these peoples. After establishing what First Nation Leadership is, we will implement the Participative Leadership style of Dr. Kenneth Leithwood to remedy these issues. b.) Establishing colleges and universities based on First Nation world-view and teaching styles is very important. This will bring them hope, excitement and a vision of a better tomorrow for their peoples. This policy directive is located in the Assembly of First Nation Education Action Plan as well. The result will be, that First Nations will be able to help Canada in the labor market, and to richly contribute to the overall identity of Canada as a nation. c.) Having courses from a First Nations perspective has shown great results from my case study in Big Trout Lake, Ontario, and Kasabonika Lake, Ontario. What was the key factor was the rise in attendance because of curriculum focused on their world-view, and naturally success was inevitable when students attended school on a consistent basis. and d.) Provide funding for summer school courses for First Nation youth. There is critical issue of retention in these communities. In these communities there is a greater obstacle to maintaining and sustaining academic success from the previous year because of lack of educational, academic and mental stimulation for these students. Parents are generally have low literacy skills, who speak their mother tongue, Oji-Cree and do not read to the children in English, do not create study room for the children to study,(housing is very small and cramped, many living under one roof), so they need a positive place to maintain their knowledge base throughout the summer months. There is the added obstacle of FAS, ADD, and ADHD so having programs to help the children retain knowledge, skills and to make sure they are constantly improving like the rest of the students in Ontario, Canada.

5. **Display and distinguish among alternative policies:**

Policy Studies Today:

After discussing with my colleagues at Aglace Chapman Education Centre (Big Trout Lake, Ontario) I was told that my current students all failed but one the year before and that many have become depressed and none thought they could successful complete grade 8. I was completing my long-range plans for the grade 8 academic year and realized that most of the objectives in the curriculum guidelines did not mesh well with the reality of these children. However, I understood that my goal was to catch these students up to the rest of the standards of Ontario and that I must cover all the curriculum objectives of the province. However, I started off every class: geography, history, English, Language Arts, and science from a First Nation perspective. As my goal was to keep attendance high, as if the students attended school regularly this increased their chances of graduating. Everything was from the First Nation perspective focusing on First Nation stories, legends, history, achievement, invention, and special contributions they have had to the country of Canada. The staff, principal and community were amazed at the high attendance levels and achievement of the students. Many variables may have came into play as in math and other areas themes and objectives were repeated from last year, but the attendance was strikingly higher than the year before and thus all 25 students passed their examinations in Literacy and Math that year.

Big Trout Lake: Grade 8 Results 2004-2005 (First Nation Focused Curriculum)

Standard Ontario Curriculum 2003-2004	# of Students in Grade 8	# of Students Failed Grade 8	# of students passed onto Grade 9
Teacher taught standard Ontario Curriculum	24	23	1
Teacher taught from a First Nations World-View Focus	26	1	25

These types of findings are critical in understanding the mind-set of First Nation Leaders. As we will see the Assembly of First Nations Education Policy Document reiterates these types of objectives and expectations throughout their education documents. If the Ministry, teachers and Ontario College of Teachers are cognizant of the importance of this we can make many positive change for these peoples, and ultimately Canada will benefit.

Why all this emphasis on leadership in educational policy? Is it really this important?

"Leadership is second only to teaching in its impact on student outcomes." (Putting Ontario's Leadership Framework Into Action, pg. 5)14

Leadership has a critical role to play when discussing change and policy development in school systems. Leadership is directly linked to administration, community, power, authority, change, diversity, and value systems. The stumbling block encountered while teaching at these two separate First Nation schools is the lack of leadership and specifically the absence of First Nation leadership. Policy makers who want to improve the education of these communities should research the leadership styles described by Dr. Kenneth Leithwood and Daniel Duke. The six types of leadership are: Instructional, Transformational, Moral, Participative, Managerial, and Contingent forms of school leadership. Therefore what of the six styles fit within the First Nation world-view? What type of leadership is congruent with the environment and culture of your school? When first assessing these two First Nation schools one thought that the Transformational Leadership style was best suited for these schools. This type of leadership has seven vital dimensions for genuine change in school systems:

"building school vision, establishing school goals, providing intellectual stimulation, offering individual support, modeling best practices, and important organizational values, demonstrating high performance expectations, creating a productive school culture, and developing structures to foster participation in school systems." (Leithwood, 1994). 15

This type of leadership eventually becomes a moral force in maintaining and sustaining these very high standards.

"Transformational leadership eventually becomes moral leadership in that it raises the standards of human conduct and ethical grounding to both the leaders and the lead, and thus a true culture of change can occur." (Burns, 1978)16

Fundamentally it is important to be mindful of these diverse types of leadership when creating policy to improve school systems. Also, what is more important is to genuinely understand the school culture and community that these schools exist in. Specifically the field of First Nation leadership is quite complicated. Not only is there a systematic way in which First Nation leaders have obstacles in securing power, and authority in school systems but once they do they are brought down by their very own community and members. Having studied Paulo Freire's monumental book: <u>The Pedagogy of the Oppressed</u> one should not be surprised of these happenings. Most colonized peoples he explained have difficulty securing power in their own communities because they already begin to doubt each other and leadership amongst their own peoples. We will return to this theme later. But the <u>Aboriginal Peoples Collections</u> findings were:

Aboriginal communities that have been traumatized display a fairly predictable pattern of collective dysfunction in the form of rampant backbiting and gossip, perpetual social and political conflict and in-fighting, a tendency to pull down the good work of anyone who arises to serve the community, political corruption, lack of accountability and transparency in governance, widespread suspicion and mistrust between people, chronic inability to unite and work together to solve critical human problems, competition and turf wars between programs, a general sense of alienation and disengagement from community affairs by most people (what's the use?), a climate of fear and intimidation surrounding those who hold power and a general lack of progress and success in community initiatives and enterprises (which often seem to self-destruct)." (Aboriginal Peoples Collection, pg.4)17

Change and policy implementation must be intimately linked with their community, resources, beliefs and needs. The policy objectives must be linked with the Elders and other cultural leaders. Viewing these events and realities from a macrocosmic level we can see a relationship between the colonized and colonizer directly when investigating leadership, policy discourse, and divide and rule ideologies of imperialism.

"Those members of the communities who show sufficient leadership capacities to be chosen for these courses necessarily reflect and express the aspirations of the individuals of their community. They are in harmony with the way of living and thinking about reality which characterize their comrades, even though they reveal special abilities which give them the status of 'leaders'. As soon as they complete the course and return to the community with resources to control and submerge and dominate consciousness of their comrades, or they become strangers in their own communities and their former leadership position is thus threatened. In order not to lose their leadership status, they will probably tend to continue manipulating the community, but in a more efficient manner." (Paulo Freire, (1970.)Pg.138-139)[18]

Policy makers who comprehend all these hindrances and issues in First Nation communities it is wise to incorporate the Participative Leadership Style of Dr. Kenneth Leithwood. Since, there is a tendency to attack and ridicule leadership that arises and that community has more weight and power than individual leaders this is the most suitable type of leadership style to apply to educational policy. Leadership in First Nation and other non-western cultures is a bottom-up trajectory. Meaning the society or community will raise the leader who best serves the community. The community members choose the leader in contrast to the individual deciding he or she should be a leader and authority figure. According to First Nation legend the greatest leader would be the hunter. The hunter was not seen as a leader because he could catch the most prey or because of his athletic ability, or intelligence. He was seen as a leader of the community because after hunting for weeks he would return to the community and share all his prey with the community equally. This is why he was seen as a leader because of his altruism and his sharing nature.

Another obstacle mentioned earlier facing teachers who teach on in these communities is that the Ontario curriculum does not relate to the community, people, world-view, or day to day life of people living in third world conditions. Therefore, the Participative Leadership is best suited for First Nation communities.

"Is that curriculum of the school ought to directly reflect the values and preferences of parents and the local community." (Leithwood, year, pg.52)[19]

This type of leadership focuses on the school professionals need to be responsive to local beliefs, concerns and values and preferences(Leithwood). This type of leadership involves all members of the community and this is critical in a community still battling the negative effects of colonization. This type of leadership distributes leadership:

"Community-control SBM aims to increase the authority and influence of parents and community members." (Leithwood, pg.52). Parents and community members who already question and doubt the intention of schools because of indoctrination, genocide, and assimilation practices of the past need to be given some power and control. The Participatory Leadership style will give parents and the community the power and authority to make decisions for their future generations.

"That professionals are willing to be quite responsive to the values and preferences of parents and the local community under conditions in which parents are in a position to act as partners with schools in the education of their children." (Leithwood,1999, pg. 52)[20]

Current Situation:

Academic Administration Today:

If the policy document created by the Ministry of Education was clear and genuine, we would know what First Nation leadership is. As the Education document created by the Assembly of First Nations discussed First Nation leadership in education throughout their document. First Nation lineages are passed down orally through the generations. The belief that the Great Spirit created the Earth and is the Mother of all creation. Plants and animals have spirits that must be venerated, honoured, and cared for. It is a holistic system that centers not only on human life but also the life of the world and all things in it. The medicine wheel symbolizes how all life is interconnected and embarked on in a circular journey. The four cardinal directions, each of which as a guiding spirit and special attributes, reflects the stages of the life journey.

From listening to Elders, one can see the change in the children and see the many negative aspects effecting their children. Children involved in gangs, loss of identity, drug use, and being sent to mental health centres is an aspect of everyday life in these communities.

"What is needed is funding that encourages and supports comprehensive long-term planning and action. Such funding must address both healing as recovery (crisis intervention) and community health and a healthy community and nation." (Aboriginals Peoples Collection, pg.52)[21]

Policy makers should have these aspects in mind when creating policy documents concerning First Nations. The future of a people depends on their children. Their children are raised in dysfunction where alcoholism, drug abuse, smoking in elementary grades, are daily occurrences. Their loss of identity, hopelessness, and loss of language has had serious negative effects on their confidence and self value. Families trying to understand and cope with the injustices and confusion of the past resorted to drugs and alcohol to deal the pain, suffering and confusion. Not knowing that these negative habits would be passed onto their children who are now affected with many disorders of Attention Deficit Disorder (ADD), Attention Deficit Hyperactivity Disorder(ADHD) and Fetal Alcohol Syndrome (FAS).

"If the goal is to heal the nation, it is critical to invest heavily in healing the nations children." (Aboriginal Peoples Collection, pg53).[22]

These alternative policies out-lined in this paper will truly help First Nations get back on their feet and help them heal their past and move them forward into the future.

6. **Monitor the implementation policy**: One key aspect that this study is trying to convey is the sense of urgency of this issue. This is also vital in monitoring and implementing this alternative policy. If there is no sense of urgency or importance of this alternative policy then nothing substantial will result for the First Nations Peoples of Ontario, Canada. Policy makers and Canadians must see the inherent value of creating policy that gives First Nation students a successful path to educational aims and goals. Furthermore, Canadians must see the value this will have on making us more competitive in the labor market, provincially, nationally, and internationally. The benefits are higher still, when seeing that our countries ancient soul will be reborn and revitalized to bring a much needed balance to our current fast paced capitalistic world.

   The important thing is that these schools will be given as much importance and respect as other colleges and universities in Canada. This will not be an easy solution, but these peoples will have genuine hope and excitement of going to college and university in the future. As for right now they view their future as hopeless. As evident by the rising rates of youth suicide in First Nation Communities. Suicide is not a failure of the individual, ultimately it is a failure of the society.

IV) Scholarly Research: Works cited are: Assembly of First Nations Education Action Plan Policy, First Nation, Metis, and Inuit Education Policy Framework by the Ministry of Ontario, First Nation, Metis and Inuit Eduacation Policy Framework from the Ministry of Alberta, Dr. Michelle Goldberg (Forming, Reforming, and Performing Education: Using Foucault to Rethink Canadian Schooling.), Martin Carnoy (Education as Cultural Imperialism), Sue Winton, (2007). (Rhetorical Analysis and of Character Education Policy), Kenneth Leithwood: Studies in Leadership Styles, Paulo Freire (Pedagogy of the Oppressed), Aboriginal Policy Research, Thomas Educational Publishing, Inc., and Carl V. Patton, David S. Sawicki (Basic Methods of Policy Analysis and Planning).

V) Independent Critical Discussion and Analysis:

Reflections, personal responses, interview analysis, case-study of my teaching experience on two separate First Nation Communities in Ontario, Canada: Big Trout Lake, Ontario and Kasabonika Lake, Ontario.

VI) Discussion of Implications and Significance of the Topic:

This was a policy analysis of the Ontario First Nation, Metis, and Inuit Education Policy Framework. The policy framework employed was the Policy Genealogy Framework when discussing: Who makes the policy? Whose voices are being heard? Especially when analyzing how truth and knowledge are relative to the historical context. Finally, the analysis was from the Critical Policy approach when displaying how the policy decisions are made and how power is exerted in the process. Does this educational policy really address the educational road blocks that First Nation students face on a daily basis living in Ontario, Canada?

This policy analysis has successfully proven that this policy created by the Ministry of Education in Ontario does not provide a genuine remedy of solving the inequality and absence of voice of the First Nations peoples and leaders in the realm of education. This policy analysis was six-fold in organization: I) Introduction, II) Context or Background, III) Framework, IV) Scholarly Research, V) Independent Critical Discussion and Analysis and VI) Discussion of Implications and Significance of the Topic.

Summary:

This study compared and contrasted these two policy documents. Thereby formulating four critical alternative policies that will truly achieve the aims of the Ministry of Education document.

The Ontario Ministry of Education Mission Statement:

"First Nation, Metis, and Inuit students in Ontario will have the knowledge, skills, and confidence they need to successfully complete their elementary and secondary education in order to pursue postsecondary education or training and/or enter the workforce."23

After this study we are well aware of the obstacles to this statement are. We are also aware that the Ministry of Education document does not address any of these obstacles facing First Nation students in Ontario. The four policy alternatives outlined in this vital study were: 1) Establishing Leadership, specifically empowering First Nation Leadership in schools, and school systems, 2) Create their own First Nation College and University school system, 3.) Modify Ontario Curriculum to have a First

Nation perspective option, and 4) Implement a Summer School System in these communities so students can maintain, sustain, retain, and build on knowledge bases acquired the year before.

Canadians of conscience and our political leadership should see that in order for Canada to be a strong and respected nation we must heal and reconcile First Nation communities and issues. This can only derive from genuine understanding, dialogue and compassion. We must understand and respect our First Nation brothers and sisters view in regards to history, self-determination, values and education. We must make sure our policies are just, genuine and fair to all peoples who belong to the nation of Canada.

CHAPTER NINE

Infusing Art Therapy into the Digital Classroom (Revised)

⌘

In this chapter we will discuss some practical solutions we can generate in the world of academic administration, school systems, curriculum and learning. Art is very critical for Change Management in Education to take place. Since our present curriculum is rooted in the Industrial Revolution we have successfully become fully functional robots. We are perfectly molded to be excellent robots on production lines and to be in compartments in workplaces throughout the world. We seek to receive more programs, more programs that can be downloaded into our hard drives (our brains) and from there we constantly converse with others by reciting our program to others. Our colleagues recite their program and we have very mechanical dealing with human beings for the majority of our time in academia and the work place. Our professors download the programs into our hard-drives and we memorize the data until it is hardwired into our brain like a computer chip. This is similar to the "banking concept" Paulo Freire talked about.

We need to become more fully human, we need to unplug this program from time to time and feel fully human. Can we share a hug or have a genuine laugh in the classroom or the workplace? Of course not! Robots do not laugh, robots do not hug. Change Management in Education looks at making us more fully alive, more human, and to recognize what education truly is.

From my personal experience I was not exposed to Art Education until I reached University. At University I was introduced to the Indigenous art of the sub-continent of India. My final grade was so high that I was able to transfer to the University of Toronto the next academic year scoring a very high GPA from this one course in Art Education. Imagine if Art Education was given more importance in our high schools today. Imagine the confidence and academic success of some our marginalized students if courses and departments gave importance other subjects. Mainstream curriculum designers and policy makers are beginning to see their importance, but it is taking a long time to implement in our schools. What they are finally understanding is that we are all visual learners. Meaning we learn more effectively through art. Indigenous peoples of this land specifically the: First Nations, Metis and Inuit have known this for thousands of years. All Indigenous education has a visual component, a tactile component because this added in the retention of knowledge. In this piece I realize that the Indigenous art of India has many of the same educational components of

Indigenous education still yet to be appreciated in our schools. In one piece of Indigenous art, we can meet the curriculum standards, expectations and strands of the Ministry set standards. Imagine the retention rates of our Indigenous students, marginalized students and low socio-economic students if we implemented courses that related to their worldviews, their learning style? Could it be that some of our students are placed in special needs, and modified programming simply because our staff, curriculum, and delivery is not reaching these students? Think about how many lives we can save by delivering courses that all students can relate with throughout their high school careers?

Here we will look at a simple piece of Indigenous art from India, and see how we can spark the critical thinking skills, research, and imagination of students through a simple piece of Indigenous artwork.

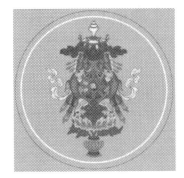

A Curriculum of Joy:

The Emergence of the Buddha Image: Indigenous Art of India

The earliest Buddhist art of Bharhut and Sanchi is aniconic: meaning Buddha is represented only in symbols. We will look at the factors that brought about this change from aniconism to iconism are of great importance and interest. Our purpose is a complicated one; we will examine the scholarship in this field of study and discuss the main factors for the emergence of the Buddha image. In this condense version of the paper we will look at I) The factors responsible for the absence of the Buddha images in early Buddhist art, and II) The eventual origin of the Buddha image.

I)   The Factors Responsible for the Aniconic Phase in Early Buddhist Art:
One of the most prominent aspects of early Buddhist art is this so called 'aniconic' phase. It can be seen at the Buddhist sites of Sanchi, Bharut, Bodhgaya, Amaravati, and Sarnath. This art was created between approximately the second century BCE, and second century AD. Recently, Susan Huntington has arrived at an interesting conclusion regarding this very issue. She believes she has seen something we all missed and basically believes that we have it all wrong. She believes that most of the reliefs in Bharhut, Sanchi, and Amaravati represent worship at sacred Buddist sites and aniconic representations pointing to Buddha.

What is aniconism? The Buddha is not seen in human form, he is only depicted by the use of symbols in early Buddhist art. So, the term in our cases why: is the Buddha never represented in human form, but only by symbolic representation? These sacred symbols are utilized to represent the actual presence of the Buddha instead. A vital point to understand in this complicated area of research is to comprehend Buddhist Indigenous art as a very gradual process. The early symbols on the Buddhist stupa for example were symbols from a shared Indigenous Indian culture. Therefore, we see that most symbols, animals, trees in formative Indigenous Buddhist art definitely have a pre-Buddhist origin. These Indigenous symbols are part of a shared cultural, religious milieu of popular Indian culture. We will now examine and discuss the main symbols that we believe represented the Buddha in the early aniconic period of early Buddhist art. The Bodhi-tree, Stupa, Chakra and the Lotus (will now be appraised).

The Bodhi-Tree:

During the early Indus Valley Civilization, it seems that the worship of trees and tree spirits was common. On several seals from both ancient Harappa and Mohenjo-daro this is seen. So these sacred trees were not originally Buddhist signs. The sacred tree was what was really important in ancient times, similar to the beliefs of Indigenous peoples in Canada. This particular tree called the Bodhi-tree is important because this is the tree Buddha attained enlightenment under. As well we notice that the same kind of sacred tree is depicted in Indigenous Jain art. So both Buddhists and Jains borrowed this early tradition of ancient tree worship.

The Medicine Wheel (Chakra)

The chakra is an ancient symbol as well. The chakra is the Sanskrit word for wheel. The wheel is also found in the Harappa and Mohenjodaro. But, in the Buddhist perspective this artistic symbolism is linked with the 'Chakravartin' (Wheel turner). Buddhist wheels have eight or twelve spokes owing to the adherence to Buddhist doctrine: Eight-fold path and Twelve-Links of dependent origination (pratitya-samutpada). A chakra on any Buddhist stupa is always linked with the First Teaching of the Buddha at the Deer Park in Sarnath, the Buddha turning the wheel of dharma (Dharma-chakra). The main point is that the wheel was already a vital and popular symbol well before it became connected with event of the First Teaching.

The Stupa:

The stupa contains the holy remains of the Buddha and this the reason why it is venerated. A practitioner of this Indigenous spirituality of India treats or perceives the stupa just as one would act towards a Buddha. In the early sutras we finds disciples and followers circumambulating the Buddha when departing from his presence, so too we find practitioners returning the same respect to the stupa. One should walk around the stupa, with the right shoulder facing the stupa. The stupa together with the sacred tree, and the wheel became associated with the three main events in the life of the Buddha.

The Flower (Padma):

The symbol is very intriguing. This Padma: Lotus flower has held a major importance in Buddhism, especially in philosophical concerns. This artistic symbol is used to describe supreme awakening. A lotus (awakening) that is unsoiled by the dirt and water (samsara) from which it is created rises above radiant and sublime. The lotus flower has always signified purity and sacredness in the Indigenous Buddhist Tradition. We see the lotus flower in early Buddhist art and on stupas. Early Jain art also utilized the lotus flower. So we can infer that the lotus must have been common to all Indigenous spiritual movements in India. The main point emphasized here is how these ancient symbols evolved into distinct Buddhist symbols that now represent the Buddha and his teaching.

The Theory of Aniconism and the Major Players:

In the early twentieth- century (a scholar by the name of) Alfred Foucher was the pioneer who first expressed the theory of aniconism. He also adhered to the belief that the earliest Buddha images were those created in Gandhara in the early centuries of the Christian era- more than half a millennium after the Buddha lived. In Gandhara, he concluded that superior sculptural background influenced Indigenous Indian artists, which was of Greek influence. This Greek influence was the reason that stimulated the creation of the Buddha in human form. But, we will examine the question of origins later, we will now return to the real issue at hand: the reason for the absence of Buddha images in early Buddhist art. Susan Huntington believes we have it all wrong and suggests that while it is true that Buddhist tenets on impermanence are central to Buddhist thought, they may not be relevant to the issue of aniconism. Even though such doctrines occur over and over again throughout the sutras, this does not to her, directly influence the issue of whether the Buddha should be depicted in human form. Susan Huntington's main argument can be summed up as this: she believes that most, if not all these works of art do not represent the events of Buddha at all, but rather portray devotion and worship at sacred historic Buddhist sites. Her conviction is not without warrant, since Buddha in fact did instruct his disciples in the Mahaparinibbana sutra, to visit the sacred sites of his major life events. She believes the chakra, Bodhi-tree, and stupa should be seen as depictions of actual sites, not events with the Buddha missing. Essentially she puts forth the claim that early Buddhist art of India was not predominantly concerned with the life story of the Buddha. Instead, an important emphasis was placed on the practice of lay devotion and worship at the sacred sites of Buddhism. She further emphasizes that since devotion to the memory of the Buddha was a practice specifically associated with laypeople rather than with monks, the prominence of lay devotees in the thematic scheme in the carvings is fitting.

However, this belief has now been put to rest by Coomaraswamy. We examined the reasons and rationalizations that were considered for the absence of the Buddha image in early Indigenous Buddhist art. This aniconic mode of depiction was a part of the milieu of the time. The sixth century BCE was an age of tremendous spiritual and philosophical investigation. The Indigenous Indian milieu of the time was divided into two main groups: the Brahmana and the Shramana. The Brahmans conceived of their deities aniconically. Thus, they had no need for image making and worship. Buddhism originated after the later Vedic period and the second current emerging within the Vedic fold at the time was that of the Upanishads. They criticized the old Vedic sacrificial religion, the worth of tis over-grown ritualism and its various ideas concerning the universe. The Upanishadic sages were engaged in metaphysical and philosophical enquiries about Brahma through supernatural insight gained from austerities and meditation. They also had no need for images. Thus, the Vedic, was one of the higher religions at that time in India with mass appeal and was opposed to iconism. The Shramana tradition to which Buddhism and Jainism belonged, was as great as the Vedic Brahmana tradition. It is interesting to note here that over 40% of the elite monks and nuns listed in the Theragatha and Therigatha belonged to the Brahmana caste; 29% to the Vaishya and 22% to the Kshatriya varnas. So owing to their previous background too they followed the same mode of traditional aniconism. On the whole image making and worship had not in general been a part of the milieu for the most part in India. Coomaraswamy has correctly observed that the artists of Pre-Kushana period were not incapable of carving images of the Buddha in human form. To him Indigenous artists who were fully capable of producing Yaksha and Yakshi images on the reliefs at Bharut and Sanchi would have no problems at all depicting Gautama Buddha in human form, if they had been required to do so. This belief that it was the Buddhist injunction that was responsible for the aniconic period in early Indigenous Buddhist art is well founded. The next issue we must consider is the obvious question of why did the Buddhists commence the making of Buddhist images and where did the Buddha image originate? We will now tackle this issue in the next and final section.

II) <u>The Emergence of the Buddha Image:</u>

There was a great debate at the beginning of this century about whether the first image of the Buddha was created as a result of 'alien' western influences, or if it had its origin in

Indigenous Mathura. As we know it was Alfred Foucher who first put forth the idea of the Greek influence for Gandhara art and that the oldest Buddha images from Gandhara were made by Greek artists. It was Ananda Commaraswamy who held the belief that Mathura invented the Buddha image. He clarified many misconceptions we had in this field. This dispute however about the geographical origin of the Buddha image did not end with Coomaraswamy. In 1951 W.W. Tarn powerfully put emphasis on Gandhara as the origin of the Buddha image. Tarn based his contention on a single coin with a human figure seated in the lotus position. This coin belongs to the rule of Maues in the middle of the first century BCE. His identification of the unknown figure with the Buddha is highly debatable and has not many supporters. The quarrel is based on a 'line' to the right of the figure. Tarn describes this horizontal line as part of a seat or throne. But others have gone, as far as to say this line is a sword or some kind of weapon. The Gandhara theory does have some validity. As we discussed earlier, the human form in early Buddhism was seen as 'Putikaya' a body full of impure matters. Thus the body of the Buddha should not be worshipped. In fact the human body in Buddhism is the very cause for all the suffering we face in this samsaric existence. This body is forever linked with the false notion of "I" and "not-I". Buddhism adheres to the unique doctrine of anatman (no-self), so ultimately the is no "I", no ego, the body is in a constant state of change; therefore it is impermanent and ultimately empty. These are the basic tenets of the Buddhadharma, but the Greeks who had no philosophical problems in depicting their highest gods in human form, so we see how this plays out to favour the Gandharan Greek origin of the Buddha image.

In 1981 van Luhuizen-de Leeuw discussed Mathura as the possible origin of the Buddha image. A.K Narain, however, agreed with Tarn that the seated figure on the Maues coin did represent a Buddha or at least a Bodhisattva. But to A.K. Narain this identification of the Buddha on the Maues coin does not favour Gandhara as the birthplace of the Buddha image. A.K. Narain believes it was the Sarvastivadins of the Swat Valley and Kashmir that produced the first image of the Buddha. He believes that the time frame between Maues (circa 95-75 BCE) and Kanishka (AD 78) was a time of trial and error before the real standardization took place both in Mathura and Gandhara. Ultimately we have found that this is a never-ending debate and any new archaeological evidence may change our viewpoints. What we do know for certain is that images of the Buddha were created in both Gandhara and Mathura at the beginning of the Kushana dynasty.

Our purpose was to discuss and examine the scholarship of early Indigenous Buddhist art and we discovered that scholars are still in disagreement in their findings about, why, where, when or even how the images of the Buddha evolved.

From the student perspective, having slides and artwork examined through class slides, commentaries and discussions would be fascinating. As we can see the majority if not all the curriculum strands for the Humanities if not the English curriculum as well were covered in examining one piece of art of the Indigenous spiritual systems of India. Next we look at the rise of international students in community college campuses and universities and make the claim that education is not a business. We need to create quality and inclusive curriculum for our International students as well.

CHAPTER TEN

Weaving the Self-Care Age with Modern Education

⌘

This latest research looked at the origin and purpose of education. The constant rise of anxiety, mental health issues, depression and even suicide in our school systems will be addressed. The growing rates of student suicide in Japan for instance for just receiving a "B" grade is something was as educators and citizens should be concerned about. This extreme competition and labelling of students is highly unhealthy for our students. The label that we give our students will follow them into adulthood.

Real education takes care of the human spirit; like medicine it nurtures the spirit and emotions. Currently if a student displays emotion or has a behavioral issue that student would be put into the hall or sent to the office. In Indigenous societies the educational setting would begin a circle. Sacred Medicines would be passed around by an Elder where students could discuss their feelings, and emotions before the class begins. In Western Education systems the student is viewed as an empty vessel where knowledge must be bestowed. In Indigenous Education systems the learner already possesses knowledge that she or he can share with the circle of learners. This leads to confidence, empowerment, and reassurance that the spirit is pure, and complete. This was the basis of holistic education learning styles found in Indigenous Education systems, human nature is good, not defiled in some way. Indigenous education was also Medicine for the body since the school day would start with Traditional songs and dances for which scientists are now discovering that singing and dancing are recognized as Medicine as this practice leads to lowered stress levels, lower blood pressure, and lowers anxiety levels in all who participate.

This research looks at the origin of the modern education system as rooted in the Industrial Age. There is a reason why our current education system is "Robotic" in nature. For what is better in a factory than an employee that acts like a robot? A human being who acts like a robot who does not require washroom breaks, no breaks, no sick days, no emotion, no conflicts, striving to conform to the system. She or he becomes the perfect employee; but not the perfect Human Being.

Real education looks at educating the whole Human Being. How can we be a happy Human Being? Indigenous Educational Systems has this as their fundamental pedagogy. What was unique and healing is that the Human Being is not the center of their Educational Systems. The Natural Law was the teacher. The Elders of Indigenous systems utilized analogies found in Natural Law. They observed the animal kingdom, and as scientists tested and experimented on what was wholesome and unwholesome.

Through their observations as scientists they discovered that everything is interconnected, not disconnected. Modern education divides all disciplines into separate fields or sectors. If one had the good fortune of listening to an Indigenous Elder one would begin to see that: psychology, anthropology, sociology, biology, medicine, and epistemology are all discussed in scientific precision in one oral teaching.

This is the hope of this latest research. We must heal our relationship with Indigenous Peoples in Canada and the world. Our world needs healing, and Indigenous Education is Medicine that can help alleviate many of our self-created human sufferings we experience today.

CHAPTER ELEVEN

An Elder's Wellness Advice to Students

⌘

Author pictured here with Elder Choeje Namse Rinpoche of the Kagyu Lineage Tibet. They are enjoying traditional barley soup and home made bread (Amdo Paley/ Bannock style bread).

The Four Dharmas of Gampopa

བློ་ཆོས་སུ་འགྲོ་བར་བྱིན་གྱིས་བརླབ་ཏུ་གསོལ།

ཆོས་ལམ་དུ་འགྲོ་བར་བྱིན་གྱིས་བརླབ་ཏུ་གསོལ།

ལམ་འཁྲུལ་པ་སེལ་བར་བྱིན་གྱིས་བརླབ་ཏུ་གསོལ།

འཁྲུལ་པ་ཡེ་ཤེས་སུ་འཆར་བར་བྱིན་གྱིས་བརླབ་ཏུ་གསོལ།

~ Grant blessings for the mind to turn towards the Dharma
Grant blessings for the Dharma to go along the right path
Grant blessings to dispel confusion along the path
Grant blessings for the confused perceptions to arise as wisdom. ~

Short Biography:

The Knowledge Holder Choeje Namse Rinpoche lak was sent to Canada by Head of the Kagyu Lineage the Gyalwa Karmapa the 16th Ranjung Rigpe Dorje. This Traditional Oral Lineage of the Kagyu Order commenced in Tibet starting with Marpa Lotsawa. Marpa Lotsawa passed down his Teachings which he secured from India to his student Jetsun Milarepa, who then passed them down to Gampopa. Gampopa was the first Teacher to the line of Karmapas who Dusum Khyenpa was the first Gyalwa Karmapa. Today the line has 17 lineage masters the current Gyalwa Karmapa is the 17th Orgyen Dodul Thinley Dorje. This lineage history is important in Traditional societies because it brings authentic energy to a teaching because like electricity there is a direct link or wire to the original battery the source of power. Therefore, before commencing a Traditional Teaching the Knowledge Holder or practitioner of Traditional Ceremony or Teaching would share the oral lineage of the Teaching and significance today. I am fortunate to my parents who took me to see the Knowledge Holder 16th Gyalwa Karmapa while he was on a tour and visited Belleville, ON and received an audience with His Holiness Gyalwa Karmapa. Also, I am very grateful to my parents for inviting and having the Elder Choeje Namse Rinpoche who has a direct connection to the Kagyu Lineage of ancient Tibet stay over at our home during my formative years.

Knowledge Holder Lama Namse Rinpoche lak was born in Tsurphu, Tibet in 1930 and became a monk at the age of fifteen. From ages 16 to 21, he did intensive studies of the basic fundamentals of Tibetan religious language, etymology, grammar, and poetry. He underwent the serious studies of the Tripitaka, Vinaya, Sutra and Abhidharma, and also the Prajna Paramita, Utara Shastra, Sutra Lankara, the five states of Madhyamika and many other versions and commentaries as well as schools of Buddhist thought and teachings.

From ages 21 to 24, Lama Namse did a three-year, three-month, three-day retreat with intensive practice of the core of the Kagyu teachings such as the Six Yogas of Naropa, the meaning of Mahamudra, and other related practices. From ages 24 to 26, especially the Five Treasuries of Jamgon Kongtrul the Great. From ages 27 to 30, Lama Namse went on an intensive pilgrimage to many sacred places and private retreats. When he was thirty years old, Lama Namse left Tibet as a refugee. He travelled to India, and from ages 32 to 35, did another three-year retreat. At this time he also became a retreat master for many new retreatants. At age thirty-seven, he travelled to Sikkim to Rumtek and received the collections of the empowerments of the Kag Ngagzod, Damgang Ngagzod practices.

Since 1974, Lama Namse has served as a teacher of the Kagyu lineage all over Europe, particularly in France, and helped many students understand the nature of the path. Lama Namse Rinpoche is His Holiness Karmapa's official representative in Canada and head of Karma Sonam Dargye Ling, the Canadian centre for His Holiness the Seventeenth Karmapa, Ogyen Trinley Dorje. The centre is located in Toronto, ON Canada.

This Teaching shared here the Elder Choeje Lama Namse Rinpoche gave was short but profound. The four lines were:

~ Grant blessings for the mind to turn towards the Dharma
Grant blessings for the Dharma to go along the right path
Grant blessings to dispel confusion along the path
Grant blessings for the confused perceptions to arise as wisdom. ~

In terms of academics and the lens of Theory and Practice we will look at the fourth line:
"Grant blessings for the confused perceptions to arise as wisdom."

The first three lines are quite spiritual in nature but this fourth line is the most powerful in terms of Indigenous Mental Health and Wellness for his students and contemporary students alike. There is no doubt our students will face confusion, doubts, hindrances, roadblocks and setbacks in their academic, personal, family and work lives. But here the Elder focuses much of the teaching on the fourth line: "Grant the blessings for the confused perceptions to arise as wisdom."

The Elder had us reflect on our own experience of seeing glimpses of our spirit, nature or mind being innately pure. We have all had glimpses of great joy, happiness and also at time sorrow. This roller-coaster of emotion what is the cause? The teaching very scientific in nature tries to find the root cause of happiness and suffering. Like a scientific experiment can we produce happy feelings and sad feelings? Can we calm the waters of disturbing emotions? The core belief or lens of this teaching is that our spirit, nature, or mind is always pure like a calm lake and able to see things clearly when the waves are settled. But, what causes the waves of disturbing emotions? The Elder continued to provide examples and analogies that might strike home the point to the diversity of students in the audience. The blazing sun was used that would peak behind dark rain clouds, the sun of awareness is always there sometime hidden behind clouds sometimes clouds of obscuration are absent. One main tenet was "Matikpa" impermanence change was a constant truth in this scientific experiment. Impermanence is to be accepted, but impermanence and change must lead to unhappiness because we cannot hold onto anything. Not being able to hold onto anything which its nature must be change brings joy. Joy at not grasping at unhappiness or happiness brings the practitioner to a bliss of awareness higher than the dualistic labels of " happy" or " sad".

What the Elder was describing was in academic circles was *theory* not practice. So, some students would say this sounds very nice, but how can we students apply this theory into real life? The Elder always asked us to revisit the life story of Jetsun Milarepa the main student of Marpa Lotsawa. Milarepa passed this oral teaching onto Rechungpa and Gampopa and now this Elder Choeje Namse Rinpoche is passing it down to us. Milarepa says that theory and practice must be combined:

The Elder stated: " Is everyone sleepy? Is everyone hungry? I am hungry! My final advice that has been passed down on how to blend this theory into practice is to welcome the disturbing emotions. Does it sound odd to welcome thoughts, anxieties that frighten us? However, through practice we see we cannot run from them. We must face the anxiety, the fear do not look for outside short-term remedies of alcohol or other pleasures that distract us from our fears. The remedy is to welcome these fears, anxieties as ' Old friends'. Are they not very old friends? Welcome old friend you are visiting me again, I welcome you, I label you, and you disappear like a wave into beautiful ocean. Please make friends with your fear and anxiety: this is the blessing of turning confused perceptions into peerless wisdom. Then the teaching ended, the Elder made the following aspiration to dedicate to the happiness of all sentient beings and he went upstairs for lunch.

The Elder recites: Theory and Practice combined in this dedication aspiration:

དགེ་བ་འདི་ཡིས་སྐྱེ་བོ་ཀུན། །བསོད་ནམས་ཡེ་ཤེས་ཚོགས་རྫོགས་ནས། །
བསོད་ནམས་ཡེ་ཤེས་ལས་བྱུང་བ། །དམ་པ་སྐུ་གཉིས་ཐོབ་པར་ཤོག །

"May all virtue that is created by accumulating merit and wisdom
Be dedicated to attaining the two truth bodies that arise from merit and wisdom."

Reflection Question:

1. How can we connect with Knowledge Holders and Elders in a classroom environment?

2. What are the protocols to inviting an Elder into your classroom?

3. What are some of the lasting benefits of inviting Elders into your classroom for the long-term wellness and success of your students?

Notes:

_____

_____

_____

_____

_____

_____

_____

_____

_____

_____

_____

Intercultural Education Woven into Lesson Planning Templates and Grading Sheets

Subject: _____ Name: _____									
_____									
_____									
_____									
_____									
_____									
_____									
_____									
_____									
_____									
_____									

_____									
_____									
_____									
_____									
_____									
_____									
_____									
_____									
_____									
_____									
_____									
_____									
_____									

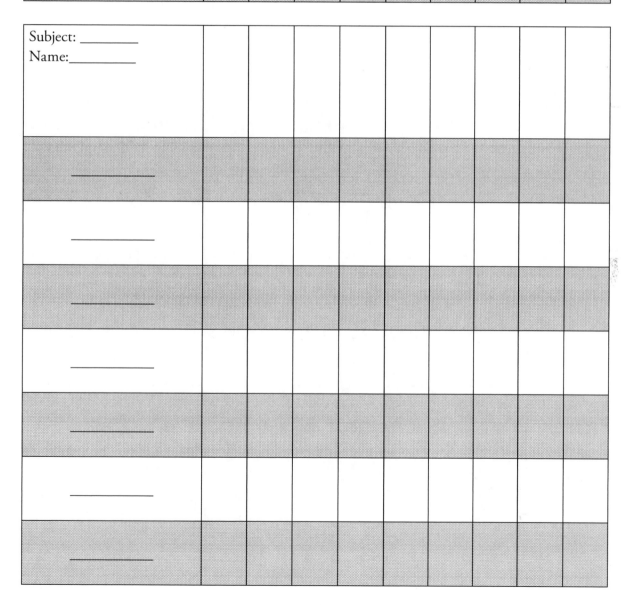

_____									
_____									
_____									
_____									
_____									
_____									
_____									
_____									
_____									
_____									
_____									
_____									

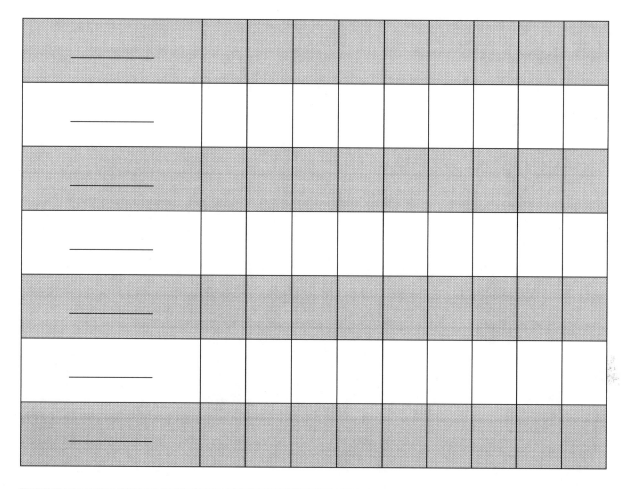

Subject: _____
Name:_____

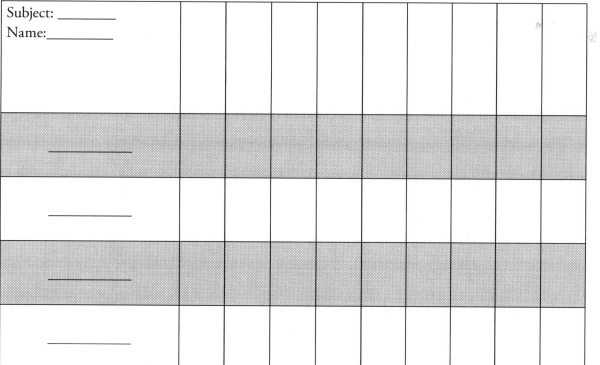

_____									
_____									
_____									
_____									
_____									
_____									
_____									
_____									
_____									
_____									
_____									
_____									

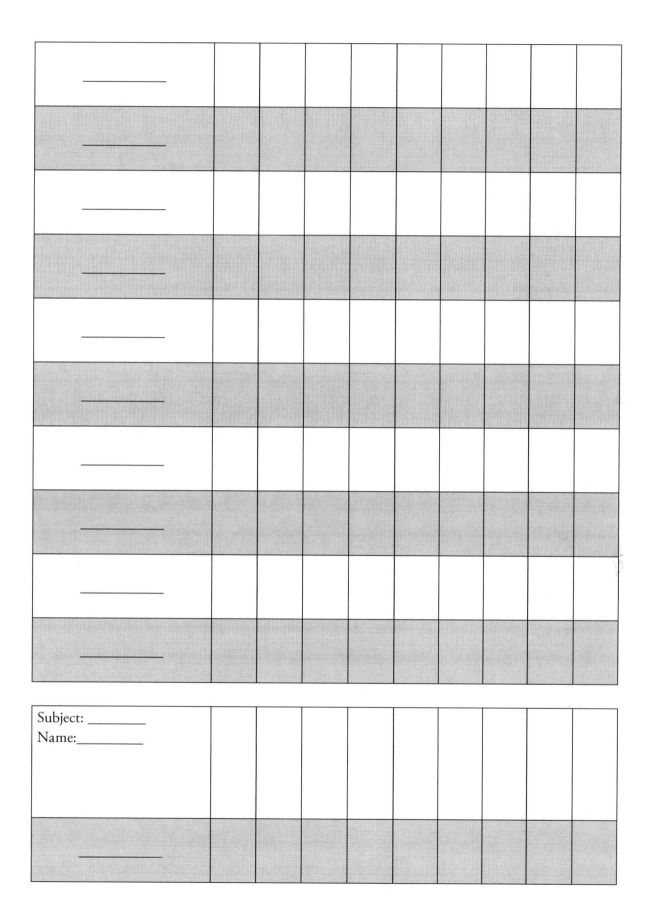

Subject: _____
Name:_____

———— ————									
———— ————									
———— ————									
———— ————									
———— ————									
———— ————									
———— ————									
———— ————									
———— ————									
———— ————									
———— ————									
———— ————									

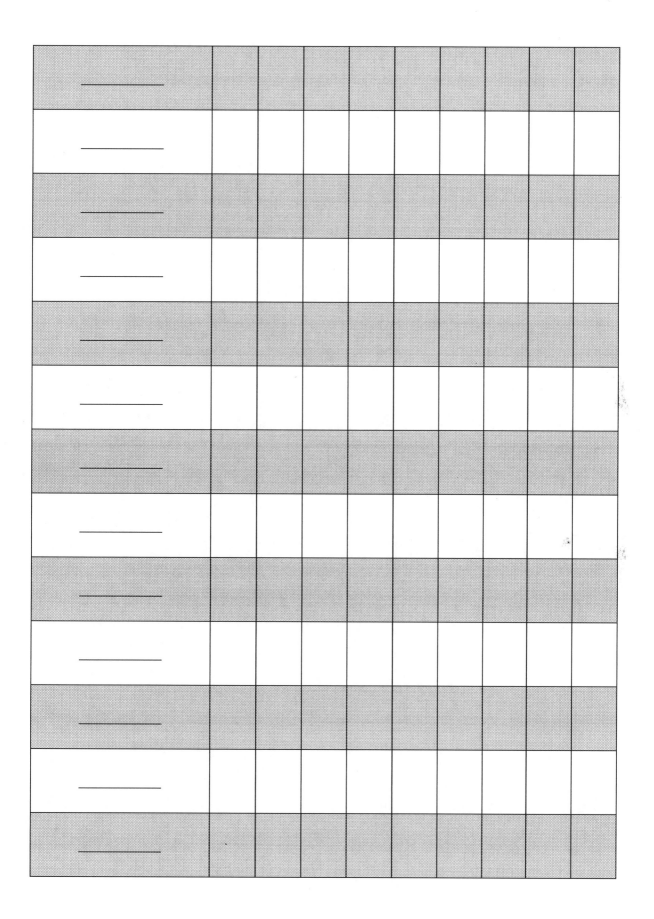

145

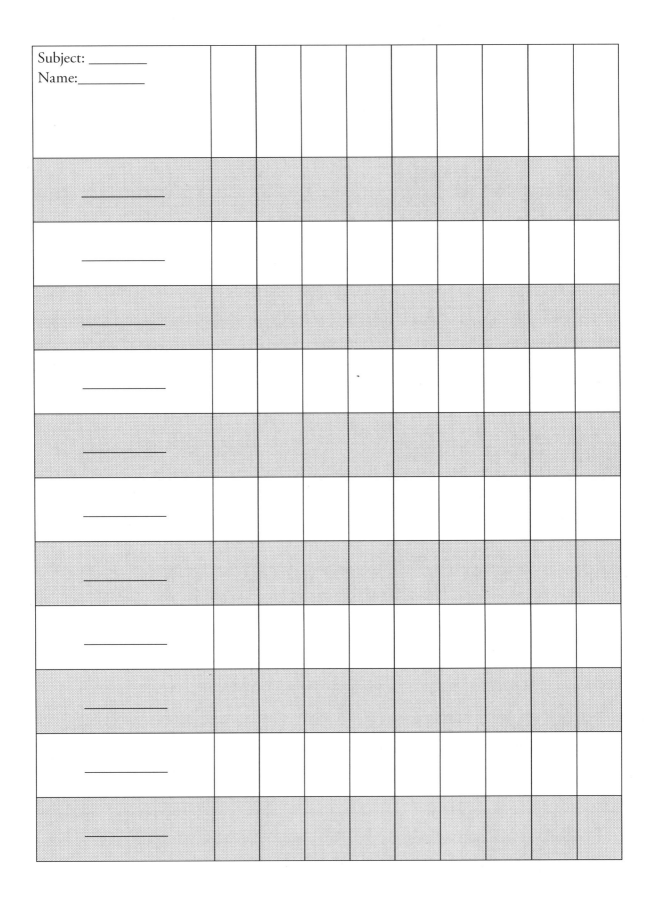

Subject: _____
Name:_____

146

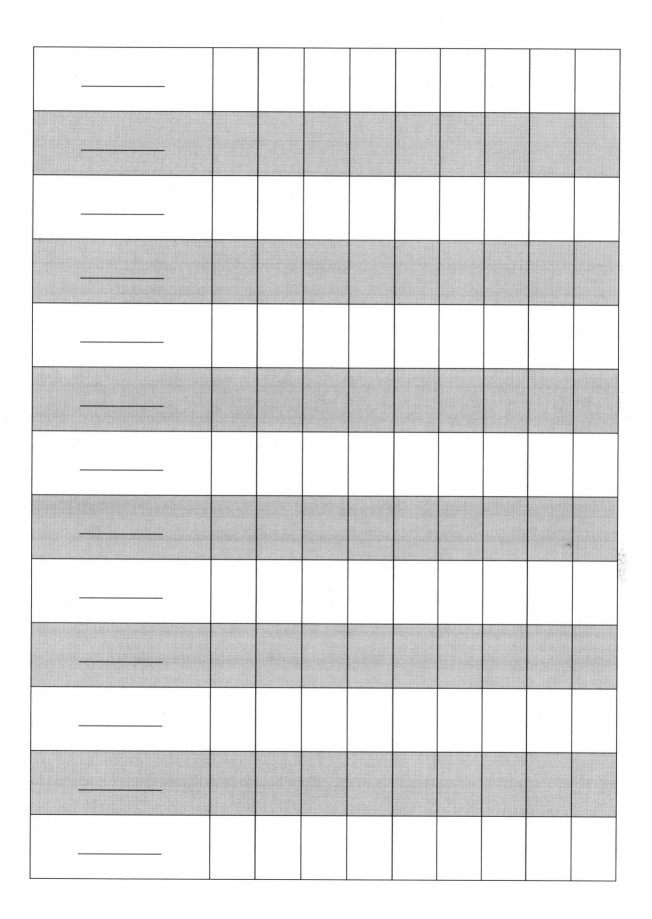

_____									
_____									
_____									

Subject: _____ Name:_____									
_____									
_____									
_____									
_____									
_____									
_____									
_____									
_____									

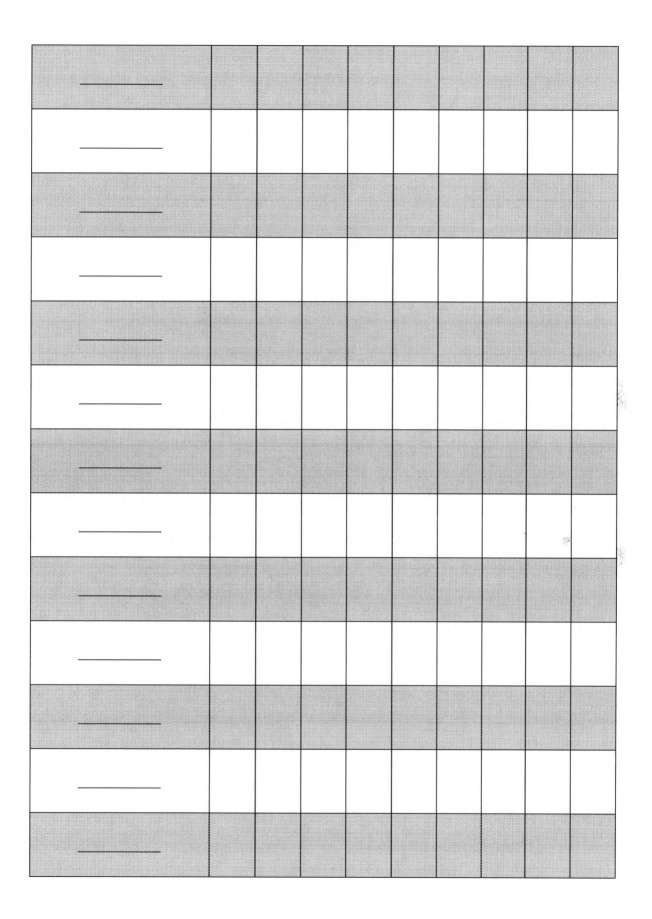

149

————									
————									
————									
————									
————									
————									

Subject: ———— Name:————									
————									
————									
————									
————									
————									

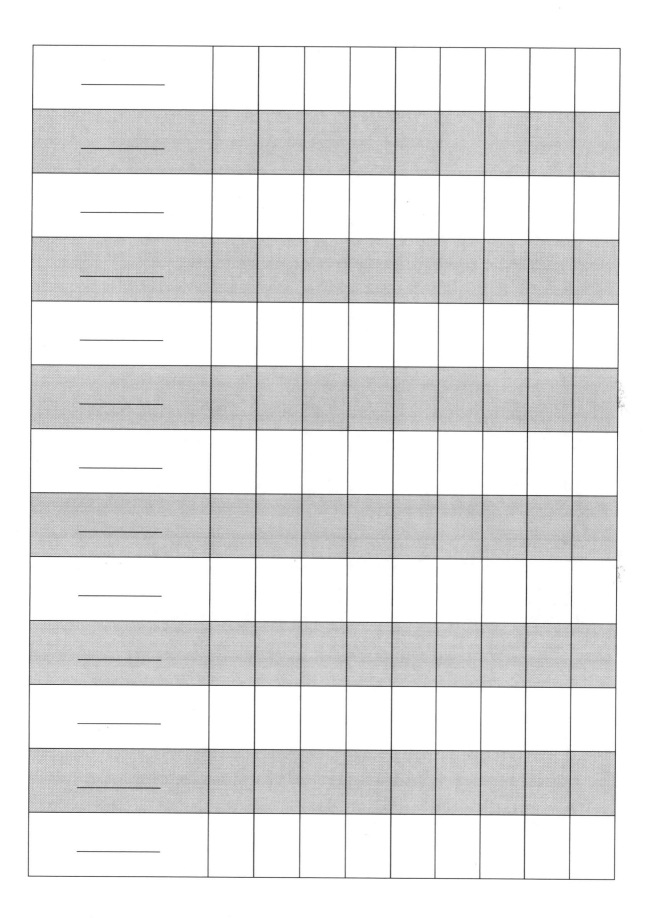

151

_____									
_____									
_____									
_____									
_____									
_____									
_____									
_____									
_____									

Subject: _____ Name:_____									
_____									
_____									

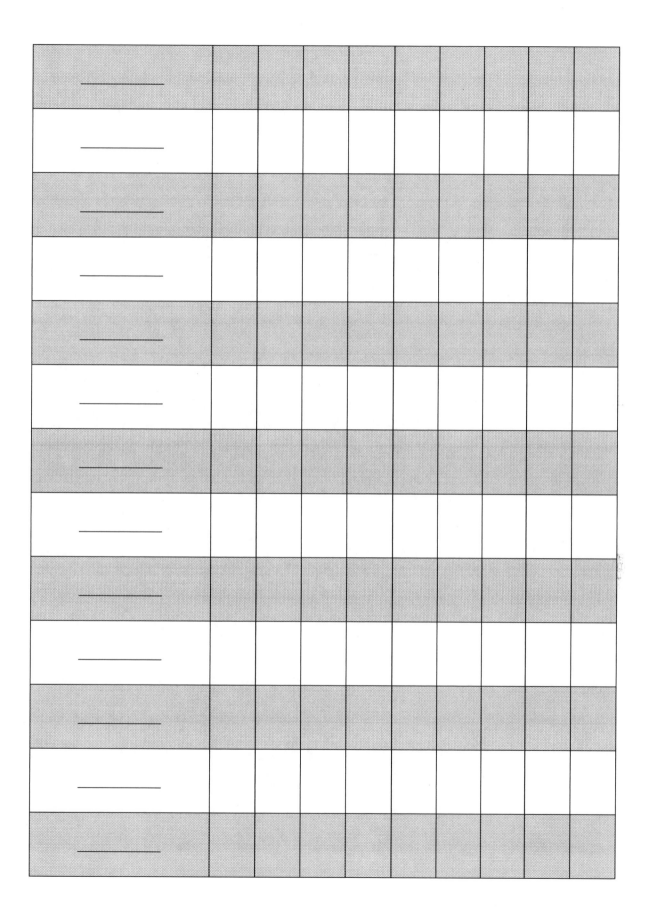

153

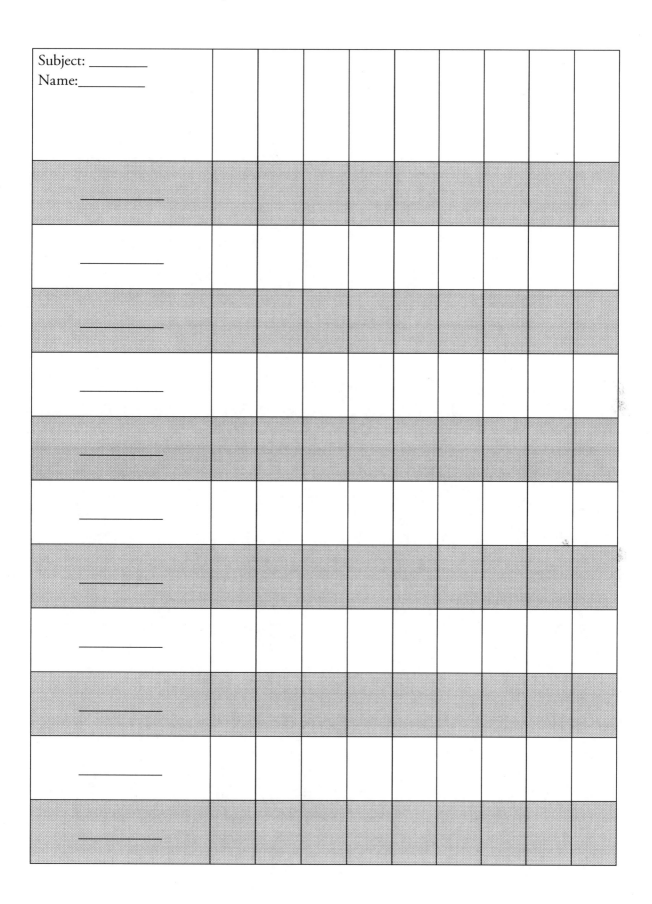

Subject: _____
Name:_____

—————— ————								
—————— ————								
—————— ————								
—————— ————								
—————— ————								
—————— ————								
—————— ————								
—————— ————								
—————— ————								
—————— ————								
—————— ————								
—————— ————								

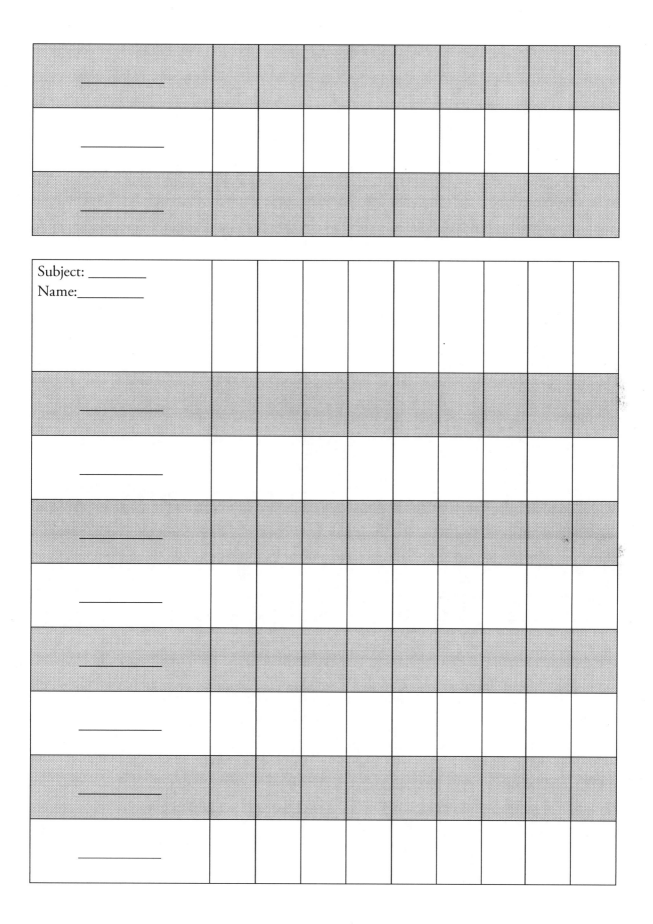

_____										
_____										
_____										
_____										
_____										
_____										
_____										
_____										
_____										
_____										
_____										
_____										

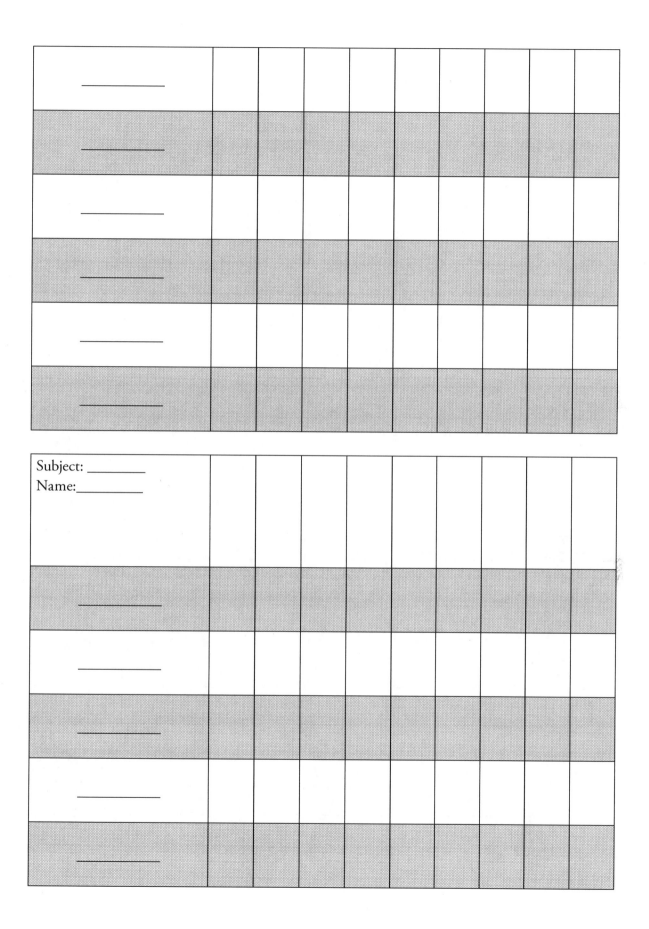

Subject: _____
Name:_____

_____										
_____										
_____										
_____										
_____										
_____										
_____										
_____										
_____										
_____										
_____										
_____										

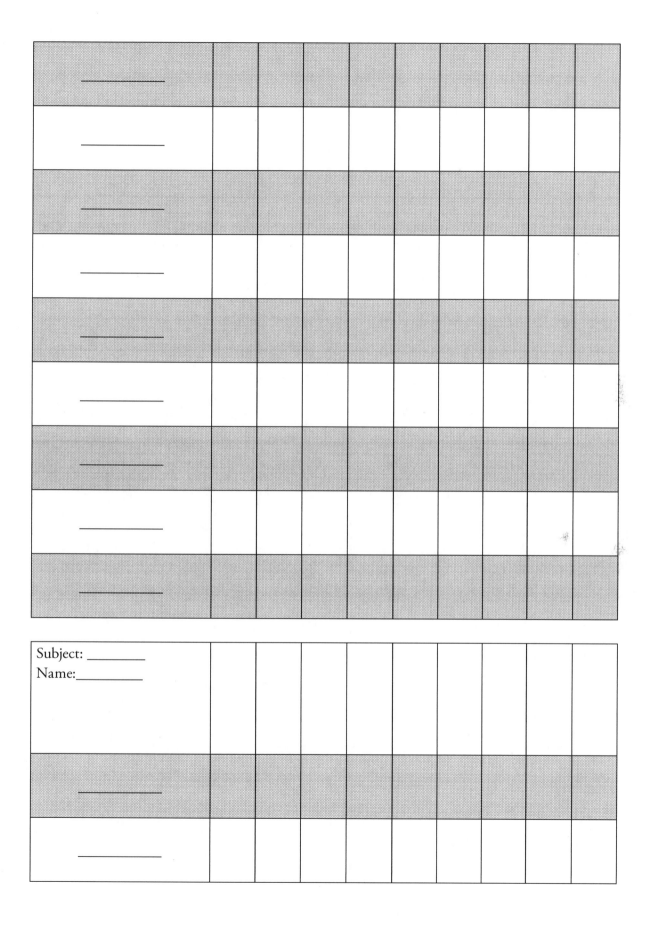

Subject: _____
Name:_____

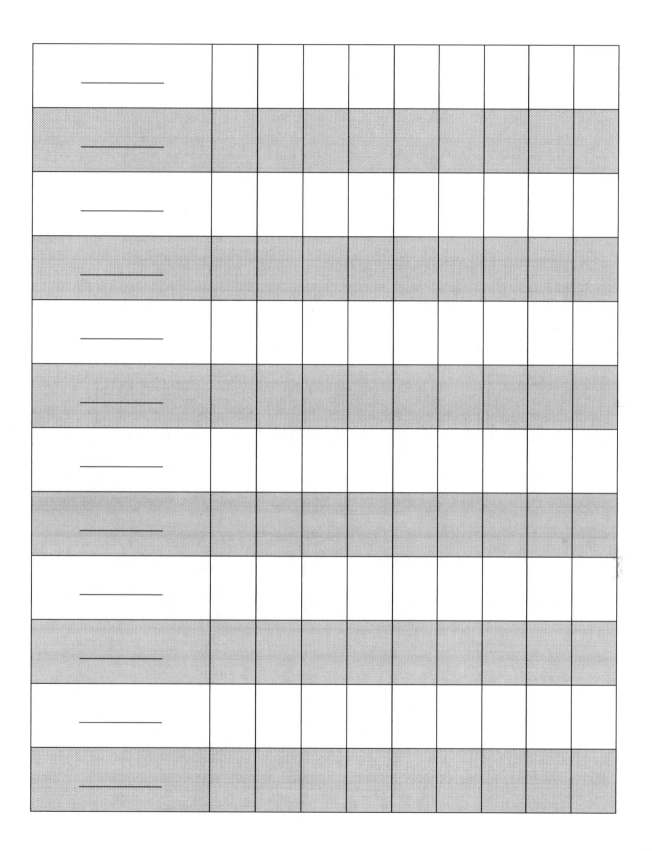

163

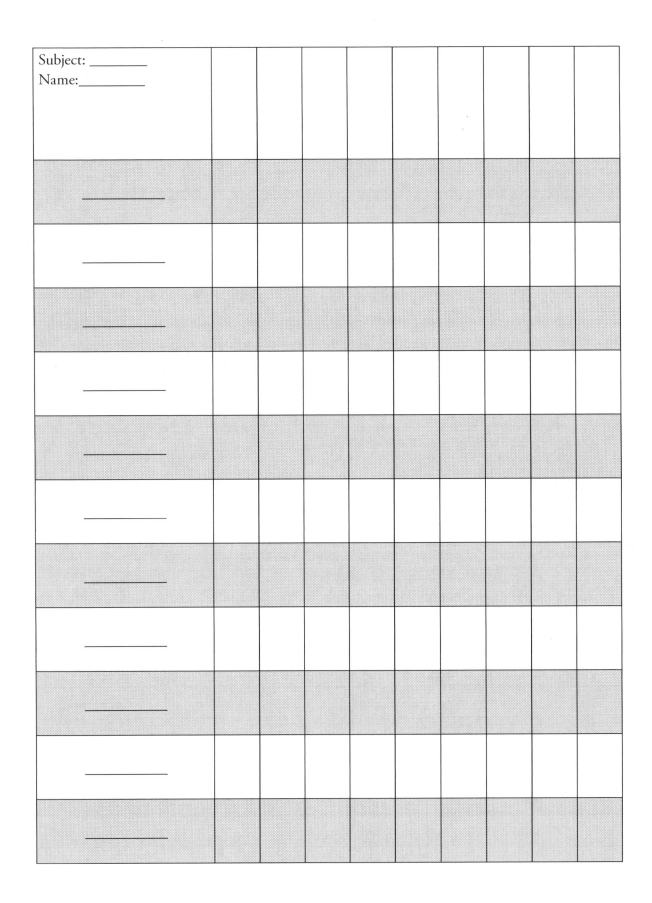

Subject: _____
Name:_____

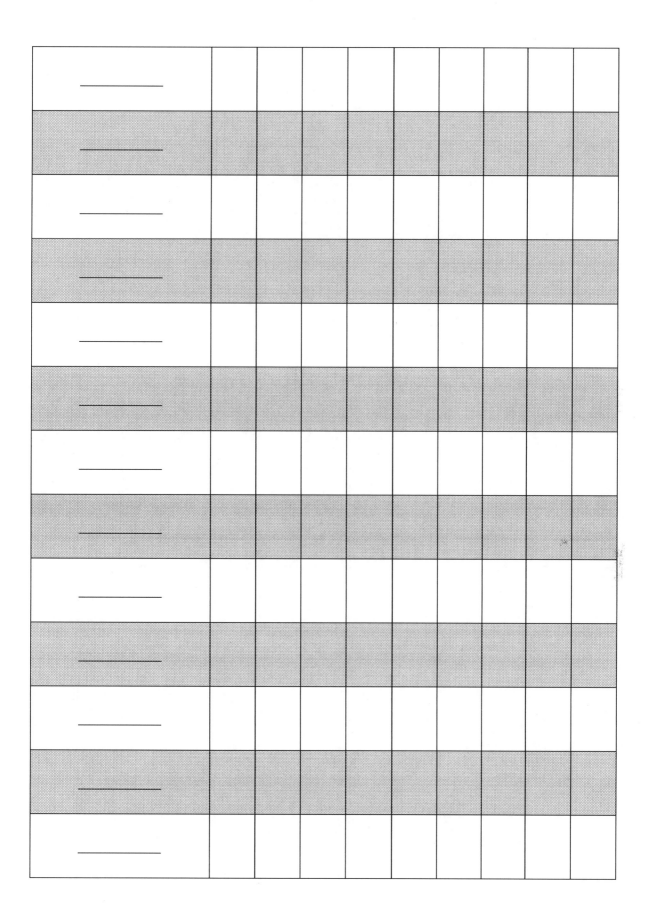

165

_____									
_____									
_____									

Subject: _____ Name:_____									
_____									
_____									
_____									
_____									
_____									
_____									
_____									
_____									

166

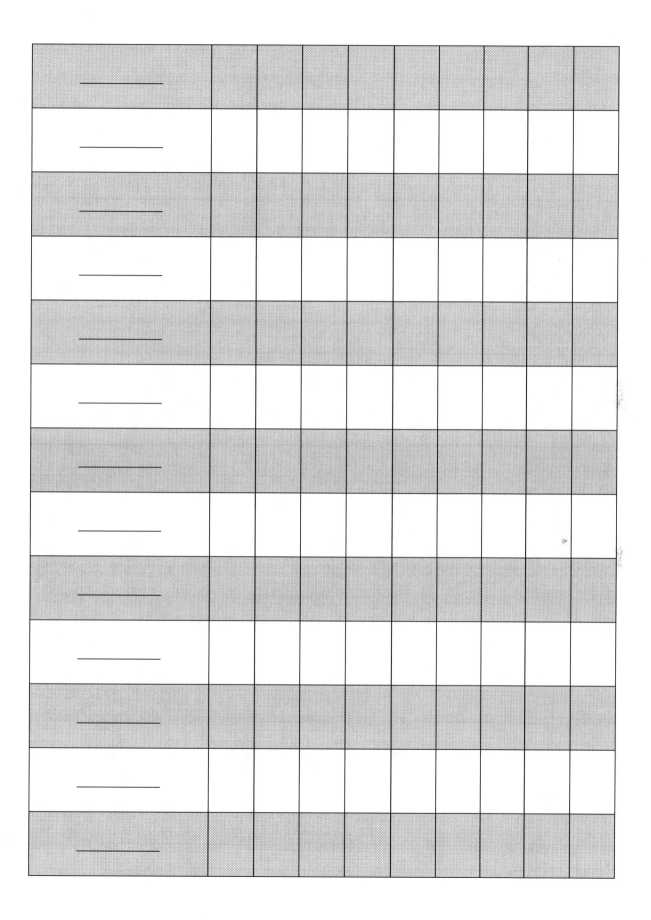

167

_____									
_____									
_____									
_____									
_____									
_____									

Subject: _____ Name:_____									
_____									
_____									
_____									
_____									
_____									

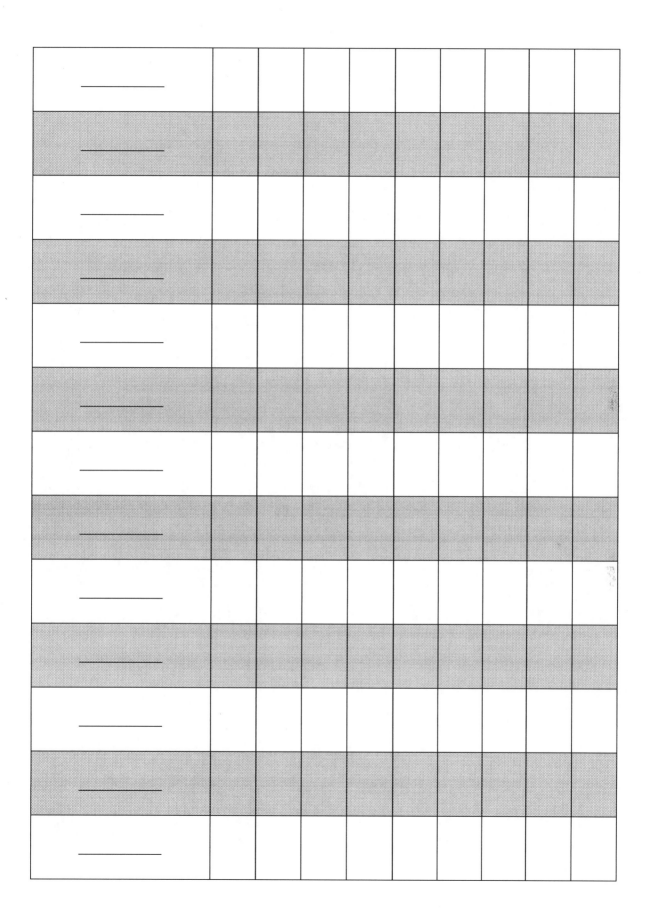

169

_____									
_____									
_____									
_____									
_____									
_____									
_____									
_____									
_____									

Subject: _____ Name:_____									
_____									
_____									

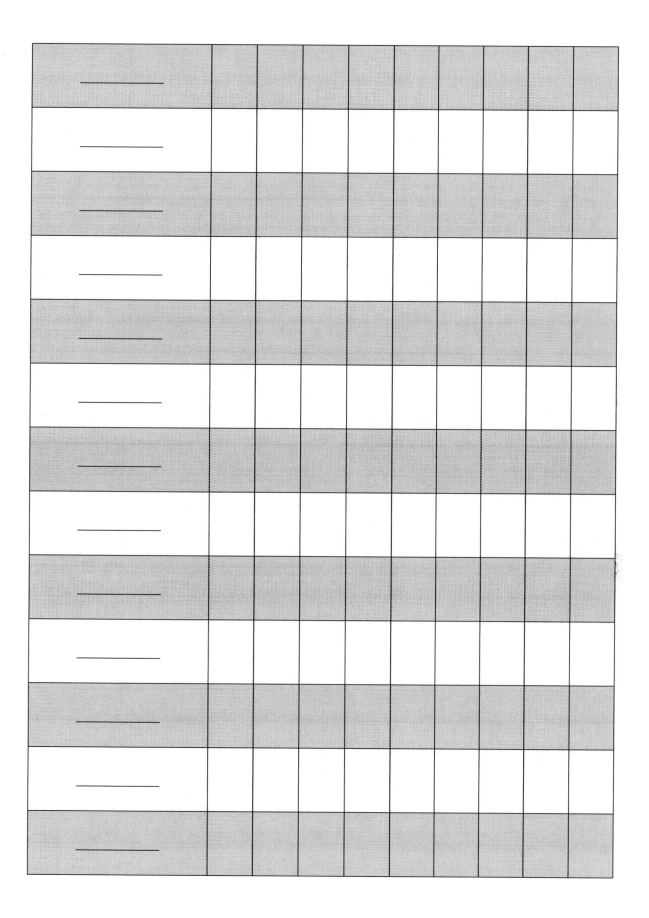

171

_____									
_____									
_____									
_____									
_____									
_____									
_____									
_____									
_____									
_____									
_____									

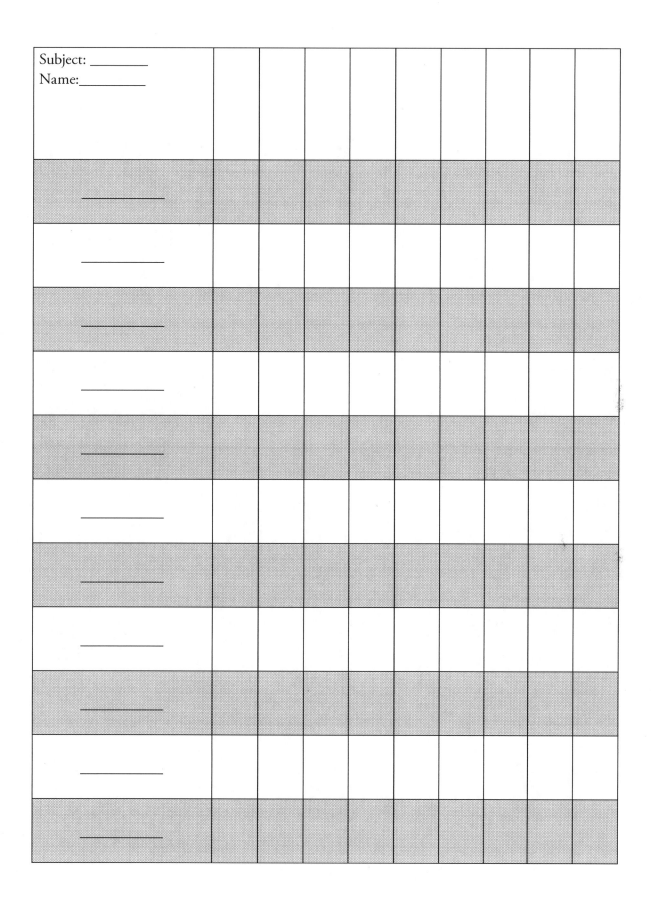

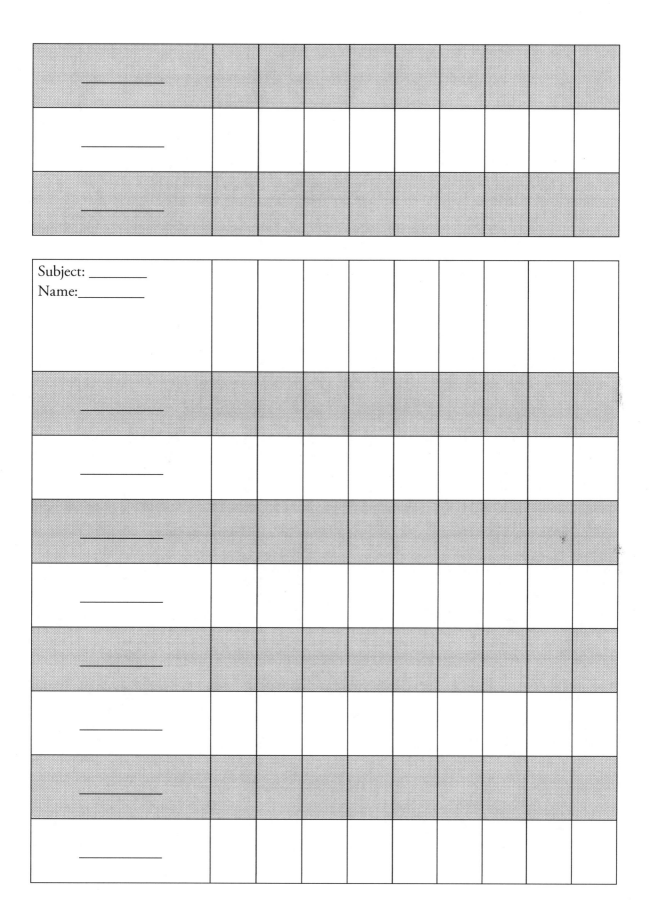

Subject: _____
Name:_____

175

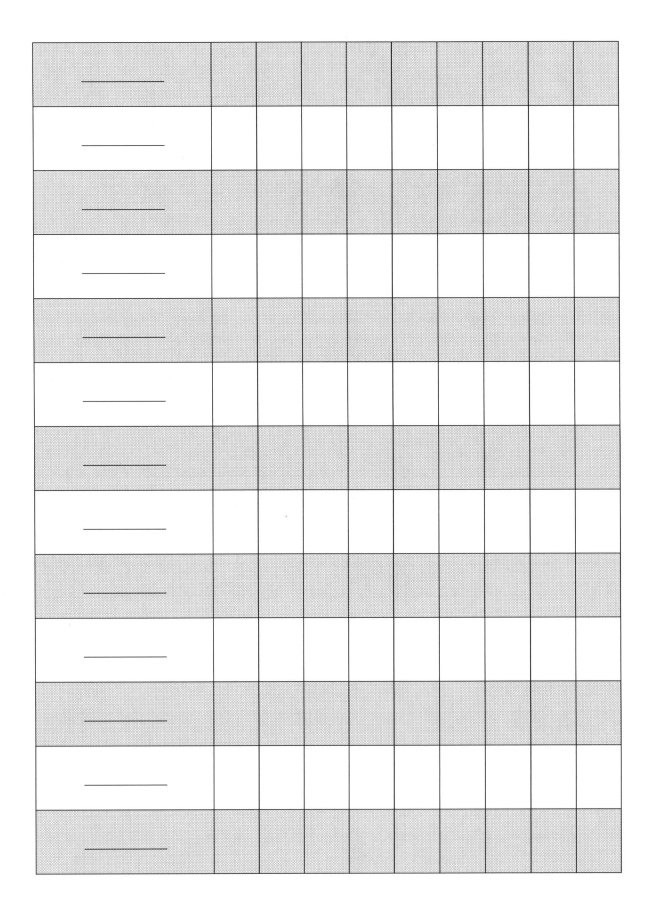

176

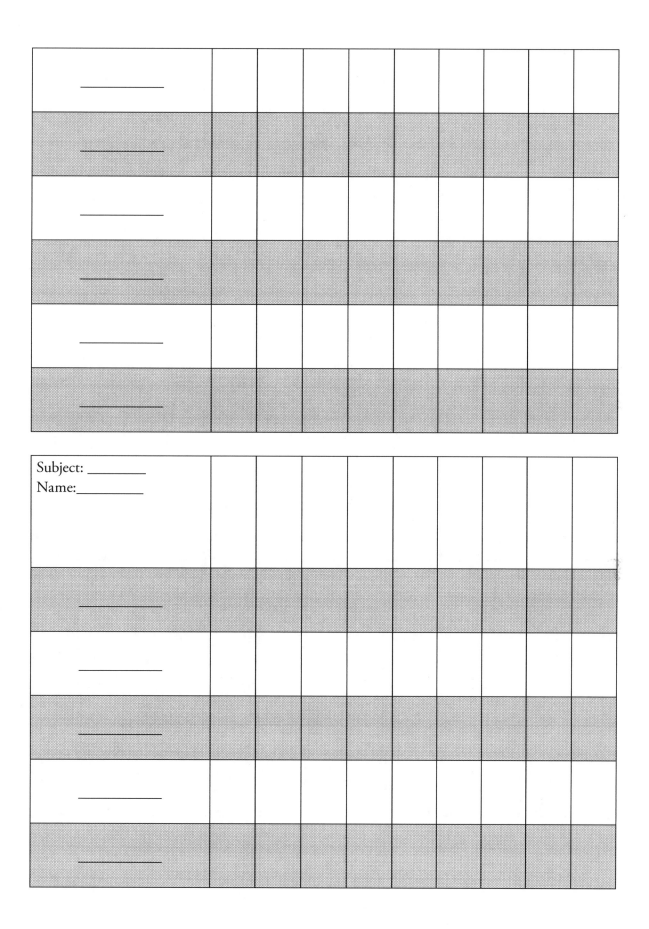

_____									
_____									
_____									
_____									
_____									
_____									
_____									
_____									
_____									
_____									
_____									
_____									

_____									
_____										
_____										
_____										
_____										
_____										
_____										
_____										
_____										

Subject: _____ Name: _____								
_____								
_____									

_____									
_____									
_____									
_____									
_____									
_____									
_____									
_____									
_____									
_____									
_____									
_____									
_____									

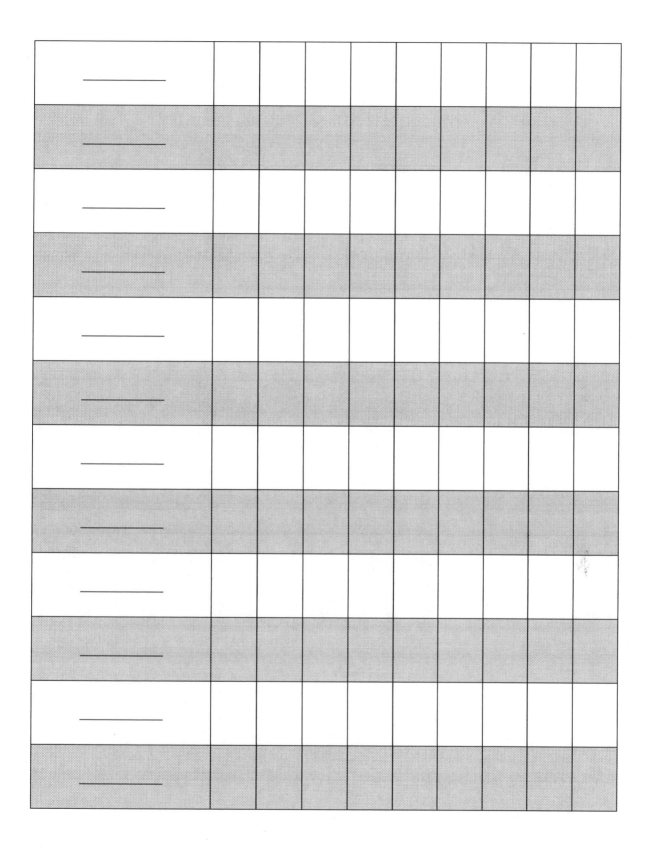

Montly Planning: Weaving Intercultural Education into Planning

Month						
Sunday	**Monday**	**Tuesday**	**Wednesday**	**Thursday**	**Friday**	**Saturday**

Month						
Sunday	Monday	Tuesday	Wednesday	Thursday	Friday	Saturday

Month						
Sunday	Monday	Tuesday	Wednesday	Thursday	Friday	Saturday

Month						
Sunday	Monday	Tuesday	Wednesday	Thursday	Friday	Saturday

Month						
Sunday	Monday	Tuesday	Wednesday	Thursday	Friday	Saturday

Month						
Sunday	Monday	Tuesday	Wednesday	Thursday	Friday	Saturday

Month						
Sunday	Monday	Tuesday	Wednesday	Thursday	Friday	Saturday

Month						
Sunday	Monday	Tuesday	Wednesday	Thursday	Friday	Saturday

Month						
Sunday	**Monday**	**Tuesday**	**Wednesday**	**Thursday**	**Friday**	**Saturday**

Month						
Sunday	Monday	Tuesday	Wednesday	Thursday	Friday	Saturday

Month						
Sunday	**Monday**	**Tuesday**	**Wednesday**	**Thursday**	**Friday**	**Saturday**

Month						
Sunday	Monday	Tuesday	Wednesday	Thursday	Friday	Saturday

Month						
Sunday	Monday	Tuesday	Wednesday	Thursday	Friday	Saturday

Month						
Sunday	Monday	Tuesday	Wednesday	Thursday	Friday	Saturday

Lesson Plans

Time	Lesson	Resources
How to improve for next time.		
What went well in this lesson?		
Who did not complete their worksheet in the class time provided.		

Time	Lesson	Resources
How to improve for next time.		
What went well in this lesson?		
Who did not complete their worksheet in the class time provided.		

Time	Lesson	Resources
How to improve for next time.		
What went well in this lesson?		
Who did not complete their worksheet in the class time provided.		

198

Time	Lesson	Resources
How to improve for next time.		
What went well in this lesson?		
Who did not complete their worksheet in the class time provided.		

Time	Lesson	Resources
How to improve for next time.		
What went well in this lesson?		
Who did not complete their worksheet in the class time provided.		

Time	Lesson	Resources
How to improve for next time.		
What went well in this lesson?		
Who did not complete their worksheet in the class time provided.		

Time	Lesson	Resources
How to improve for next time.		
What went well in this lesson?		
Who did not complete their worksheet in the class time provided.		

Time	Lesson	Resources
How to improve for next time.		
What went well in this lesson?		
Who did not complete their worksheet in the class time provided.		

203

Time	Lesson	Resources
How to improve for next time.		
What went well in this lesson?		
Who did not complete their worksheet in the class time provided.		

Time	Lesson	Resources
How to improve for next time.		
What went well in this lesson?		
Who did not complete their worksheet in the class time provided.		

Time	Lesson	Resources
How to improve for next time.		
What went well in this lesson?		
Who did not complete their worksheet in the class time provided.		

Time	Lesson	Resources
How to improve for next time.		
What went well in this lesson?		
Who did not complete their worksheet in the class time provided.		

Time	Lesson	Resources
How to improve for next time.		
What went well in this lesson?		
Who did not complete their worksheet in the class time provided.		

Time	Lesson	Resources
How to improve for next time.		
What went well in this lesson?		
Who did not complete their worksheet in the class time provided.		

Time	Lesson	Resources
How to improve for next time.		
What went well in this lesson?		
Who did not complete their worksheet in the class time provided.		

Time	Lesson	Resources
How to improve for next time.		
What went well in this lesson?		
Who did not complete their worksheet in the class time provided.		

Time	Lesson	Resources
How to improve for next time.		
What went well in this lesson?		
Who did not complete their worksheet in the class time provided.		

Time	Lesson	Resources
How to improve for next time.		
What went well in this lesson?		
Who did not complete their worksheet in the class time provided.		

Time	Lesson	Resources
How to improve for next time.		
What went well in this lesson?		
Who did not complete their worksheet in the class time provided.		

ABOUT THE ARTIST

Jim Oskineegish

First Nation Art within the text: "**Let's Work Together**"

Jim comes from Nakina, a small town in Northern Ontario. His mother comes from the Eabametoong First Nation in Ontario, Canada and his Father came from Poland where he lived in the city of Lwow. Both of Jim's parents suffered traumatic experiences as children. Jim's mother was forced to attend and suffer the treatment of Residential Schools and his father survived the concentration camps during WWII. Jim's early childhood was full of traumatic experiences that no child should ever have to go through. Jim was taken from his home during the sixties scoop at the age of five and went through the foster care system where he endured emotional and physical trauma. Through all the tribulations Jim went through as a child there was a silver lining in the field of Art.

Jim gravitated towards art at an early age and was proud of what he could draw and paint. Jim finished high school and attended University in the Visual Arts program at Lakehead University in Thunder Bay, Ontario. He used the artistic skills he had developed at Lakehead to help the children and families he worked with in the mental health field.

Jim went into hiatus to support and provide for his family. In the spring of 2005 Jim picked up the brush once again with the encouragement of his nephew Mark Anthony Jacobson who is a third generation woodland artist based out of Vancouver BC. Jim painted three works of art in the Ojibwe Woodland Style and these three paintings were blessed by Norval Morrisseau while Mark Anthony Jacobson and Norval were doing a show together in Nanaimo BC.

Norval Morrisseau gave Jim his blessing that he could paint in this style and tradition. Jim has been painting on a fulltime basis in the Ojibwe Woodland style since 2005. Jim is a born medicine man and artist along with being a traditional drum keeper, eagle staff carrier as well as pipe carrier as these sacred items were given to him by the creator. Jim has been learning from traditional elders from the treaty #3 area and was adopted into the Atik (caribou) clan of Siene River and Eagle Lake. As Jim continues on his journey through life his focus has been painting and sharing his life experiences through his paintings. He paints his dreams and thoughts, hoping this can help another human being in some way. Jim uses solid bold colors and tries to achieve a visual balance of color and feeling in his work.

Jim wants to promote Ojibwe culture to the world by painting stories and legends, as well as traditional teachings and values. Jim draws inspirations from 1st generation woodland artists like Norval Morrisseau, Roy Thomas and Benjamin Chee Chee to name a few. Jim is painting his life and these paintings are spiritual based as he believes that inner soul consciousness is to be shared and feels that this style of art can help beautify the world we live in.

Artist Statement

"I believe that Woodland art can promote healing and understanding amongst all of mankind. Color, I believe is a power that the creator gave us to communicate traditional values and teachings. Ojibwe culture is alive and well as long as we express it in a good way"

View all his collections here: https://jimi-oskineegish.pixels.com/

Andy Weber

Traditional Tibetan artwork within this latest text belongs to the artist Andy Weber.

Artist Andy Weber spent seven years living and studying the iconographical art of Tibetan Buddhism under the guidance of accomplished masters in India and Nepal.

His unique style of authentic images for visualization are highly respected not only by the growing number of Western Buddhists but also by Tibetan Lamas of all traditions, many of whom have commissioned his work.

His thangka paintings (Tibetan scroll paintings) can be seen in Buddhist centres and temples throughout the world including the Potala Palace in Lhasa and his images have become well known and popular through numerous publications.

With over 35 years of experience Andy Weber and his students offer their artwork, their services, and their experience to the wider Dharma community. Andy Weber Studios makes most of the artwork directly available through this web site for everybody to see.

You can also acquire high quality reproductions of Andy's artwork through our online store. Andy also teaches all over the world.

ABOUT THE AUTHOR

Karma M. Chukdong

Professor Karma Chukdong holds a master's in arts and science and a bachelor of education and honors BA. After working in school systems for a few years, he wanted to earn some further qualifications to make more concrete positive change in school systems in terms of management. He has taken many courses at the doctor of education level and eventually acquired a second master's degree from the University of Toronto in education.

This master of education degree focused on curriculum, policy, teaching, leadership, and education management. Karma Chukdong prepared these practical solutions found in this book. With the current understandable stress of parents teaching from home, student mental health and teacher fatigue this academic text was created to assist in being a wellness and empowerment resource as we return to a re-imagined school environment.

These are the most immediate concerns in education management that can be implemented by any administrator or educator who holds compassionate leadership as her or his philosophical pedagogy. This text is presented in a way that is accessible and connected to the practicing education specialist and the passionate parent preparing for the academic life of their child.

Presently, Professor Chukdong serves Indigenous community schools and provides Quality Assurance for Canadian College programming. Other titles by this author are: The Human Family, Educational Leadership: A Student-Centered Approach, Education Management: Building Student Success, Curriculum Teaching and Learning Today, and Social Justice Education.

BIBLIOGRAPHY

Aboriginal Peoples Collection (2002). The Final Report of a First Nation Research Project on Healing in Canadian Aboriginal Communities.

Aboriginal Policy Research. (2003). Setting the Agenda For Change. Thompson Educationa Publishing Inc.

Aiyangar, Krishna. Edicts of Ashoka. The Adyar Library. Madras, 1950.

Ambedekar, The Buddha and His Dhamma, Siddarth Pub., 1974.

Assembly of First Nations. (May 31,2005). First Nations Education Plan. Educational Policy created by First Nation Leaders, Elders and Chiefs. First published in 1971.

Bowles, S., Gintis, and Gintis and Groves, M. (2005). Unequal Chances: Family Background and Economic Success. Intergenerational Inequality Matters.

Burns, J. (1978). Leadership. New York: Harper and Row.

Carnoy, Martin. (1974). Education as Cultural Imperialsim. New York: Longman.

Chukdong, Karma.(2008). The Human Family: A Modern Tibetan Buddhist Perspective.

AuthorHouse Publications. Bloomington Indiana.

Dundas, Paul. Jainism. Routledge, London and New York. 1992.

Fullan, M. (1998). The Meaning of Educational Change: A Quarter Century of A Century of Learning. International Handbook of Educational Change. Dordecht, The Netherlands: Kluwer.

Freire, Paulo. (1970). Pedagogy of the Oppressed. New York: Continuum.

Gillborn, David.(2006). Citizenship Education as Placebo: 'Standards', institutional racism, and educational policy. Sage Publications.

Goldberg, Michelle. (2006). Forming, Reforming, and Performing Education: Using Foucault to Rethink Canadian Schooling.

Goleman, Destructive Emotions. (2002)

Gorski, P. (2008). Good Intentions Are Not Enough: A Decolonizing Intercultural Education. Intercultural Education.

Hamza, H. (2004) Decolonizing Research on Gender Disparity in Education in Niger: Complexities of Language Culture and Homecoming. Critical Personal Narratives. New York Suny Press.

Harris, A. (2006) Distrubition of Successful Leadership. Successful School Leadership: What is it and how it influences student learning. Deptartment for Education and Skills, London.

Hay, Stephen, Sources of Indian Tradition, Penguin Books. 1988.

Horner, Women Under Primitive Buddhism. Dutton, New York. 1930

Iqbal, Saeeda, Islamic Rationalism in the Subcontinent, Islamic Book Service, 1984.

Joshi, Studies in Buddhist Culture, Patiala Punjabi University, Delhi. 1969

Kanu, Y. (2005). Tensions and Dilemmas of Cross-Cultural Knowledge: Post-Structural/ Post-Colonial Reflections on an Innovative Teacher Education in Pakistan. International Journal of Educational Development.

Korth, B. (2004). Education and Linguistic Division in Kyrgyzstan. The Challenges of Education in Central Asia. Information Page Publishing.

Laskmi, The Essence of Buddhism, Bharatiya Pub. House, Delhi. 1976.

Leithwood, K. (1999). A Century's Quest To Understand School Leadership. Handbook of Research on Educational Adminstration, Second Edition (San Francisco: Jossey-Bass.)

Leithwood, K. (2005). Accountable Schools and The Leadership They Need. International Handbook of Educatoinal Policy, (pp. 439-456). Drodrecht, The Netherlands: Springer.

Lipsky, Michael, (1993). Street Level Bureaucracy: Dilemmas of the Individual in Public Services. New York: Russell Sage Foundation.

Mohammad, Shan, Writing and Speeches of Sir Syed Ahmad Khan, Nachiketa Publications Limited, 1972.

Mulford, B. (2005). Accountability Policies and Their Effects. International Handbookof Educational Policy, Part 1. (pp.281-294). Dordecht, the Netherlands: Springer.

Munro, John C. Hon. (1981). Minister of Indian Affairs and Northern Development. In All Fairness: A Native Claims Policy. Ottawa.

Munro, John C. Hon. (1982). Minister of Indian Affairs and Northern Development. Outstanding Business: A Native Claims Policy. Ottawa.

Niyozov, S (2009). Teacher's Perspectives on the Education of Their Muslim Students: A Missing Voice in Educational Research. Curriculum Inquiry.

Ontario Advisory Council on Senior Citizens (1993). Denied Too Long. The Needs and Concerns of Seniors Living in First Nation Communities in Ontario.

Ontario First Nation, Metis, Inuit Education Policy Framework. (2007). Aboriginal Education Office. Minstry of Eduction.

Patton, Carl V.(1986). Basic Methods of Policy Analysis and Planning. Prentice-Hall, Englewood Cliffs, N.J.

Perley, D. (2001). Aboriginal Education in Canada as Internal Colonialism. Canada Journal of Native Education.

Raina, V. (1999). Indigenizing Teacher Education in Developing Countries: the Indian Context. Prospects.

Rothstein, William (1991) Identity and Ideology: Socio-cultural Theories of Schooling. Greenwood Press.

Stone, Deborah (2001). The Policy Paradox: The Art of Political Decision Making. New York: W.W. Norton.

Suzuki, David. (1996). Wisdom of the Elders with Peter Knudtson. Native and Scientific Ways of Knowing about Nature. Mountain Man Graphics, Australia.

Thrupp, Martin (1999). The Social Limits of Reform: Open University Press.

Willis, Paul, The Elements of a Culture, Learning to Labour: How working class kids get working class jobs, 1977.

Winton, Sue. (2007.) Rhetorical Analysis and of Character Education Policy.

Zine. J. (2001). Muslim Youth in Canadian Schools. Education and the Politics of Religious Identity. Anthropology and Education Quarterly.

Printed in the United States
By Bookmasters